SELECT POEMS OF CATULLUS

SELECT POEMS OF
CATULLUS

EDITED, WITH INTRODUCTIONS, NOTES, AND
APPENDICES, BY

FRANCIS P. SIMPSON

BALLIOL COLLEGE, OXFORD

MACMILLAN AND CO., LIMITED
ST. MARTIN'S STREET, LONDON
1948

PRINTED IN GREAT BRITAIN

THE present edition has been carefully revised, in accordance with the opinion of high educational authorities, in order to render this volume of selections from Catullus perfectly suitable for school reading.

At the same time, from the scholar's point of view, a thorough recension has been made of the text, and the Appendices have been verified and augmented. The Notes also have been reviewed and improved, and include observations furnished by Mr. Munro, to whose kind criticism I am much indebted.

I am also obliged to Mr. T. Agar (late Junior Student of Christ Church) for valuable corrections.

F. P. S.

October, 1879.

CONTENTS.

GENERAL INTRODUCTION.

I.

'Venias hedera juvenalia cinctus
Tempora cum Calvo, docte Catulle, tuo.'

EVERLASTING gratitude is due to the notary of Verona who rescued from the dust the sole manuscript, so long lost, of his compatriot Catullus; for, possessing this,[1] we possess a diary vividly picturing the life of Rome, just before it was overcast with the grey monotone of Imperialism, in the colours which it wore to the feelings of a young Republician, man of the world, and poet. Catullus had many friends who lived and wrote like himself; but their works met the fate of the authors, and perished before their time. It is most fortunate for us, therefore, that one has escaped, by a hair's-breadth, the general mortality; and it is most fortunate that the survivor is Catullus. For he was especially fitted to represent to us the daily world he lived in, both because his sensibility was singularly pure—embalming its experience in crystal, without stain, shadow, or distortion—and because he belonged

[1] Or rather transcripts of it. See Advertisement to Text.

to those natures which look neither before nor after,
but people and perceive only the present.

Before we consider his works, we may for a moment
consider the man.   Born after the convulsions of
private ambition had begun to shake the over-built
Republic, he died at thirty, in time to escape its final
downfall.   For though a man of letters and of pleasure
rather than a politician, and an Italian not a Latin by
birth, he had the Roman spirit of independence, and
was a good Republican.   A verse is quoted to indicate
that he apologised for his lampoons on Caesar; the truth
is, while he might be proud of Caesar's conquests, he
never saw their consequences without passionate dis-
gust.   So far from regarding him as anything more
than a Roman citizen, he declared that he could sleep
comfortably in ignorance whether Caesar had a white
skin or a black.   But his bile is hottest to see Caesar's
minions, Mamurra, 'the Formian cheat,' Porcius and
Socration, 'murrain and lean kine of the earth,' prosper and grow sleek on Gallic and British plunder,
while men of birth cringed for a dinner.   He went
himself to Bithynia, to find better tenants for his
purse than its old inhabitants 'the cobwebs,' in the
train of the Praetor Memmius—who, if our poet is to
be believed, was the last person in the world to have a
poem like that of Lucretius dedicated to him,—but
returned poorer in every sense except in his vocabulary
of curses.   Catullus was a good hater, and never
shrank from plain speech ; but his attachment to his
friends was as strikingly sincere—clever spendthrifts,

prodigal poets, like himself. The great passion, however, and the poison of his history was his love of Lesbia, or, to take off the mask, Clodia. The sister of Cicero's enemy Clodius, the wife—but suspiciously soon the widow—of Metellus Celer, among three sisters who were the wickedest and most beautiful women in Rome, she bore the palm. Catullus' blind passion lasted long ; and, when his eyes were opened, only changed into infatuation. We do not know that he ever was entirely cured of his lunacy ; but, if so, when he ceased to be lover he ceased to be poet.

The existing poems cannot be arranged in order of composition. Probably Catullus, like most other poets, began with imitation and translation. But it is necessary to suppose that his brother's death occurred quite early in Catullus' short life—a supposition in which there are difficulties—if we would place the extant translations among his first compositions. As, however, the 'Lock of Berenice's Hair,'[1] the 'Dialogue with a Door,' and the rest of these pieces, are not the best works of Catullus, we must praise them as clever exercises, and pass on to his other poems.

The longest of these is the idyll on the 'Marriage of Peleus and Thetis.' The argument is very simple : the Argo breaking for the first time the silence of the seas—the sea-nymphs rising to the strange sight—the

[1] Once called the best of Catullus' works ; but that was by a Dutch pedant, who had probably spent a life-time in emending the text.

mutual passion of Peleus and Thetis—the solemn be-
trothal and the marriage scene.   First, all Thessaly
throngs to see the palace and to admire the marvellous
coverlet of the bed, on which was wrought in colours
the whole of the story of Ariadne—her winning and
desertion—her standing desolate on the shore of Dia,
where she utters words of despair and reproach against
Theseus—the fulfilment of her curse at Athens—the
advent of Bacchus and his train, and her assumption
into heaven.   Then the tide of humanity passes, and
the gods enter : Chiron with garlands of every flower
that blows, Peneus with laurel branches, Prometheus
still wearing faint scars of his ancient doom—followed
by Jove and all the great gods, except Phoebus and
his sister.   The venerable Fates spin their threads
and sing a prophetic song of the great Pelides, while
the divine guests sit round and banquet.   Alas, that
human degeneracy had now banished the gods from
earthly scenes !   The versification of the poem is as
little elaborate as the tale, but is everywhere felicitous.
As with the Endymion, to begin this idyll is to read
it through ; and no quotation would convey the true
character of the poem, which is that of perfect
continuity.

The ' Attis ' shows the orgiastic madness and wild
flight of some worshippers of Cybele from their homes
in Greece to the sacred forests of Phrygia.   The
rapidity and vehemence of the verse, corresponding
to the subject, make no pause until the end.   No
English metre gives any such impression of intensity

and speed.   A few lines, when the passion is quieter,
may be translated :

> ' As soon as the wayworn company set foot on Cybele's
> demesne, spent with travel and fasting they fell asleep ; and
> while their eyelids were steeped in dull slumber's relaxing
> swoon, rest gently charmed away the fever and frenzy of their
> souls.   But when the golden-visaged sun flashed forth his eyes
> and began his survey of clear white sky, solid lands and the
> waste of ocean, and routed the shades of night before the
> rattling hoofs of his new-risen steeds,—that moment Sleep
> hastily took flight from the waking Attis, and rested not till
> he found a haven in Queen Pasithea's bosom.'

Waking brings repentance ; but repentance is re-
bellion against the goddess, who appears in her chariot,
drawn by lions, to execute vengeance. The poem
thus closes :—

> ' Cybele spoke in anger ; her hands drew back the yoke,
> and the monster, summoning his might, sprang furiously
> forward. Roaring in the chase, crashing through the under-
> wood in his wild career, he came to the moist expanse of the
> foam-fringed beach, discovered unmanned Attis by the bright
> waters' edge, and rushed upon him.   Blind with terror he fled
> into the fastnesses of the forest, and there remained in bondage
> for ever, until he died.
>
> Great goddess, goddess Cybele, goddess and queen of Dindy-
> mus ! Grant, dear mistress, that thy fever may never light
> upon my house : choose others for that headlong rout, drive
> others on that passionate pilgrimage.'

The ' Peleus ' and ' Attis ' have been thought to
be translations ; if this be so, they have entirely
superseded their originals.

The two ' Marriage Songs ' may now be mentioned. One of these has no special occasion, or at least contains no names. The form is that of a dialogue between the parts of a double chorus—the young men invoke, the maidens reproach, the evening star ; the latter sing the beauty of virginity, the former the praises of the married state.   Maidenhood, the maidens say,

> ' is a flower that grows in a corner within garden walls, never discovered by flocks, never bruised by the plough ; to which the breezes add sweetness and the sun strength and the rains stature.'

Not so, their antagonists reply ; say rather—

> ' an unwedded vine, struggling on an unsheltered soil— never able to raise her head, or rear the mellow cluster, but bowing her delicate frame in drooping heaviness until the topmost tendril almost clasps the root.'

Catullus' mastery of the language of flowers brings him nearer than any other classical poet to modern feeling.   For in the other Epithalamium, written for the marriage of Manlius to Vinia, the bride stands pre-eminent among the beauty of the world—

> ' as the stately hyacinth-bloom rises in a rich man's many-coloured garden of flowers.'

And again—

> ' He shall be folded in thy embrace as closely as the limber vine flings her tendrils about the elm that is planted by her side.'

Continuous rapid music characterizes this Hymeneal

as it characterizes the 'Attis.' The verse is of the lightest texture known to Latin poetry. The invocation of the deity, the welcome of the bride, the assurance of a happy future and the adieu, are full of delicate imagination, simply and gracefully expressed. The whole is unique in Latin if not in all literature.

We are sometimes inclined to assume that certain capacities and feelings, generally such as may be considered laudable, are peculiar to our own age or even to our own country. Thus the interpretative sympathy with inanimate nature has been thought to be a modern faculty, and the sentiment of home an English virtue, exclusively. Both of these insularities of opinion are reproved by Catullus ; for both the qualities were elements of the old Italian spirit which he breathed. Tongues in trees and the passions of the flowers were as intelligible to him as to us, although they played a properly subordinate part, and were not allowed perpetually to intrude themselves, in his poetry. A few passages will be sufficient to show that he could understand the language of nature. He proved his possession of the power of interpretation when he wrote of

'the woods of Cytorus, where the leaves talk in whispers,'

or showed how, in the agony of destruction,

'the oak flings her arms aloft, and drops of sweat stand on the bark of the pine.'

The bride, in the Epithalamium, is as fair and dear

' as the myrtle branches, blossom-laden, which the wood-nymphs feed with honey-dew, to be their toy.'

When he himself was disenchanted, his love

' fell, as the flower on the skirt of a meadow falls, when the passing ploughshare has swept over it.'

In earlier times, while he still drank of the ' bitter-sweet ' cup of passion, he sang of kisses

' multitudinous as the stars which, while night holds her breath, peer upon stolen loves.'

Finally, the fineness of his susceptibility to natural effects is established by this description, even if it stood alone, of the sea at daybreak :—

' At first, as the waves move in slow procession at the command of the lenient breath of morning, they ring muffled chimes of laughter ; but, when the gale freshens, they crowd faster and faster on, and fling back the splendour as they float far away in front of the crimsoning day.'

In the second place, the creditable weakness, which we are not ashamed to impute to ourselves, of fondness for home, was freely confessed and tenderly exemplified by Catullus in the following poem, which he composed on returning, fatigued with travel, to his retreat on the Lago di Garda :—

' Sirmio, brightest jewel of all forelands or islands that have been begotten, in pellucid mere or on the illimitable ocean, by either water-god, how willing and how pleased am I to come home to you ! My senses scarcely persuade me that I have escaped from Thynia and the Bithynian steppes ; that all is safe, and I am looking upon you. Can there be a greater blessing than when the cords of care are snapt, and the mind lets slip its burden—when, spent with toil in far-off places, we come to our home sanctuary and find rest on the long-dreamed-of couch ? This moment is cheaply bought even by such costly pains. Welcome, lovely Sirmio ! make merry before your master ! make merry too, ye waves of the water of Lydia ! and let every jocund echo with which home is haunted break into laughing ! '

II.

' Odi et amo.'

WE pass now to the consideration of the personal poems of Catullus, in which he has immortalized, by truthfully recording, his sincere affections, passionate love, genuine hatreds, clear wit, and hearty merriment.

It was truly felt at this period, by all who were not content to pass their lives in lethargy, that there was only one place on earth where active existence was possible to a man ; that it was better to struggle and starve at Rome than batten on the pastures of all the rest of the world. There, and there alone, could be found news, amusement, political agitation, society— in a word, a life worth the trouble of living. How much more enjoyment than could be afforded by the stalled ox of provincial dulness was promised to himself by Catullus, when he invited his friend to dine with him off wit and a bare cupboard, in these lines :—

' You shall dine nobly at my table, Fabullus, in a few days, granting your stars are favourable, if you bring a noble and ample dinner with you—sunny maiden, and wine, and salt,

and funds of laughter. Bring only these, as I bid you, our
prince of good fellows, and you shall dine nobly : for your
Catullus' purse teems—with cobwebs. But you shall get in
return the essence of delight, or a something still more fragrant
and dainty. For I will give you a balm, vouchsafed to my
mistress by the Loves and Joys : once you catch its odour,
you will fall on your knees to the gods, and beg them to trans-
form you into absolute nose ! '

We are told by Juvenal that the worst of poverty
is that it makes men ridiculous. Following the canon
that most satire is as untrue as it is uninteresting,
we may believe that the absurdity of poverty is its
only palliative, and sense of humour the best fortitude.
At any rate Catullus, with empty and disappointed
pockets, could laugh at himself :—

' As I idled in the square, my friend Varus carried me away
to see his mistress ; whom I rather abruptly discovered to
be as full of wit as she was charming. When we arrived, we
talked after a desultory fashion, until Bithynia came on the
carpet—its present state and prospects, and how my purse had
prospered there. I answered, with simple truth, that there
was absolutely nothing to be got by native, governor, or subal-
tern. Why, I asked, should any of us come home with larded
locks, especially when our governor was a scoundrel, and did
not care a straw for his staff ? " But still," said they, " at any
rate you provided yourself, with what is believed to be a natural
product of your province. bearers for your chair." Adopting the
tone of a man of means in presence of the lady, " No," said I, " I
was not quite so miserably off, although I had fallen into a poor
province, as not to set up half-a-dozen straight-backed fellows.'
That was a bounce : for I never had a creature, at home or
abroad, able to shoulder an old bed leg. Upon this she asked
me, playing her wicked part to perfection, " Dear Catullus,

may I beg the loan of your bearers for a little while ? for I want to go in state to the feast of Serapis." "Truce !" cried I to the lady, "when I spoke just now of chattels of mine I was not thinking. My dear friend, Caius Cinna, is the nominal purchaser : but whether things are his or mine is all one to me ; for I use them as freely as if I bought for myself. You, however, are a mischievous dunce and a plague, for you do not forgive a slip of the tongue." '

Catullus' firm and close attachment to his friends is one of the leading traits of his character. The feeling of friendship was elevated by him into devotion, demanding a complete and fervent faith on both parts, and imposing in action a circle of attentions as obligatory as religious exercises. Breach of duty was not a sentimental injury, but sacrilege ; an unfaithful friend was not fickle, but an apostate. Such an apostate the Varus [1] of the preceding poem proved to be. Catullus shows in the following lines how deeply he felt the blow :—

' Unfaithful Alfenus, betrayer of companions so linked together, has your hard heart no compassion left for your once-cherished friend ? Do you not tremble to cast me off, and break your vows, like a traitor ? Treachery is irreligion, and finds no favour with the gods. Despising this truth, you abandon me to my fate in a sea of troubles. What now must poor humanity do ? Where can its faith be placed ? Did you not yourself bid me give my heart to you, ingrate, inveigling me into Love's perilous land by promises of perfect security ?

[1] Alfenus Varus, friend of the poets of this period, orator, and leading lawyer, had been a cobbler at Cremona. He rose to the consulate (39 B.C.) ; but Horace tells us that he remained a potential cobbler all his life.

Now, in spite of the past, you fall back, and suffer wind and rack to sweep into nothingness all that you have said and done ! Mark ! tho' you have forgotten, the gods remember, Honour remembers, and one day she shall overwhelm you with remorse for your crime.'

Catullus was happier in his friendship with Licinius Calvus. Calvus was a poet, and the two friends are always mentioned together. Had he lived longer—we have the testimony of Cicero as well as of Quintilian —he would have become one of the greatest of the world's orators. The extraordinary vehemence of his style is illustrated by the story according to which Vatinius, whose several prosecutions were conducted by Calvus, on one occasion sprang from his seat and appealed to the judges, exclaiming—" Am I to be damned just because that man has an eloquent tongue ? " The effect of this passionate oratory was heightened by the small stature and childish appearance of the man, as we learn from a few hendecasyllables of Catullus :—

'A fellow in the crowd made me laugh the other day, when Calvus had completed his magnificent impeachment of Vatinius : for, lifting both hands in amazement, " Great Gods ! " cried he, " little Cupid is an orator." '

Calvus must have exercised a great influence on the poetical culture of his friend ; we find the two in the habit of writing against one another in friendly rivalry and raillery. A wicked Christmas present from Calvus evoked these verses :—

'Calvus, you prince of wits, I would hate you, for your

wicked present, with all the spleen of Vatinius—if you were not more precious to me than my own eyes. What have I done or said to justify you in cruelly poisoning me with such a dose of poets? May the gods visit with a thousand plagues the vile client of yours who has sent you this horde of outcasts! But if (as I shrewdly guess) this original and exquisite offering was made you by the pedant Sulla, I do not murmur, but thank the stars that you have not thrown your pains away. I hold up in the sight of the great gods this portentous and predestinate volume, which you sent of all men to your friend Catullus, designing that he should die on the morrow, on the Saturnalia, the brightest day of the year! But no, jester! this act must bring you its consequences: for, at the first streak of day, I will fly to the publisher's shelves, make a packet of Caesii, Aquini, Suffenus—every literary drug—and send these tortures to pay you in kind.

You—in the meantime—hence and God speed ye, away to the regions from which you made your base egress, curse of our times, most vile poetasters!'

A much sadder theme, the early death of Calvus' young wife, Quintilia, called from his friend an expression of most tender sympathy and delicate consolation:—

'Dear Calvus, if any pleasure or any satisfaction can steal into the silent tomb out of our sense of loss, when with tender memory we recast our old passions and weep for the friendships we bade adieu to long ago, then surely Quintilia's sorrow for her summer fading cannot compare with her joy in the knowledge of your love.'

The aversions of Catullus were as strong as his attachments, and suffered no diminution of vivacity and no loss of colour when reflected in the mirror of his verse. Invective is now to be numbered among

the lost arts ; and perhaps can only enjoy true vitality
in a synthetic language.   Even among the ancients
but few grand masters of this art arose, separated by
wide intervals of time and place.   The last truly gifted
artist in opprobrium, if we may believe a profound
critic,[1] was Catullus.   Some of the most vigorous pro-
ductions affect our altered taste with no pleasure
or admiration.   Aurelius, the ' father of Inanition,'
Mamurra, whose gluttony would have swallowed the
British Isles at a meal, Furius, too miserly to board
a flea or a spider, are pilloried with indignities peculiar
to the older world.[2]   But we can sympathize with an
indignation that stigmatizes the practical joke, when
wit is conspicuous by its absence.   The fop, too, who,
because nature had decorated him with a white set of
teeth, grinned on every occasion down to a funeral,
received an appropriate castigation.   The absolute
stupidity of the Veronese boor, incapable of appre-
ciating the treasure he possessed in his beautiful
young wife, would have justly provoked his towns-
men to pitch him headlong from the bridge into the
bluest of the mire.   The terrible atrocities committed
on a helpless language by the mutilation of aspirates
is still unrepressed, and everybody knows the modern
replica of ' Arrius.'   But the most awful seals of
Catullus' wrath are opened against the bad poets, with
whom all times abound.   The direst curses are invoked

---

[1] Iambus cujus acerbitas in Catullo reperietur : Quint., *In.* x.
[2] See Munro on XXIX. for an appreciation of the meaning and
value of ancient defamation.

by him, or hecatombs are vowed, in the shape of execrable poems ; and they are relentlessly doomed to the death by fire or fish, or to fates still more horrible.

Chivalry was a flame that never burned in classic Greece or classic Rome. Its first spark was struck when the spirit of Christianity met the northern spirit in the west. Chivalrous love was a world into which not even our passionate poet ever broke, although there were times when he hovered on the verge. Deep personal affection he knew, for that was his ruin. Self-abnegation was the motive of the old Roman constitution. But affection was still sensuous, and devotion confined to patriotism, in ancient feeling. No brighter picture of the former exists than the 'Acme and Septimius' of Catullus, which by itself (and, indeed, his love-poems are but few) would place him in the front rank of the 'poets of love.' The greatest of English scholars has said, 'I look on Catullus as the peer of Alcaeus and Sappho' and bids us, to find his match in after-times, 'jump over the ages and come at once to Burns and Goethe.' Again he affirms, 'No love poems yet written are so exquisite, to my mind.' We may also borrow here the fine words of his criticism of the 'Acme and Septimius': 'Note the perfect unity and harmony of the thought, the magnificent motion of the rhythm. . . . Here again we have the ring of true passion. At the moment when the poem was written Caesar was invading Britain, and Crassus was off " partant pour la Syrie," to annihilate the Parthians. The youth of Rome were flocking east and west, some to share in the conquest and pillage of the new America : others to seek the gold and jewels of Asia. Septimius heeds it not. What is gain and glory to him, when Acme is on his bosom ? The whole of this exquisite poem well illustrates the fine observation of Hermogenes : ἡ δὲ γλυκύτης οἷον κάλλος τι τῆς ἀφελείας ἐστί.' Whenever Catullus speaks of love, there is nothing artificial, nothing strained in the tones ; no skilled analysis of emotion, no introduction of intellectual afterthoughts ; nothing but the simple and natural expression of strong excitement, nothing but what is becoming in one, like himself, who ' loved not wisely, but too well.'

In his own history there is no doubt that he lavished on Lesbia a love painfully out of proportion to the worth of its object. The praises of other women he heard with scornful incredulity, wondering at the obtuseness of the world. The restitution of his mistress' smile left him without a desire. The death of her linnet was a grave calamity and a theme of pretty pathetic verse to him, as it would have been to a romantic poet. In herself and in all that belonged to her she was dearer to him than his own eyes. He must certainly have sacrificed the use of his eyes in her presence, when he could believe that in her presence alone the medicine of life was to be found.

When Catullus fell from favour he made no stay at the intermediate fields of sighing now set apart for unhappy lovers : he leaped from heaven to hell, from love to hate. When he finally woke from the deception, he confronted the reality. He knew the delusion was of his own creation; and his detestation of the cause was almost mixed with wonder at its power. But he cannot forgive Clodia; much less Rufus, the author of his destruction. He persecutes both with a venom and brutality of purpose only explicable on the principle that the corruption of the best thing is the worst.

Yet in spite of the blight which thus fell upon the life of Catullus, there were some feelings which still remained fresh and healthy. His tender attentions to his friends and to his brother's memory still remained in leaf. The brother died at an early age, and was buried in the Troad—'that neutral graveyard of Europe and Asia.' Catullus made a pilgrimage to the tomb, where all that made his life worth living was laid, and his words then spoken will make a fitting conclusion :—

'Dear brother, I have passed through many peoples, I have crossed many seas, and I am here, at these untimely obsequies, that I may deliver to thee death's last tribute, and waste fruitless words on dust that cannot answer. For I know that blind chance has stolen away from me thy living self, O my poor brother, so loved and yet lost by me ! Behold ! these despairing sacrifices, which old custom on this soil enjoins, take, I pray thee—they are made wet with a brother's tears. And thus I greet thee and bid thee farewell, brother, for evermore.'

III.

' Quid est, Catulle ? quid moraris emori ?

THE secret of immortality can be learned more easily from Catullus than from any one, for he possessed nothing beside. To express a conceived object of sense or form of emotion in some plastic material which can be made to present an image, such as stone, metal or pigment, or words, which are images of images, with the simplicity of truth and the grace always accompanying true simplicity, is the conclusion of the whole duty of art. Of making many additions to this duty, some more and some less incongruous, but all supererogatory and laborious, there is no end among artists of every kind. But Catullus stands clear of this imputation. His experience of a passion or a conception is direct, spontaneous, and so free from superfluous pains and any appearance of effort. He reproduced with precision what he saw and felt with an unconfused sensibility ; and was successful because he did not strain to do more. The peculiar merit of his poetry consists in what we might call *incuriosa felicitas*. If he is one of the most perfect of poets, why then is he not one of the greatest of poets ? Because, when the power of execution is assumed, rank and precedence among artists is determined by the comparative elevation of their subject-matter; and Catullus' subjects are not of the highest sublimity. But whatever title we give him must be perpetual, for his works have the immortality of truth.

QUAESTIO I.

CATULLUS IN RELATION TO GREEK LITERATURE.

'Saepe tibi studiose animo venante requirens
Carmina uti possem mittere Battiadae.'

IF the web of history could be unravelled, and we
might speculate afresh on what is past, nothing would
appear so certain as this : that Rome, but for her
contact with Greece, instead of producing a literature
whose influence has pervaded and ruled the later
world of letters with almost sovereign authority, would
have had no literature whatsoever worthy of the
name. Whatever native inspiration the Italians
possessed, they wanted the proper forms of expression.
Greek genius had created these forms for itself : the
Roman borrowed them, and used them, in his own
way, to supply his need. Roman poetry is far from a
lifeless imitation of Greek poetry ; but the Roman
poet could not work without a model. At first wrong
models were chosen. The earlier and greater Greek
literature rather defied than assisted Latin literary
effort. It was too spontaneous for conscious endeavour

to learn from it ; its Hellenic characters were too
deeply stamped to be effaced or changed in order to
suit Roman purposes. As long therefore as only the
earlier Greek epic and drama were studied by the first
Latin poets, so long—men of genius though they
were—they failed. But the last generation of the
Republic turned for instruction to the school of
Alexandria. There, by royal command, a cosmopolitan
university of letters had arisen, whose members had
specially devoted themselves to the critical examination of the modes of literary composition, and had
provided a series of ' studies ' in almost every literary
form. Alexandrine poetry was not written by men of
the highest order of genius : it was artificial, unreal,
often spoilt by over-precision and pedantry. Its power,
though indeed it has left much which the world will
not willingly let die, lies in execution rather than
creation. But the Roman poets seized the forms which
the Alexandrines taught them, made them their own,
and breathed into them the freshness of a newer life.
More than this, they were enabled by Alexandria to
reach and reap with profit the older literature of
Greece. Thus Roman literature, in its best originality,
became possible ; but the debt of Rome to Alexandria
is ever shown by a constant searching after the right
model, discernible in all Latin poetry from its beginning to its close.

This debt was freely confessed by Propertius, Ovid,
Virgil ; but by none so frankly as by the most original
of Roman poets, Catullus. He had learned enough

from the Alexandrine poets to respect them as masters
of style. How much he depended on them for guid-
ance (far greater poet as he was than they) is curiously
illustrated by the lines (CXVI. 1-2) prefixed to these
remarks. There, wishing to find a means of winning
over Gellius and appeasing his hostility, he does not
send him a poem written from his own heart and
appealing to the heart of his enemy, but tries *to find
poems of Callimachus* (for translation or imitation)
that will serve the same end. In LXV., also, he seems
to imply that he does not care to compose without his
books.

But Catullus is no mere disciple of Alexandria. He
is a student also of the grand classical writers of
Greece, and rises nearer to their elevation than any
Alexandrine had done. Still further, throughout all
his employment of acquired culture, he is a great
original poet.

[1] ' In what then, we may ask, is Catullus a follower

[1] I venture to borrow these eloquent words from the Commentary of Professor Ellis, of whose work on Catullus it may
truly be said, κτῆμα ἐς ἀεὶ μᾶλλον ἢ ἀγώνισμα ἐς τὸ παραχρῆμα
ἀκούειν ξύγκειται, and I take this opportunity of acknowledging
my obligations to him. Most of the views expressed in this
volume were formed before the appearance of his valuable
commentary : where I have borrowed from him I have
religiously stated my debt, where I have found myself in
accordance with him I have felt both pleasure and confirma-
tion, where I have differed from him I have done so with
diffidence. In the following tables I have obtained a certain
number of parallelisms, which I had not before known, from
his notes.

of the Alexandrine poets ? Not in their pedantry, for he is without a trace of it ; nor in their obscurity, for he is rarely obscure ; nor in their scrupulous choice of the least obvious expression, for all he says is simple and straightforward, . . . nor in their cosmopolitan Hellenism which has ceased to think of individual autonomy and cares only to influence the world, for he can never forget that he is an Italian, a Veronese, above all a Roman citizen ; nor in their flattery of the great, for he is never happier than when he is scoffing at worthless nobles or reviling Caesar : nor even in the tone of their love poetry, for, with some unimportant exceptions, he expresses not a Theocritean sentimentalism, which feeds on the thought of a beloved object, and half contents itself with the shadow when the reality is away ; but rather a full feeling of the enjoyment of life, the sensuous even coarse delights of a love present and palpable, the melancholy which attends the thought of death as ending them, and the various episodes of a lover's life, its quarrels, reproaches, and reconciliation, or despair. So far as these love-poems are Greek at all, they are like the early Greek lyrics, not the latest compositions of Alexandria ; and we are left to the conclusion that Catullus is, except in the elegies, and to some extent in the " Peleus and Thetis," less indebted to Alexandrine models than is generally supposed : amongst his personal friends Cinna, in the succeeding generation, Virgil and Propertius, show far clearer proofs of direct and conscious imitation.'

We do not know how much Catullus modelled upon originals now lost; but parallelisms—which do not seem accidental—between him and extant Alexandrine writers (A), and between Catullus and the older Greek writers (B), are shown in the following tables.

A.

CALLIMACHUS.

Cat.	Call.	Cat.	Call.
with III. 5	cf. Hym. Di. 211	with LXIV. 283	cf. Hym. Ap. 81
,, LXI. 76	,, Hym. Ap. 5	,, ,, 389	,, ,, ,, 76 sqq.
,, ,, 88	,, Hym. Di. 249	,, LXVI.	,, Βερ. Πλοκ.
,, LXII. 37	,, Frag. 52	,, LXX.	,, Epig. 26
,, LXIV. 62	,, Hym. Ap. 22		

APOLLONIUS.

Cat.	Apoll.	Cat.	Apoll.
with LXIV. 4	cf. III. 347	with LXIV. 132	cf. IV. 361
,, ,, 9	,, I. 111	,, ,, 160	,, III. 677
,, ,, 51 sqq.	,, I. 730 sqq.	,, ,, 172	,, ,, 773
,, ,, 53	,, IV. 433	,, ,, 174	,, IV. 523
,, ,, 87 sqq.	,, III. 275 sqq.	,, ,, 261	,, I. 290
,, ,, 95 sqq.	,, IV. 445 sqq.	,, ,, 296 sqq.	,, II. 1250 sqq.
,, ,, 199	,, ,, 1683	,, ,, 319	,, III. 254

PHILETAS.[1]

Cat.	Phil.
with III. 12	cf. Frag. (Sch.)

LYCOPHRON.[2]

Cat.	Lyc.
with LXIV. 165	cf. Alex.

[1] Probably oftener than we know from the remains of Philetas.
[2] Probably oftener than we know from the remains of Lycophron.

THEOCRITUS.

Cat.	Theoc.	Cat.	Theoc.
with III. 12	cf. { XVII. 120 / XII. 19	with LXIV. 97	cf. XV. 100
,, XI. 1.	,, XXIX. 37	,, ,, 155	,, XXIII. 9
,, XVII. 15	,, XI. 20	,, ,, 260	,, XXVI. 13
,, XXX. 10	,, XXIX. 35	,, ,, 261	,, III. 51
,, XLV. 20	,, XII. 15	,, ,, 272	,, XIII. 11
,, LXI. 5	,, XVIII. 58	,, ,, 292	,, XXII. 41
,, LXIV. 94	,, III. 17	,, LXVIII B. 77	,, III. 41

BION.

Cat.	Bion.
with III. 14	cf. I. 55

MOSCHUS.

Cat.	Mos.	Cat.	Mos.
with V. 4-6	cf. III. 106	with LXIV. 13	cf. II. 118

B.

HOMER.

Cat.	Hom.	Cat.	Hom.
with IX. 9	cf. O. XVI. 15	with LXIV. 225	cf. Il. XVIII. 23
,, XXV. 11	,, Il. IV. 139, XI. 388	,, ,, 229	,, Il. V. 260
,, XXX. 4	,, O. XIV. 83	,, ,, 240	,, Il. V. 522 sqq.
,, L. 9 sqq.	,, Il. XXIV. 3-6, 127	,, ,, 260	,, H. C. 476
,, L. 12	,, Il. IX. 240	,, ,, 268	,, O. IV. 47
,, LXI. 92	,, Il. XI. 68	,, ,, 270	,, { Il. IV. 422 sqq. / Il. VII. 63
,, ,, 198	,, Il. IV. 127	,, ,, 299	,, O. III. 381
,, LXII. 26	,, Il XXII. 316	,, ,, 309	,, H. C. 182
,, LXIII. 39	,, { H. C. 69 / O. XI. 16	,, ,, 340	,, Il. XIII. 289
,, LXIV. 9	,, H. Aph. 12	,, ,, 350	,, Il. XVII. 122
,, ,, 13	,, O. XII. 171	,, ,, 354	,, Il. XI. 67
,, ,, 20	,, Il. XVIII. 132	,, ,, 360	,, Il. XXI. 16, 218
,, ,, 22-4	,, H. M. 579	,, ,, 368	,, Il. XVI. 100
,, ,, 64	,, H. C. 40	,, LXV. 13	,, O. XIX. 518
,, ,,106sq.	,, Il. V. 560	,, LXVIII B. 20	Il. XV. 681
,, ,, 132	,, O. IV. 103	,, ,, 74	{ O. XI. 621 / H. C. 164 sqq.
,, ,, 155	,, Il. XVI. 33	,, LXVIII B. 101	cf. Il. V. 440
,, ,, 162	,, Il. III. 409	,, ,, 120	cf. O. XXIV. 435
,, ,, 180	,, Il. I. 157	,, LXXIII. 3	,, O. IV. 695
,, ,, 206	,, Il. I. 528		

HESIOD.

Cat.	Hes.	Cat.	Hes.
with LXI. 20	cf. Fragment.	with LXIV. 398 sqq.	cf. Ἔργ.
,, LXIV. 88	,, Ἔργ. 517		171 sqq.

PINDAR.

Cat.	Pind.	Cat.	Pind.
with LXI. 206	cf. Ol. II. ad fin.	with LXVIII B. 79 sq.	cf. Ol. XI. 8(
,, LXIV. 323	,, Ol. X. 56		

SAPPHO.

Cat.	Sap.	Cat.	Sap.
with LI.	cf. Fragment.[1]	with LXXIII. 5	cf. Fragment.[1]
,, LXI. 88	,, ,,		

AESCHYLUS.

Cat.	Aesch.	Cat.	Aesch.
with LXIV. 9	cf. P. V. 475	with LXVIII B. 21	cf. Ag. 901
,, ,, 276	,, Ag. 1150	,, CVII. 3	,, Choe. 372
,, ,, 297	,, P. V. 6, 112 sqq.		

SOPHOCLES.

Cat.	Soph.
with LXII. 15	cf. Trach. 272
,, LXX. 4	,, Fragment.[1]

EURIPIDES.

Cat.	Eur.	Cat.	Eur.
with XXII. 18 sq.	cf. Frag. 1029	with XIV. 21	cf. I. A. 700
,, LX.	{ Med. 1343 ,, { Bac. 988	,, ,, 30	,, Or. 1377
,, LXI. 10	,, I. A. 1041	,, ,, 95 sq.	,, Frag. Aeol.
,, ,, 18	,, And. 275	,, ,, 149 sq.	,, Med. 476
,, ,, 88	,, Hec. 635	,, ,, 153	,, Tro. 450
,, LXII. 16	,, Phoen. 728	,, ,, 178	,, Med. 502
,, LXIII. 53	,, Tro. 1066		sqq.
,, LXIV. 4	,, Med. 1. sq.	,, ,, 257	,, Bac. pass.
		,, ,, 351	,, Supp. 826 [2]

[1] Given in note.

[2] We may here add, *with* XXVII. *cf.* DIPHILUS Frag. (Mein. IV. 402); *wit*
XXXIX. 16 *cf.* MENAND. (IV. 342) ; *with* L. 21 *cf.* ANTIMACHUS, 588.

On all these passages it is to be remarked, in the words of Ellis, ' that Catullus, even when he translates most literally, transfuses his own nature into the words, and remains as Italian as before.'

QUAESTIO II.

CATULLUS' POSITION IN LATIN LITERATURE.

'Lepidum novum libellum.'

EARLIER Roman poetry, as we have seen, failed for the most part for lack of form. It was also confined in subject, and attempted only the epos, the drama, satire, and (in a limited sense) the epigram. In the age of Catullus, better directed study resulted in a truer and larger sense of the various forms of literary composition; and the lyric, the idyll, and the elegy were added to Roman literature. This new birth of Latin poetry is represented to us by Catullus alone. The works of all the other writers of his time have been lost; and the same irony of fate, which gave us Hesiod in place of Archilochus and the Greek lyrists, has preserved Cicero's translation of Aratus, instead of the works of Bibaculus and Calvus. Catullus was, however, as far as we can learn, far greater than the rest of his contemporaries; and should be regarded, therefore, as the first in time, as well as in genius, of Roman lyric, elegiac, idyllic, and epigrammatic poets.

That he should have shown much literary resemblance to the more ancient Roman verse-writers is, therefore, as unlikely in itself as it is disproved by his writings. But he shared their native boldness and independence of spirit ; and his wide reading did not leave him ignorant of what they had done. With LXIV. 163 compare PACUVIUS' *Niptra ;* with LXIV. 191 compare PACUVIUS *Il.* fr. ix. ; with LXIV. 291 compare Ennius, quoted by Gellius, N. A. XIII. xx. 13.

With PLAUTUS and TERENCE Catullus had more in common. Like them (but without their archaic colour) he employed the idiom of ordinary life, which, with but little change, he elevated into the language of poetry. Parallelisms are—

PLAUTUS.

Cat.		Plaut.	Cat.		Plaut.
with X. 23	cf.	Asin. III. iii. 67	with XXVII. 5	cf.	Mil. Gl. IV. i. 27
„ „ 29	„	Amph. I. i. 230	„ LXIII. 46	„	Epid. v. i. 36
„ XIII. 7	„	Aul. I. ii. 156	„ „ 78	„	Men.v.ii.109 sq.
„ XVII. 22	„	{ Asin. II. iv. 59	„ LXV. 4	„	Epid. IV. i. 4
		{ Capt. III. iv. 28	„ LXVIII B. 84	„	Trin. 100
„ XXV. 11	„	Pseud. I. v. 131			

TERENCE.

Cat.		Ter.	Cat.		Ter.
with III. 5	cf.	Ad. IV. v. 67	with XXX. 6	cf.	And. II. v. 14
„ IX. 10	„	Eun.v.viii.1, &c.	„ LXI. 62	„	Ph. IV. v. 12
„ XI. 17	„	And. v. iii. 18	„ „ 211	„	Ph. II. ii. 33
„ XVII. 12 sq.	„	Eun. v. viii. 49	„ LXXVI. 20	„	Ad. II. i. 34
„ XXX. 5	„	Eun. II. iii. 17			

LUCRETIUS, between whom and Catullus there are parallelisms which cannot have been accidental, died less than a year before the younger poet, and his poem

" could not have been published in the author's life-
time " (Munro). Yet Munro affirms that Catullus
imitated Lucretius. Before this view can be accepted
we must believe that in the course of a few months,
and during the illness which proved fatal to Catullus
(unless he died a violent death, for which there is no
evidence), he studied Lucretius' great philosophical
work throughout—for the parallelisms are found in
every book of that work—and then wrote his longest
and most elaborated poem,[1] the ' Peleus and Thetis,'
if not also XXXIV. and (this would be incredible) LXI.
Munro admits that the philosopher Cicero himself
could not have read the ' " De Natura " four months
after the death of Lucretius,' if he had not ' had
anything to do with preparing it for publication.'
Catullus, too, shows no taste for philosophy, no liking
for the more archaic Roman poetry. Still further,
there is no reason to think that he wrote his idyll last
of all his writings ; it was quite as probably one of his
earliest creations. Munro himself admits that ' many
of Catullus' occasional poems on the other hand had
in all likelihood been seen by Lucretius.' Most probably, then, Catullus never read Lucretius ; who, it
must also be remarked, if he imitated Catullus at all,
would be most likely to confine himself chiefly to the
hexameter poem. The parallelisms are given below :—

---

[1] Or, at least, the ' Ariadne ' episode, which could not have
been at all suggested by Lucretius, and (see LXIV. introduction) is not as much out of place as is generally supposed.

LUCRETIUS.

Cat.	Lucr.	Cat.	Lucr.
with XXXIV. 15	*cf.* V. 575	*with* LXIV. 179	*cf.* I. 718
,, LX. 2	,, V. 892	,, ,, 187	,, I. 110
,, LXI. 127	,, II. 368	,, ,, 208	,, III. 304
,, LXIV. 63	,, VI. 34, 74	,, ,, 210 ⎱	
,, ,, 126 ⎫	⎧ III. 57	,, ,, 232 ⎰	,, II. 581
,, ,, 196 ⎬	,, ⎨ ,, 81	,, ,, 239 ⎰	
,, ,, 203 ⎬	⎩ VI. 16		⎧ II. 618, 636
,, ,, 222 ⎭		,, ,, 262	⎨ IV. 546
	⎧ I. 631	,, ,, 263	,, I. 11
,, ,, 166	,, ⎨ III. 626, 630	,, ,, 295	,, III. 824
	⎩ IV. 460		

The relative position of HORACE and Catullus in
Latin lyrical poetry has, in recent discussions, been
made one of rivalry for the first place.   That Horace
was strongly adverse to the Alexandrine school, of
which no imitative trace is found in him, cannot be
doubted.   But (Epist. I. i.) it is equally certain that he
was at least as strongly adverse to the earlier and
untutored Latin poetry.   In his literary criticisms and
in his odes he omitted to mention Catullus with honour
as a lyric poet, partly because Catullus was a Republican, partly because the elder poet wrote mostly in
metres unused by the Augustan ; chiefly because
Horace [1] devoted himself specially to imitation of the
elder Greek lyrics.   Catullus, however, was of infinitely higher lyrical genius than Horace, and this is
shown in the conscious imitations by the latter
exhibited in the following table.

[1] It is, however, curious that Horace, the anti-Alexandrine,
was more Alexandrine in his artificial, unreal and elaborate
lyrics than Catullus, the student of Alexandria.   See Munro
'Elucidations of C.' ad fin., for a comparative criticism of the
two poets.

HORACE.

Cat.	Hor.	Cat.	Hor.
with IV.	cf. Od. I. xiv. 12 sq.	with XXXVI. 5	cf. Od. I. xvi.
„ v. 46	„ Od. IV. vii. 13	„ XLIII. 1 sq.	cf. Sat. I. ii. 93
„ XI. 1 sq.	„ Od. II. vi. 1 sq.	„ XLIV. 12	cf. Sat. I. vii. 1
„ „ 11	„ Od. I. xxxv. 29	„ XLV.	„ Od. I. xxii.
„ XXII. 16	„ Epis. II. ii. 106	„ LI. 5	„ Od. I. xxii. 23
„ „ 21	{ Sat. II. iii. 299 / cf. Persius IV. 24	„ LII. 1	„ Od. III. xxvii. 5.
„ XXV. 8	„ Sat. I. vi. 79	„ LXI. 20	{ Epod. X. 1 / Od. I. xv. 5
„ XXVII.6	„ Epis. I. xix. 10	„ LXII. 53	„ Od. IV. v. 30
„ XXX. 9	„ Epis. I. xviii. 58	„ LXIV. 27	„ Od. II. xvii. 4
„ XXXIV.	„ Od. I. xxi.	„ „ 358	„ Od. IV. iv. 37
„ „ 13	{ C. S. i. 3 / Od. III. xxii. 2	„ „ 367	„ Od. II. iv. 11
		„ LXVI. 48	„ Sat. II. i. 43

The imitations of Catullus by the other Augusta[n] writers were very numerous. In VIRGIL, PROPERTIUS, TIBULLUS and OVID, we find at least the following :—

VIRGIL.

Cat.	Virg.	Cat.	Virg.
with IV. 12	cf. Ec. VIII. 22	with LXII. 56	cf. G. II. 299
„ „ 13	„ G. II. 437	„ LXIII. 2, &c.	„ A. IX. 616 sq.
„ VII. 12	„ Ec. VII. 28	„ „ 41	„ A. IV. 135
„ IX. 4	„ A. VII. 335	„ „ 53	„ A. VI. 179
„ XI. 7	{ A. VI. 800 / G. IV. 292	„ „ 83	„ A. XII. 6
„ „ 11	„ Ec. I. 66	„ LXIV. 4	„ A. VIII. 518
„ „ 22	„ A. IX. 435	„ „ 12	„ G. I. 97
„ XXX. 8	„ A. IV. 298	„ „ 22	„ A. VI. 649
„ LX. 2	„ Ec. VI. 67	„ „ 44	„ A. II. 299
„ LXI. 7	„ A. I. 694	„ „ 47	„ A. I. 637
„ „ 28	„ Ec. X. 12	„ „ 51 sq.	„ A. VIII.625,&
„ „ 54	„ A. III. 514	„ „ 63	„ A. IV. 532
„ „ 131	„ Ec. VIII. 30	„ „ 77 sq.	„ A. VI. 29 sq.
„ „ 208	„ G. II. 105	„ „ 108	{ G. I. 481 / A. IV. 442
„ „ 216	„ A. IV. 328	„ „ 109	„ A. V. 449
„ „ 219	„ Ec. IV. 61	„ „ 114	„ A. VI. 29 sq.
„ „ 231	„ Ec. III. 111	„ „ 116	„ A. V. 591
„ LXII. 1	„ Ec. VI. 86	„ „ 142	„ A. IV. 316
„ „ 7	„ Ec. VIII. 302	„ „ 157	„ A. VII. 302
„ „ 15	„ A. IV. 285	„ „ 163	„ A. V. 566
„ „ 24	„ A. II. 746	„ „ 167	„ A. I. 408

Cat.		Virg.	Cat.		Virg.
with	LXIV. 172	cf. A. IV. 657	with	LXIV. 400	cf. G. II. 510
,,	,, 180	,, A. IV. 508	,,	LXV. 12	,, G. III. 518
,,	,, 188	,, A. I. 91	,,	,, 23	,, G. I. 203
,,	,, 206	,, A. IX. 106	,,	LXVI. 23	,, A. IV. 66
,,	,, 217	,, A. V. 724	,,	,, 39	,, A. VI. 460
,,	,, 227	,, A. IX. 500	,,	,, 47	,, Ec. III. 16
,,	,, 228	,, A. IX. 582	,,	,, 55	,, A. V. 838
,,	,, 289	,, G. I. 20	,,	LXVIII B, 30	,, A. I. 566
,,	,, 327	,, Ec. IV. 46	,,	,, 79	,, A. IV. 599
,,	,, 342	{ ,, A. VII. 807	,,	,, 109	,, Ec. III. 70
		{ ,, A. XII. 345	,,	,, 111	,, G. I. 495
,,	,, 384	,, A. III. 373			

PROPERTIUS.

Cat.	Prop.	Cat.	Prop.
with XIII. 12	cf. II. xix. 17	with LXIII. 65	cf. I. xvi. 30 sq.
,, XXV. 12	,, I. xi. 9	,, LXIV. 9	,, II. xii. 7
,, XL. 6	,, I. v. 3	,, LXV. 14	,, III. x. 8
,, XLV. 9	,, II. iii. 23	,, LXVI. 74	,, I. viii. 21
,, ,, 21	,, II. xiv. 3	,, LXVIII. 31	,, I. xi. 19
,, LX. 2	,, IV. iv. 40	,, LXVIII B. 10	,, II. vi. 35
,, LXII. 24	,, IV. viii. 55		

TIBULLUS.

Cat.	Tib.	Cat.	Tib.
with XXII. 5 sq.	cf. III. i. 9	with LXIV. 193	cf. III. vi. 41
,, LX. 2	,, III. iv. 89	,, ,, 314	,, II. i. 64
,, LXIV. 157	,, III. iv. 85 sq.		

OVID.

Cat.		Ovid.	Cat.		Ovid.
with	IV.	cf. Trist. I. x.	with	LXIV. 115	cf. M. VIII. 159 sq.
,,	XVII. 16	,, M. XIII. 790, 798	,,	,, 128 sq.	,, H. X. passim
,,	XL. 5	,, Tr. III. xiv. 23	,,	,, 178	,, M. VIII. 113 sq.
,,	LXII. 46	,, M. III. 353	,,	,, 261	,, A. A. II. 601
,,	LXIII. 10	{ ,, F. IV. 342	,,	,, 314	,, M. VI. 22
		{ ,, Ib. 458	,,	,, 324	,, Pont. I. viii. 17
,,	,, 92	,, F. IV. 116			
,,	LXIV. 21	,, M. XI. 224	,,	,, 340	,, M. X. 706
,,	,, 45	,, M. II.	,,	LXVIII. 29	,, A. III. v. 42
,,	,, 68	,, M. IV. 342	,,	LXVIII. B. 109	,, H. VIII. 3
,,	,, 72	,, M. I. 641	,,	LXXVI. 12	,, R. A. 657
,,	,, 92	,, M. VII. 86 sq.	,,	,, 23 sq.	,, A. III. xiv.
,,	,, 99	,, F. I. 417	,,	CVIII. 6	,, Ib. 167

Imitations of Catullus in the VIRGILIAN CATA-
LECTA and in MARTIAL are incessant, and are too
numerous to admit or require statement in this place.
Outlines of poems, ideas, phrases, and words are borrowed freely and constantly from Catullus, whom the
authors seem wisely to regard as the first Latin poet
who struck out the true lines in which Latin poetry
might run with success.

LIFE.

GAIUS VALERIUS CATULLUS was born at Verona (87 or 84 B.C.) of a good family. We hear of his father as the friend and frequently the host of Julius Caesar. The poet came to Rome as soon as he became his own master, and there made his settled home. There he had the society of Calvus, Cinna, Cornificius, young Asinius Pollio, Alfenus Varus, Caelius Rufus, and, perhaps, Cicero; and there he fell into the toils of Clodia, the wife of the consul Metellus Celer, and the Lesbia of the poems. We hear of visits to his villa at Tibur, to another villa at Sirmio, and also to Verona. The pleasures of the town seem to have kept him always poor; and he followed the praetor Memmius to Bithynia, which had newly become a Roman province, in the vain hope of mending his fortunes (57 B.C.). On his homeward journey he went to see his brother's grave in the Troad, passed through the famous cities of Asia, and returned in his yacht to Sirmio (56 B.C.). This retreat he left for Rome, where he seems to have spent the remainder of his short life. We know that he died young, perhaps (as is said) at the age of thirty; and, as his poems contain no certain allusion to events of later date than 54 B.C., we may believe that to have been the year of his death.

ADVERTISEMENT TO TEXT.

THE Gothic malice of mice and men has played havoc with the manuscripts of Catullus. No MS. containing any of his works now exists of earlier date than the *Thuanean* (in the Paris Library), considered to have been written about 900 A.D., which is an anthology of Latin poems, but of Catullus includes only LXII. About fifty years later the French monk Rather, Bishop of Verona, speaks of having read our poet for the first time. Soon after 1300 A.D. a MS. of Catullus was brought to Verona, discovered, apparently, in some distant place, hidden under a bushel-measure:—

Versus domini Benevuti de Campexanis de Vicentia de resurrectione Catulli, poetae Veronensis :

    Ad patriam venio longis de finibus exul :
      Causa mei reditus compatriota fuit,
    Scilicet a calamis tribuit cui Francia nomen
      Quique notat turbae praetereuntis iter.
    Quo licet ingenio vestrum celebrate Catullum,
      Cujus sub modio clausa papyrus erat.

These verses are found in the MS. called *Sangermanensis* (now in the Paris Library), written 1375 A.D. ; which the writer says he copied ' a corruptissimo ex emplari,' (his original being perhaps the Veronese MS. above mentioned, which, unfortunately, was soon lost again), that being the only MS. extant to which he could have access.   The only other MS. which may be ascribed to the fourteenth century is one in the Bodleian Library, Oxford (generally known as O).   Although these are our best authorities, yet both contain *variae lectiones*, and are often wrong.   Some dozen other MSS. date from 1411 to 1463 A.D.—the first printed edition was published 1472 A.D.—but all are obscured by corrections, interpolated, and full of errors.   There are many, still less valuable, of later date.

Even the agreement of Catullus' best MSS.[1] is not enough to establish a doubtful reading. Many necessary corrections were made by the early Italian scholars, and much too has been done by scholars of the present century, whose attentions have at least atoned for the neglect of the previous hundred years.   Many passages still admit conjecture, which, however, in recent editions has been perhaps too largely employed.   The old maxim, indeed, that an emendation ' must account for every letter,' cannot fairly be applied in the present state of our manuscript evidence; and perhaps the *ipsis-*

---

[1] Even in these words are wrongly divided ; syllables are wrongly doubled or not doubled ; there are mutilations or confusing contractions of the ends of words ; proper names are constantly corrupted ; and among commoner interchanges of letters we find confounded a—co, a—e, a—ei, c—r, c—s—sc, c—t, d—cl, d—p, e—o, i—y, l—n—u, li—ll, n—ni—m, n—r, m—s final, p—t, r—t—rt—tr, c—i, t—s final.

sima verba of Catullus are in some cases very different from the mutilated presentations of the extant codices. But it would be inadvisable to admit into a text even attractive readings which differ widely from those of our best, if still inadequate, authorities. The following text will be found to adhere (except in undoubted corrections) to the best MSS. ; which have been made accessible by recent and most valuable *apparatus critici*, especially that of ELLIS.

In spelling, all peculiarities have been avoided. These occur largely in the extant MSS., and some of them *may* have been derived from early MSS., but the probability is infinitely remote that they are Catullian. For the purposes of the present edition, their retention would be worse than useless. The use of *j* and *v* for the consonantal *i* and *u* may be pardoned on the score of convenience.

SELECT POEMS

CATULLUS.

I.

Cui dono lepidum novum libellum
Arido modo pumice expolitum ?
Corneli, tibi ; namque tu solebas
Meas esse aliquid putare nugas,
Jam tum cum ausus es unus Italorum   5
Omne aevum tribus explicare cartis
Doctis, Juppiter, et laboriosis.
Quare habe tibi quicquid hoc libelli ;
Qualecumque (quidem,) patrona virgo,   *quod o*
Plus uno maneat perenne saeclo.   10

II.

opanow   *pet*
Passer, deliciae meae puellae,
Quicum ludere, quem in sinu tenere,
Cui primum digitum dare appetenti
Et acres solet incitare morsus,
Cum desiderio meo nitenti *bright-eyed*   5
Carum nescio quid libet jocari
Et solaciolum sui doloris.
Credo : ut, cum gravis acquiescet ardor,
œ

Tecum ludere sicut ipsa possem
Et tristes animi levare curas.   10
Tam gratum est mihi quam ferunt puellae
Pernici aureolum fuisse malum,
Quod zonam soluit diu ligatam.

emoft

III.

Lugete, o Veneres Cupidinesque
Et quantum est hominum venustiorum.
Passer mortuus est meae puellae,
Passer, deliciae meae puellae,
Quem plus illa oculis suis amabat :   5
Nam mellitus erat suamque norat
Ipsam tam bene quam puella matrem,
Nec sese a gremio illius movebat,
Sed circumsiliens modo huc modo illuc
Ad solam dominam usque pipilabat.   10
Qui nunc it per iter tenebricosum
Illuc, unde negant redire quemquam.
At vobis male sit, malae tenebrae
Orci, quae omnia bella devoratis :
Tam bellum mihi passerem abstulistis.   15
O factum male, io miselle passer,
Tua nunc opera meae puellae
Flendo turgiduli rubent ocelli.

pretty

IV.

Phaselus ille, quem videtis, hospites,
Ait fuisse navium celerrimus,

Neque ullius natantis impetum trabis
Nequisse praeterire, sive palmulis
Opus foret voláre sive linteo.   5
Et hoc negat minacis Adriatici
Negare litus insulasve Cycladas
Rhodumque nobilem horridamque Thraciam
Propontida, trucemve Ponticum sinum,
Ubi iste post phaselus antea fuit   10
Comata silva : nam Cytorio in jugo
Loquente saepe sibilum edidit coma.
Amastri Pontica et Cytore buxifer
Tibi haec fuisse et esse cognitissima
Ait phaselus : ultima ex origine   15
Tuo stetisse dicit in cacumine,
Tuo imbuisse palmulas in aequore,
Et inde tot per impotentia freta
Erum tulisse, laeva sive dextera
Vocaret aura, sive utrumque Juppiter   20
Simul secundus incidisset in pedem ;
Neque ulla vota litoralibus deis
Sibi esse facta, cum veniret a mari
Novissime hunc ad usque limpidum lacum.
Sed haec prius fuere : nunc recondita   25
Senet quiete seque dedicat tibi
Gemelle Castor et gemelle Castoris.

V.

Vivamus mea Lesbia atque amemus,
Rumoresque senum severiorum
Omnes unius aestimemus assis.

Soles occidere et redire possunt :
Nobis, cum semel occidit brevis lux,   5
Nox est perpetua una dormienda.
Da mi basia mille, deinde centum,
Dein mille altera, dein secunda centum,
Deinde usque altera mille, deinde centum.
Dein, cum milia multa fecerimus,   10
Conturbabimus illa, ne sciamus,
Aut ne quis malus invidere possit,
Cum tantum sciet esse basiorum.

VII.

Quaeris, quot mihi basiationes
Tuae, Lesbia, sint satis superque.
Quam magnus numerus Libyssae harenae
Laserpiciferis jacet Cyrenis,
Oraclum Jovis inter aestuosi   5
Et Batti veteris sacrum sepulcrum ;
Aut quam sidera multa, cum tacet nox,
Furtivos hominum vident amores :
Tam te basia multa basiare
Vesano satis et super Catullo est,   10
Quae nec pernumerare curiosi
Possint, nec mala fascinare lingua.

IX.

Verani, omnibus e meis amicis
Antistans mihi milibus trecentis,
Venistine domum ad tuos Penates
Fratresque unanimos anumque matrem ?

Venisti. O mihi nuntii beati.   5
Visam te incolumem audiamque Hiberum
Narrantem loca, facta, nationes,
Ut mos est tuus ; applicansque collum
Jucundum os oculosque saviabor.
O quantum est hominum beatiorum,   10
Quid me laetius est beatiusve ?

X.

Varus me meus ad suos amores
Visum duxerat e foro otiosum,
Scortillum, ut mihi tum repente visum est,
Non sane illepidum neque invenustum.
Huc ut venimus, incidere nobis   5
Sermones varii, in quibus, quid esset
Jam Bithynia, quomodo se haberet,
Et quonam mihi profuisset aere.
Respondi, id quod erat, nihil nec ipsis
Nec praetoribus esse nec cohorti.   10
Cur quisquam caput unctius referret ?
'At certe tamen,' inquiunt, ' quod illic
Natum dicitur esse, comparasti   15
Ad lecticam homines.' Ego, ut puellae
Unum me facerem beatiorem,
'Non,' inquam, ' mihi tam fuit maligne,
Ut, provincia quod mala incidisset,
Non possem octo homines parare rectos.'   20
At mi nullus erat neque hic neque illic

Fractum qui veteris pedem grabati
In collo sibi collocare posset.
Hic illa, ut decuit cinaediorem,
'Quæso,' inquit, 'mihi, mi Catulle, paulum   25
Istos commoda, nam volo ad Sarapim
Deferri.' 'Mane me,' inquii puellae,
'Istud quod modo dixeram me habere—
Fugit me ratio—meus sodalis
Cinna—est Gaius—is sibi paravit.   30
Verum utrum illius an mei, quid ad me?
Utor tam bene quam mihi pararim.
Sed tu insulsa male et molesta vivis,
Per quam non licet esse neglegentem.'

XI.

Furi et Aureli, comites Catulli,
Sive in extremos penetrabit Indos,
Litus ut longe resonante Eoa
where
            Tunditur unda,
Sive in Hyrcanos Arabesque molles,   5
Seu Sacas sagittiferosque Parthos,
Sive quae septemgeminus colorat
            Aequora Nilus,
Sive trans altas gradietur Alpes,
Caesaris visens monimenta magni,   10
Gallicum Rhenum horribilesque ulti-
            mosque Britannos,
Omnia haec, quaecumque feret voluntas
Caelitum, temptare simul parati,

Pauca nuntiate meae puellae 15
     Non bona dicta :
Nec meum respectet, ut ante, amorem,
Qui illius culpa cecidit velut prati
Ultimi flos, praetereunte postquam
     Tactus aratro est.

XII.

Marrucine Asini, manu sinistra
Non belle uteris in joco atque vino :
Tollis lintea neglegentiorum.
Hoc salsum esse putas ? Fugit te, inepte :
Quamvis sordida res et invenusta est. 5
Non credis mihi ? Crede Pollioni
Fratri, qui tua furta vel talento
Mutari velit : est enim leporum
Disertus puer ac facetiarum.
Quare aut hendecasyllabos trecentos 10
Expecta, aut mihi linteum remitte,
Quod me non movet aestimatione,
Verum est mnemosynum mei sodalis.
Nam sudaria Saetaba ex Hibere
Miserunt mihi muneri Fabullus 15
Et Veranius : haec amem necesse est
Et Veraniolum meum et Fabullum.

XIII.

Cenabis bene, mi Fabulle, apud me
Paucis, si tibi dii favent, diebus,
Si tecum attuleris bonam atque magnam
Cenam, non sine candida puella
Et vino et sale et omnibus cachinnis. *laughter*   5
Haec si, inquam, attuleris, venuste noster,
Cenabis bene : nam tui Catulli
purse Plenus sacculus est aranearum.
Sed contra accipies meros amores
Seu quid suavius elegantiusve est.   10
Nam unguentum dabo, quod meae puellae
Donarunt Veneras Cupidinesque,
Quod tu cum olfacies, deos rogabis
Totum ut te faciant, Fabulle, nasum.

XIV.

Ni te plus oculis meis amarem,
Jucundissime Calve, munere isto
Odissem te odio Vatiniano.
Nam quid feci ego quidve sum locutus
Cur me tot male perderes poetis ?   5
Isti dii mala multa dent clienti
Qui tantum tibi misit impiorum.
Quod si, ut suspicor, hoc novum ac repertum
Munus dat tibi Sulla litterator, *pedant*
Non est mi male sed bene ac beate,   10
Quod non dispereunt tui labores.
Dii magni, horribilem et sacrum libellum,

Quem tu scilicet ad tuum Catullum
Misti, continuo ut die periret,
Saturnalibus, optimo dierum, 15
Non, non hoc tibi, salse, sic abibit:
Nam, si luxerit, ad librariorum
Curram scrinia; Caesios, Aquinos, *bookcases*
Suffenum, omnia colligam venena,
Ac te his suppliciis remunerabor. 20
Vos hinc interea (valete) abite
Illuc unde malum pedem attulistis,
Saecli incommoda, pessimi poetae.

XVII.

O Colonia, quae cupis ponte ludere magno,
Et salire paratum habes, sed vereris inepta
Crura ponticuli axulis stantis in redivivis, *poole posts*
Ne supinus eat cavaque in palude recumbat,
Sic tibi bonus ex tua pons libidine fiat, 5
In quo vel Salisubsali sacra suscipiantur:
Munus hoc mihi maximi da, Colonia, risus.
Quemdam municipem meum de tuo volo ponte
Ire praecipitem in lutum per caputque pedesque, *mud*
Verum totius ut lacus putidaeque paludis 10
Lividissima maximeque est profunda vorago.
Insulsissimus est homo, nec sapit pueri instar *blockhead*
Bimuli tremula patris dormientis in ulna; *Syr old elbow*
Cui cum sit viridissimo nupta flore puella,
(Et puella tenellulo delicatior hædo, 15
Asservanda nigerrimis diligentius uvis)
Ludere hanc sinit ut libet, nec pili facit uni,

Nec se sublevat ex sua parte, sed velut alnus
In fossa Liguri jacet suppernata securi,
Tantundem omnia sentiens quam si nulla sit us-
    quam.   20
Talis iste meus stupor nil videt, nihil audit,
Ipse qui sit, utrum sit an non sit, id quoque
    nescit.
Nunc eum volo de tuo ponte mittere pronum.
Si pote stolidum repente excitare veternum,
Et supinum animum in gravi derelinquere
    caeno,   25
Ferream ut soleam tenaci in voragine mula.

XXII.

Suffenus iste, Vare, quem probe nosti,
Homo est venustus et dicax et urbanus,
Idemque longe plurimos facit versus.
Puto esse ego illi milia aut decem aut plura
Perscripta, nec, sicut fit, in palimpsesto   5
Relata : cartae regiae, novi libri,
Novi umbilici, lora rubra, membranae,
Derecta plumbo et pumice omnia aequata.
Haec cum legas tu, bellus ille et urbanus
Suffenus unus caprimulgus aut fossor   10
Rursus videtur : tantum abhorret ac mutat.
Hoc quid putemus esse ? qui modo scurra,
Aut si quid hac re tritius, videbatur,
Idem infaceto est infacetior rure
Simul poemata attigit, neque idem unquam   15
Aeque est beatus ac poema cum scribit :

Tam gaudet in se tamque se ipse miratur.
Nimirum idem omnes fallimur, neque est quisquam
Quem non in aliqua re videre Suffenum
Possis. Suus cuique attributus est error :   20
Sed non videmus manticae quod in tergo est.

XXVI.

Furi, villula nostra non ad Austri
Flatus opposita est neque ad Favoni
Nec saevi Boreae aut Apheliotae,
Verum ad milia quindecim et ducentos.
O ventum horribilem atque pestilentem.   5

XXVII.

Minister vetuli puer Falerni,
Inger mi calices amariores,
Ut lex Postumiae jubet magistrae
Ebrioso acino ebriosioris.
At vos, quod jubet, hinc abite, lymphae,   5
Vini pernicies, et ad severos
Migrate. Hic merus est Thyonianus.

XXX.

Alfene immemor atque unanimis false sodalibus,
Jam te nil miseret, dure, tui dulcis amiculi ?
Jam me prodere, jam non dubitas fallere, perfide ?
Nec facta impia fallacum hominum caelicolis pla-
cent.
Quae tu neglegis ac me miserum deseris in malis.   5
Eheu quid faciant, dic, homines, cuive habeant fi-
dem ?

Certo tute jubebas animam tradere, inique, me
Inducens in amorem, quasi tuta omnia mi forent.
Idem nunc retrahis te ac tua dicta omnia fac-
    taque
Ventos irrita ferre ac nebulas aereas sinis.   10
Si tu oblitus es, at dii meminerunt, meminit Fides,
Quae te ut poeniteat postmodo facti faciet tui.

XXXI.

(e peninsulae)

Paene-insularum, Sirmio, insularumque
Ocelle, quascunque in liquentibus stagnis
Marique vasto fert uterque Neptunus,
Quam te libenter quamque laetus inviso,
Vix mi ipse credens Thyniam atque Bithynos   5
Liquisse campos et videre te in tuto.
O quid solutis est beatius curis,
Cum mens onus reponit ac peregrino
Labore fessi venimus larem ad nostrum
Desideratoque acquiescimus lecto ?   10
Hoc est quod unum est pro laboribus tantis.
Salve, o venusta Sirmio, atque ero gaude,
Gaudete vosque, o Lydiae lacus undae ;
Ridete quicquid est domi cachinnorum.

XXXIV.

Dianae sumus in fide
Puellae et pueri integri :
Dianam pueri integri
            Puellaeque canamus.

O Latonia, maximi 5
Magna progenies Jovis,
Quam mater prope Deliam
      Deposivit olivam,
Montium domina ut fores
Silvarumque virentium 10
Saltuumque reconditorum
      Amniumque sonantum.
Tu Lucina dolentibus
Juno dicta puerperis, *women in labour*
Tu potens Trivia et notho es 15
      Dicta lumine Luna.
Tu cursu, dea, menstruo
Metiens iter annuum,
Rustica agricolae bonis
      Tecta frugibus exples. 20
Sis quocumque tibi placet
Sancta nomine, Romulique,
Antique ut solita es, bona
      Sospites ope gentem.

XXXV.

Poetae tenero, meo sodali,
Velim Caecilio, papyre, dicas
Veronam veniat, Novi relinquens
Comi moenia Lariumque litus;
Nam quasdam volo cogitationes 5
Amici accipiat sui meique.
Quare si sapiet viam vorabit,
Quamvis candida milies puella

Euntem revocet, manusque collo
Ambas injiciens roget morari,   10
Quae nunc, si mihi vera nuntiantur
Illum deperit impotente amore.
Nam quo tempore legit incohatam
Dindymi dominam, ex eo misellae
Ignes interiorem edunt medullam.   15
Ignosco tibi, Sapphica puella
Musa doctior : est enim venuste
Magna Caecilio incohata mater.

XXXVI.

Annales Volusi, cacata carta, *filthy !*
Votum solvite pro mea puella.
Nam sanctae Veneri Cupidinique
Vovit, si sibi restitutus essem
Desissemque truces vibrare iambos,   5
Electissima pessimi poetae
Scripta tardipedi deo daturam
Infelicibus ustulanda lignis ; *to be burnt up*
Et hoc pessima se puella vidit
Jocose lepide vovere divis.   10
Nunc o caeruleo creata ponto,
Quae sanctum Idalium Uriosque apertos,
Quaeque Ancona Cnidumque arundinosam
Colis, quaeque Amathunta, quaeque Golgos,
Quaeque Durrachium Adriae tabernam,   15
Acceptum face redditumque votum,
Si non illepidum neque invenustum est.
At vos interea venite in ignem,

Pleni ruris et inficetiarum
Annales Volusi, cacata carta.   20

XXXVIII.

Male est, Cornifici, tuo Catullo,
Male est, me hercule, et laboriose,
Et magis magis in dies et horas.
Quem tu, quod minimum facillimumque est,
Qua solatus es allocutione ?   5
Irascor tibi.   Sic meos amores ?
Paulum quidlibet allocutionis,
Maestius lacrimis Simonideis.

XXXIX.

Egnatius, quod candidos habet dentes,
Renidet usque quaque : si ad rei ventum est
Subsellium, cum orator excitat fletum,
Renidet ille : si ad pii rogum fili
Lugetur, orba cum flet unicum mater,   5
Renidet ille : quicquid est, ubicunque est,
Quodcumque agit, renidet : hunc habet morbum,
Neque elegantem ut arbitror neque urbanum.
Quare monendum te est mihi, bone Egnati :
Si urbanus esses aut Sabinus aut Tiburs,   10
Aut parcus Umber aut obesus Etruscus,
Aut Lanuvinus ater atque dentatus,
Aut Transpadanus, ut meos quoque attingam,
Aut quilibet, qui puriter lavit dentes,
Tamen renidere usque quaque te nollem,   15
Nam risu inepto res ineptior nulla est.

Nunc Celtiber es : *Celtiberia in terra,*

Quod quisque minxit, hoc sibi solet mane
Dentem atque russam defricare gingivam, — grin
Ut quo iste vester expolitior dens est,
Hoc te amplius bibisse praedicet loti. urine

XL.

Quaenam te mala mens, miselle Ravide,
Agit praecipitem in meos iambos ?
Quis deus tibi non bene advocatus
Vecordem parat excitare rixam ?
An ut pervenias in ora vulgi ?   5
Quid vis ? qualibet esse notus optas ?
Eris, quandoquidem meos amores
Cum longa voluisti amare poena.

XLIII.

Salve, nec minimo puella naso,
Nec bello pede nec nigris ocellis
Nec longis digitis nec ore sicco
Nec sane nimis elegante lingua,
Decoctoris amica Formiani.   5
Ten provincia narrat esse bellam ?
Tecum Lesbia nostra comparatur ?
O saeclum insipiens et infacetum.

XLIV.

O funde noster seu Sabine seu Tiburs—
Nam te esse Tiburtem autumant quibus non est
Cordi Catullum laedere, at quibus cordi est,
Quovis Sabinum pignore esse contendunt—   *will wager anything*
Sed seu Sabine sive verius Tiburs,   5
Fui libenter in tua suburbana
Villa, malamque pectore expuli tussim,   *cough*
Non immerenti quam mihi meus venter,
Dum sumptuosas appeto, dedit, cenas.
Nam Sestianus dum volo esse conviva,   10
Orationem in Antium petitorem
Plenam veneni et pestilentiae legi.
cold Hic me gravedo frigida et frequens tussis
Quassavit usque dum in tuum sinum fugi,
Et me recuravi otioque et urtica.   *nettle*   15
Quare refectus maximas tibi grates
Ago, meum quod non es ulta peccatum.
Nec deprecor jam, si nefaria scripta
Sesti recepso, quin gravedinem et tussim
Non mi, sed ipsi Sestio ferat frigus,   20
Qui tum vocat me cum malum librum legi.

C

XLV.

Acmen Septimius, suos amores,
Tenens in gremio 'mea' inquit 'Acme,
Ni te perdite amo atque amare porro
Omnes sum assidue paratus annos
Quantum qui pote plurimum perire,   5
Solus in Libya Indiaque tosta
Caesio veniam obvius leoni.'
Hoc ut dixit, Amor sinistra, ut ante,
Dextram sternuit approbationem.
At Acme leviter caput reflectens   10
Et dulcis pueri ebrios ocellos
Illo purpureo ore saviata,
'Sic' inquit 'mea vita, Septimille,
Huic uni domino usque serviamus,
Ut multo mihi major acriorque   15
Ignis mollibus ardet in medullis.'
Hoc ut dixit, Amor sinistra, ut ante
Dextram sternuit approbationem.
Nunc ab auspicio bono profecti
Mutuis animis amant amantur.   20
Unam Septimius misellus Acmen
Mavult quam Syrias Britanniasque ;
Uno in Septimio fidelis Acme
Facit delicias libidinesque.
Quis ullos homines beatiores   25
Vidit, quis Venerem auspicatiorem ?

XLVI.

Jam ver egelidos refert tepores, *balmy*
Jam caeli furor aequinoctialis
Jucundis Zephyri silescit auris.
Linquantur Phrygii, Catulle, campi
Nicaeaeque ager uber aestuosae :   5
Ad claras Asiae volemus urbes.
Jam mens praetrepidans avet vagari,
Jam laeti studio pedes vigescunt.
O dulces comitum valete coetus,
Longe quos simul a domo profectos   10
Diversae variae viae reportant.

XLVII.

Porci et Socration, duae sinistrae
Pisonis, scabies famesque mundi,
Vos Veraniolo meo et Fabullo
Verpus praeposuit Priapus ille ?
Vos convivia lauta sumptuose   5
De die facitis ? mei sodales
Quaerunt in trivio vocationes ?

XLIX.

Disertissime Romuli nepotum
Quot sunt quotque fuere, Marce Tulli,
Quotque post aliis erunt in annis,
Gratias tibi maximas Catullus
Agit pessimus omnium poeta,   5
Tanto pessimus omnium poeta
Quanto tu optimus omnium patronus.

L.

Hesterno, Licini, die otiosi
Multum lusimus in meis tabellis,
Ut convenerat esse delicatos. *to take our pleasure*
Scribens versiculos uterque nostrum
Ludebat numero modo hoc modo illoc,　　5
Reddens mutua per jocum atque vinum
Atque illinc abii tuo lepore
Incensus, Licini, facetiisque,
Ut nec me miserum cibus juvaret
Nec somnus tegeret quiete ocellos,　　10
Sed toto, indomitus furore, lecto
Versarer cupiens videre lucem,
Ut tecum loquerer simulque ut essem.
At defessa labore membra postquam
Semimortua lectulo jacebant,　　15
Hoc, jucunde, tibi poema feci,
Ex quo perspiceres meum dolorem.
Nunc audax cave sis, precesque nostras,
Oramus, cave despuas, ocelle,
Ne poenas Nemesis reposcat a te.　　20
Est vemens dea : laedere hanc caveto.

LI.

Ille mi par esse deo videtur,
Ille, si **fas** est, superare divos,
Qui sedens adversus identidem te
　　　Spectat et audit
Dulce ridentem misero quod omnes　　5
Eripit sensus mihi ; nam simul te,

Lesbia, aspexi, nihil est super mi

. . . . .

Lingua sed torpet, tenuis sub artus
Flamma demanat, sonitu suopte   10
Tintinant aures, gemina teguntur
            Lumina nocte.   *a double night*
Otium, Catulle, tibi molestum est ;
Otio exsultas nimiumque gestis.
Otium et reges prius et beatas   15
            Perdidit urbes.

LII.

Quid est, Catulle ? quid moraris emori ?
Sella in curuli Struma Nonius sedet :
Per consulatum perjerat Vatinius :
Quid est, Catulle ? quid moraris emori ?

LIII.

Risi nescio quem modo e corona,
Qui, cum mirifice Vatiniana
Meus crimina Calvus explicasset,
Admirans ait haec manusque tollens,
' Dii magni, salaputium disertum.'   *little cocky*

LX.

Num te leaena montibus Libystinis
Aut Scylla latrans infima inguinum parte
Tam mente dura procreavit ac taetra,
Ut supplicis vocem in novissimo casu
Contemptam haberes ? a nimis fero corde !

LXI.

Collis o Heliconii
Cultor, Uraniae genus,
Qui rapis teneram ad virum
Virginem, o Hymenaee Hymen,
   O Hymen Hymenaee,   5
Cinge tempora floribus
Suave olentis amaraci, *marjoram*
bridal veil Flammeum cape laetus, huc
Huc veni, niveo gerens
   yellow Luteum pede soccum, 10
Excitusque hilari die
Nuptialia concinens
Voce carmina tinnula,
Pelle humum pedibus, manu
   Pineam quate taedam. 15
Namque Vinia Manlio,
Qualis Idalium colens
Venit ad Phrygium Venus
Judicem, bona cum bona
   Nubet alite virgo, 20
Floridis velut enitens
Myrtus Asia ramulis, *sprays*
Quos Hamadryades deae
as a plaything Ludicrum sibi rosido
   Nutriunt humore. 25
Quare age, huc aditum ferens
make haste to Perge linquere Thespiae
Rupis Aonios specus,

Nympha quos super irrigat
      Frigerans Aganippe,   30
Ac domum dominam voca
Conjugis cupidam novi,
Mentem amore revinciens
Ut tenax hedera huc et huc
      Arborem implicat errans.   35
Vosque item simul integrae
Virgines, quibus advenit
Par dies, agite in modum
Dicite, o Hymenaee Hymen,
      O Hymen Hymenaee,   40
Ut libentius, audiens
Se citarier ad suum
Munus, huc aditum ferat
Dux bonae Veneris, boni
      Conjugator amoris.   45
Quis deus magis *anxiis*
Est petendus amantibus ?
Quem colent homines magis
Caelitum, o Hymenaee Hymen
      O Hymen Hymenaee ?   50
Te suis tremulus parens
Invocat, tibi virgines
Zonula soluunt sinus.
Te timens cupida novus
      Captat aure maritus.   55
Tu fero juveni in manus
Floridam ipse puellulam
Dedis a gremio suae

Matris, o Hymenaee Hymen,
        O Hymen Hymenaee.   60
Nil potest sine te Venus,
Fama quod bona comprobet,
Commodi capere, at potest
Te volente. Quis huic deo
        Compararier ausit ?   65
Nulla quit sine te domus
Liberos dare, nec parens
Stirpe vincier, at potest
Te volente. Quis huic deo
        Compararier ausit ?   70
Quae tuis careat sacris
Non queat dare praesides
Terra finibus, at queat
Te volente. Quis huic deo
        Compararier ausit ?   75
Claustra pandite januae.
Virgo adest. Viden ut faces
Splendidas quatiunt comas

.   .   .   .   .   .

.   .   .   .   .   .   80 (78)

Tardet ingenuus pudor

.   .   .   .   .   .

.   .   .   .   .   .

Quem tamen magis audiens
        Flet quod ire necesse est. 85 (81)
Flere desine : non tibi, Au-
runculeia, periculum est
Ne qua femina pulchrior

Clarum ab oceano diem
       Viderit venientem.   90 (86)
Talis in vario solet
Divitis domini hortulo
Stare flos hyacinthinus.
Sed moraris. Abit dies.
       Prodeas nova nupta.   95 (91)
Prodeas nova nupta, si
Jam videtur, et audias
Nostra verba. Vide ut faces
Aureas quatiunt comas.
       Prodeas nova nupta.   100 (95)
Tollite, o pueri, faces.
Flammeum video venire.
Ite, concinite in modum
' Io Hymen Hymenaee io,
       Io Hymen Hymenaee.'   125 (118)
En tibi domus ut potens
Et beata viri tui.
Quae tibi sine serviat,
Io Hymen Hymenaee io,
       Io Hymen Hymenaee,   160 (153)
Usque dum tremulum movens
Cana tempus anilitas
Omnia omnibus annuat.
Io Hymen Hymenaee io,
       Io Hymen Hymenaee.   165 (158)
Transfer omine cum bono
Limen aureolos pedes,
Rasilemque subi forem

Io Hymen Hymenaee io,
   Io Hymen Hymenaee. 170 (163)
Mitte bracchiolum teres,
Praetextate, puellulae.
Jam cubile adeant viri.
Io Hymen Hymenaee io,
   Io Hymen Hymenaee. 185 (178)
Vos, unis senibus bonae
Cognitae bene feminae,
Collocate puellulam.
Io Hymen Hymenaee io,
   Io Hymen Hymenaee. 190 (183)
Jam licet venias, marite :
Uxor in thalamo tibi est,
Ore floridulo nitens
Alba parthenice velut *daisy*
   Luteumve papaver. 195 (188)
At, marite, ita me juvent
Caelites, nihilo minus
Pulcher es, neque te Venus
Neglegit. Sed abit dies.
   Perge, ne remorare. 200 (193)
Non diu remoratus es.
Jam venis. Bona te Venus
Juverit, quoniam palam
Quae cupis capis et bonum
   Non abscondis amorem. 205 (198)
Ille pulveris Africi
Siderumque micantium
Subducat numerum prius.

cast up the sum

Qui vestri numerare vult
        Multa milia ludi.   210 (203)
Ludite ut libet et brevi
Liberos date. Non decet
Tam vetus sine liberis
Nomen esse, sed indidem
        Semper ingenerari.   215 (208)
Torquatus volo parvulus,
Matris e gremio suae
Porrigens teneras manus,
Dulce rideat ad patrem
        Semihiante labello.   220 (213)
Sit suo similis patri
Manlio et facile insciis
Noscitetur ab omnibus
Et pudicitiam suae
        Matris indicet ore.   225 (218)
Talis illius a bona
Matre laus genus approbet,
Qualis unica ab optima
Matre Telemacho manet
        Fama Penelopeo.   230 (223)
Claudite ostia, virgines :
Lusimus satis. At, boni
Conjuges, bene vivite et
Munere assidue valentem
        Exercete juventam   235 (228)

LXII.
Juvenes.

Vesper adest juvenes, consurgite : Vesper Olympo

Expectata diu vix tandem lumina tollit.
Surgere jam tempus, jam pingues linquere mensas
Jam veniet virgo, jam dicetur Hymenaeus.
Hymen o Hymenaee, Hymen ades o Hymenaee. 5

Puellae.

Cernitis, innuptae, juvenes ? Consurgite contra :
Nimirum Oetaeos ostendit noctifer ignes.
Sic certe est : viden ut perniciter exsiluere ?
Non temere exsiluere, canent quod visere par est.
Hymen o Hymenaee, Hymen ades o Hymenaee. 1

Juvenes.

Non facilis nobis, aequales, palma parata est :
Aspicite, innuptae secum ut meditata requirunt.
Non frustra meditantur, habent memorabile quo
    sit,
Nec mirum, penitus quae tota mente laborant.
Nos alio mentes, alio divisimus aures ;   1
Jure igitur vincemur : amat victoria curam.
Quare nunc animos saltem committite vestros ;
Dicere jam incipient, jam respondere decebit.
Hymen o Hymenaee, Hymen ades o Hymenaee.

Puellae.

Hespere, qui caelo fertur crudelior ignis ?   2
Qui natam possis complexu avellere matris,
Complexu matris retinentem avellere natam,
Et juveni ardenti castam donare puellam.
Quid faciunt hostes capta crudelius urbe ?
Hymen o Hymenaee, Hymen ades o Hymenaee.   2

Juvenes.

Hespere, qui caelo lucet jucundior ignis ?
Qui desponsa tua firmes conubia flamma,
Quae pepigere viri, pepigerunt ante parentes,
Nec junxere prius quam se tuus extulit ardor.
Quid datur a divis felici optatius hora ?   30
Hymen o Hymenaee, Hymen ades o Hymenaee.

Puellae.

Hesperus e nobis, aequales, abstulit unam.

.   .   .   .

Namque tuo adventu vigilat custodia semper.

.   .   .   .   35
Hymen o Hymenaee, Hymen ades o Hymenaee.

Juvenes.

Nocte latent fures, quos idem saepe revertens,
Hespere, mutato comprendis nomine eosdem.
At libet innuptis ficto te carpere questu : *chide*
Quid tum si carpunt, tacita quem mente re-
quirunt ? *seek, desire*   40
Hymen o Hymenaee, Hymen ades o Hymenaee.

Puellae.

Ut flos in septis secretus nascitur hortis,
Ignotus pecori, nullo contusus aratro, *bruised*
Quem mulcent aurae, firmat sol, educat imber

.   .   .   .   45
Multi illum pueri, multae optavere puellae :
Idem cum tenui carptus defloruit ungui,
Nulli illum pueri, nullae optavere puellae.
Sic virgo, dum intacta manet, dum cara suis est :

Cum castum amisit polluto corpore florem, 5(
Nec pueris jucunda manet, nec cara puellis.
Hymen o Hymenaee, Hymen ades o Hymenaee.

Juvenes.

Ut vidua in nudo vitis quae nascitur arvo
Nunquam se extollit, nunquam mitem educat uvam
Sed tenerum prono deflectens pondere corpus 5!
Jam jam contingit summum radice flagellum,
Hanc nulli agricolae, nulli coluere juvenci :
At si forte eadem est ulmo conjuncta marito,
Multi illam agricolae, multi coluere juvenci.
Sic virgo, dum intacta manet, dum inculta senes
    cit : 6(
Cum par conubium maturo tempore adepta est,
Cara viro magis et minus est invisa parenti.

Et tu ne pugna cum tali conjuge virgo,

  .   .   .   .

Non aequum est pugnare, pater cui tradidit ipse, 6
Ipse pater cum matre, quibus parere necesse est.
Virginitas non tota tua est ; ex parte parentum
    est
Tertia pars patri, pars est data tertia matri,
Tertia sola tua est ; noli pugnare duobus,
Qui genero sua jura simul cum dote dederunt. 7(

Hymen o Hymenaee, Hymen ades o Hymenaee

LXIII.

Super alta vectus Attis celeri rate maria,

Phrygium ut nemus citato cupide pede tetigit,
Adiitque opaca silvis redimita loca deae,
Stimulatus ibi furenti rabie, vagus animis,
Devolvit ili acuto sibi pondera silice.   5
Itaque ut relicta sensit sibi membra sine viro,
Etiam recente terrae sola sanguine maculans,
Niveis citata cepit manibus leve typanum,
Typanum, tubam Cybelles, tua, mater, initia,
Quatiensque terga tauri teneris cava digitis,   10
Canere haec suis adorta est tremebunda comitibus.
' Agite, ite ad alta, Gallae, Cybeles nemora procul,
Simul ite, Dindymenae dominae vaga pecora,
Aliena quae petentes velut exsules loca,
Sectam meam exsecutae, duce me mihi comites,   15
Rapidum salum tulistis truculentaque pelagi,
Et corpus evirastis Veneris nimio odio;
Hilarate aere citatis erroribus animum.
Mora tarda mente cedat; simul ite, sequimini
Phrygiam ad domum Cybelles, Phrygia ad nemora
    deae,   20
Ubi cymbalum sonat vox, ubi tympana reboant
Tibicen ubi canit Phryx curvo grave calamo,
Ubi capita Maenades vi jaciunt hederigerae,
Ubi sacra sancta acutis ululatibus agitant,
Ubi suevit illa divae volitare vaga cohors,   25
Quo nos decet citatis celerare tripudiis.'
Simul haec comitibus Attis cecinit, notha mulier,
Thiasus repente linguis trepidantibus ululat,
Leve tympanum remugit, cava cymbala recrepant,
Viridem citus adit Idam properante pede chorus.   30

Furibunda simul anhelans vaga vadit animam
    agens
Comitata tympano Attis per opaca nemora dux,
Veluti juvenca vitans onus indomita jugi :
Rapidae ducem sequuntur Gallae properipedem.
Itaque ut domum Cybelles tetigere lassulae,   35
Nimio e labore somnum capiunt sine Cerere ;
Piger his labante langore oculos sopor operit :
Abit in quiete molli rabidus furor animi.
Sed ubi oris aurei Sol radiantibus oculis
Lustravit aethera album, sola dura, mare ferum, 40
Pepulitque noctis umbras vegetis sonipedibus,
Ibi Somnus excitum Attin fugiens citus abiit :
Trepidante eum recepit dea Pasithea sinu.
Ita de quiete molli rapida sine rabie
Simul ipse pectore Attis sua facta recoluit,   45
Liquidaque mente vidit sine queis ubique foret,
Animo aestuante rursum reditum ad vada tetulit.
Ibi maria vasta visens lacrimantibus oculis,
Patriam allocuta maesta est ita voce miseriter.
' Patria o mei creatrix, patria o mea genetrix, 50
Ego quam miser relinquens, dominos ut erifugae
Famuli solent, ad Idae tetuli nemora pedem,
Ut apud nivem et ferarum gelida stabula forem,
Et earum omnia adirem furibunda latibula,
Ubinam aut quibus locis te positam, patria, reor ? 55
Cupit ipsa pupula ad te sibi dirigere aciem,
Rabie fera carens dum breve tempus animus est.
Egone a mea remota haec ferar in nemora domo ?
Patria, bonis, amicis, genitoribus abero ?

Abero foro, palaestra, stadio et gymnasiis ?   60
Miser a miser, querendum est etiam atque etiam,
    anime.
Quod enim genus figurae est, ego quod non obierim ?
Ego mulier, ego adulescens, ego ephebus, ego puer,
Ego gymnasi fui flos, ego eram decus olei ;
Mihi januae frequentes, mihi limina tepida,   65
Mihi floridis corollis redimita domus erat,
Linquendum ubi esset orto mihi sole cubiculum.
Ego nunc deum ministra et Cybeles famula ferar ?
Ego Maenas, ego mei pars, ego vir sterilis ero ?
Ego viridis algida Idae nive amicta loca colam? 70
Ego vitam agam sub altis Phrygiae columinibus,
Ubi cerva silvicultrix, ubi aper nemorivagus ?
Jam jam dolet quod egi, jam jamque paenitet.'
Roseis ut hinc labellis sonitus adiit. . . .
Geminas deorum ad aures nova nuntia referens, 75
Ibi juncta juga resolvens Cybele leonibus
Laevumque pecoris hostem stimulans ita loquitur.
' Agedum,' inquit, ' age ferox i, fac ut hunc furor
    agitet,
Fac uti furoris ictu reditum in nemora ferat,
Mea libere nimis qui fugere imperia cupit.   80
Age caede terga cauda, tua verbera patere,
Fac cuncta mugienti fremitu loca retonent,
Rutilam ferox torosa cervice quate jubam.'
Ait haec minax Cybelle religatque juga manu.
Ferus ipse sese adhortans rapidum incitat animo, 85
Vadit, fremit, refringit virgulta pede vago.
At ubi umida albicantis loca litoris adiit

Tenerumque vidit Attin prope marmora pelagi,
Facit impetum : ille demens fugit in nemora fera :
Ibi semper omne vitae spatium famula fuit.   90

Dea magna, dea Cybelle, dea domina Dindymi,
Procul a mea tuus sit furor omnis, era, domo :
Alios age incitatos, alios age rabidos.

LXIV.

Peliaco quondam prognatae vertice pinus
Dicuntur liquidas Neptuni nasse per undas
Phasidos ad fluctus et fines Aeetaeos ;
Cum lecti juvenes, Argivae robora pubis,
Auratam optantes Colchis avertere pellem,   5
Ausi sunt vada salsa cita decurrere puppi,
Caerula verrentes abiegnis aequora palmis.
Diva quibus retinens in summis urbibus arces
Ipsa levi fecit volitantem flamine currum,
Pinea conjungens inflexae texta carinae.   10
Illa rudem cursu prima imbuit Amphitriten ;
Quae simul ac rostro ventosum proscidit aequor,
Tortaque remigio spumis incanduit unda,
Emersere feri candenti e gurgite vultus,
Aequoreae monstrum Nereides admirantes.   15
Illac, haudque alia, viderunt luce marinas
Mortales oculis nudato corpore nymphas
Nutricum tenus exstantes e gurgite cano.
Tum Thetidis Peleus incensus fertur amore,
Tum Thetis humanos non despexit hymenaeos,   20
Tum Thetidi pater ipse jugandum Pelea sensit.

O nimis optato saeclorum tempore nati
Heroes, salvete, deum gens, o bona matrum
Progenies salvete iterum
Vos ego saepe meo vos carmine compellabo,   25
Teque adeo eximie taedis felicibus aucte,
Thessaliae columen, Peleu, cui Juppiter ipse,
Ipse suos divum genitor concessit amores.
Tene Thetis tenuit pulcherrima Nereine ?
Tene suam Tethys concessit ducere neptem   30
Oceanusque, mari totum qui amplectitur orbem ?
Quae simul optato finito tempore luces
Advenere, domum conventu tota frequentat
Thessalia ; oppletur laetanti regia coetu.
Dona ferunt prae se, declarant gaudia vultu.   35
Deseritur Scyros, linquunt Phthiotica Tempe
Crannonisque domos ac moenia Larissaea ;
Pharsalum coeunt, Pharsalia tecta frequentant.
Rura colit nemo ; mollescunt colla juvencis ;
Non humilis curvis purgatur vinea rastris,   40
Non glebam prono convellit vomere taurus,
Non falx attenuat frondatorum arboris umbram ;
Squalida desertis robigo infertur aratris.
Ipsius at sedes, quacunque opulenta recessit
Regia, fulgenti splendent auro atque argento ;   45
Candet ebur soliis, collucent pocula mensae,
Tota domus gaudet regali splendida gaza.
Pulvinar vero divae geniale locatur
Sedibus in mediis, Indo quod dente politum
Tincta tegit roseo conchyli purpura fuco.   50
　　Haec vestis, priscis hominum variata figuris,

Heroum mira virtutes indicat arte.
Namque fluentisono prospectans litore Diae
Thesea cedentem celeri cum classe tuetur
Indomitos in corde gerens Ariadna furores ;   55
Necdum etiam sese, quae visit, visere credit,
Ut pote fallaci quae tum primum excita somno
Desertam in sola miseram se cernat harena.
Immemor at juvenis fugiens pellit vada remis,
Irrita ventosae linquens promissa procellae.   60
Quem procul ex alga maestis Minois ocellis,
Saxea ut effigies Bacchantis, prospicit, eheu,
Prospicit, et magnis curarum fluctuat undis,
Non flavo retinens subtilem vertice mitram,
Non contecta levi velatum pectus amictu,   65
Non tereti strophio lactentes vincta papillas,
Omnia quae toto delapsa e corpore passim
Ipsius ante pedes fluctus salis alludebant.
Sed neque tum mitrae, neque tum fluitantis amictus
Illa vicem curans, toto ex te pectore, Theseu,   70
Toto animo, tota pendebat perdita mente.
A misera, assiduis quam luctibus exsternavit
Spinosas Erycina serens in pectore curas,
Illa tempestate, ferox quo ex tempore Theseus,
Egressus curvis e litoribus Piraei,   75
Attigit injusti regis Gortynia templa.
Nam perhibent olim, crudeli peste coactam
Androgeoneae poenas exsolvere caedis,
Electos juvenes simul et decus innuptarum
Cecropiam solitam esse dapem dare Minotauro.   80
Queis angusta malis cum moenia vexarentur,

Ipse suum Theseus pro caris corpus Athenis
Projicere optavit, potius quam talia Cretam
Funera Cecropiae nec funera portarentur ;
Atque ita nave levi nitens ac lenibus auris   85
Magnanimum ad Minoa venit sedesque superbas.
Hunc simul ac cupido conspexit lumine virgo
Regia, quam suaves exspirans castus odores
Lectulus in molli complexu matris alebat,
Quales Eurotae progignunt flumina myrtus   90
Aurave distinctos educit verna colores,
Non prius ex illo flagrantia declinavit
Lumina, quam cuncto concepit corpore flammam
Funditus atque imis exarsit tota medullis.
Heu misere exagitans immiti corde furores,   95
Sancte puer, curis hominum qui gaudia misces,
Quaeque regis Golgos quaeque Idalium frondosum,
Qualibus incensam jactastis mente puellam
Fluctibus, in flavo saepe hospite suspirantem.
Quantos illa tulit languenti corde timores,   100
Quanto saepe magis fulgore expalluit auri, *than gleaming gold*
Cum saevum cupiens contra contendere monstrum
Aut mortem oppeteret Theseus aut praemia laudis.
Non ingrata tamen frustra munuscula divis
Promittens tacito succendit vota labello. *offered* 105
Nam velut in summo quatientem bracchia Tauro
Quercum, aut conigeram sudanti cortice pinum,
Indomitus turbo contorquens flamine robur,
Eruit—illa procul radicitus exturbata
Prona cadit, lateque com*is* ob*it* omnia frangens—110
Sic domito saevum prostravit corpore Theseus

Nequiquam vanis jactantem cornua ventis.
Inde pedem sospes multa cum laude reflexit
Errabunda regens tenui vestigia filo,
Ne labyrintheis e flexibus egredientem   115
Tecti frustraretur inobservabilis error.

   Sed quid ego, a primo digressus carmine, plura
Commemorem, ut linquens genitoris filia vultum,
Ut consanguineae complexum, ut denique matris,
Quae misera in nata deperdita laeta*batur*,   120
Omnibus his Thesei dulcem praeoptarit amorem,
Aut ut vecta ratis spumosa ad litora Diae
Venerit, aut ut eam devinctam lumina somno
Liquerit immemori discedens pectore conjux.
Saepe illam perhibent ardenti corde furentem   125
Clarisonas imo fudisse e pectore voces,
Ac tum praeruptos tristem conscendere montes
Unde aciem in pelagi vastos protenderet aestus,
Tum tremuli salis adversas procurrere in undas
Mollia nudatae tollentem tegmina surae,   *knee*   130
Atque haec extremis maestam dixisse querellis,
Frigidulos udo singultus ore cientem.

   ' Sicine me patriis avectam, perfide, ab aris,
Perfide, deserto liquisti in litore, Theseu ?
Sicine discedens neglecto numine divum   135
Immemor a devota domum perjuria portas ?
Nullane res potuit crudelis flectere mentis
Consilium ? tibi nulla fuit clementia praesto,
Immite ut nostri vellet miserescere pectus ?
At non haec quondam nobis promissa dedisti   140
Voce, mihi non haec miserae sperare jubebas,

Sed conubia laeta, sed optatos hymenaeos,
Quae cuncta aerei discerpunt irrita venti.
Tum jam nulla viro juranti femina credat,
Nulla viri speret sermones esse fideles ;   145
Queis dum aliquid cupiens animus praegestit apisci,
Nil metuunt jurare, nihil promittere parcunt,
Sed, simul ac cupidae mentis satiata libido est,
Dicta nihil metuere, nihil perjuria curant.
Certe ego te in medio versantem turbine leti   150
Eripui et potius germanum amittere crevi,
Quam tibi fallaci supremo in tempore deessem.
Pro quo dilaceranda feris dabor alitibusque
Praeda, neque injecta tumulabor mortua terra.
Quaenam te genuit sola sub rupe leaena,   155
Quod mare conceptum spumantibus exspuit undis,
Quae Syrtis, quae Scylla rapax, quae vasta Charybdis,
Talia qui reddis pro dulci praemia vita ?
Si tibi non cordi fuerant conubia nostra,
Saeva quod horrebas prisci praecepta parentis,   160
At tamen in vestras potuisti ducere sedes,
Quae tibi jucundo famularer serva labore,
Candida permulcens liquidis vestigia lymphis
Purpureave tuum consternens veste cubile.
Sed quid ego ignaris nequiquam conquerar auris,   165
Exsternata malo, quae nullis sensibus auctae *distracted*
Nec missas audire queunt nec reddere voces ?
Ille autem prope jam mediis versatur in undis,
Nec quisquam apparet vacua mortalis in alga.
Sic nimis insultans extremo tempore saeva   170
Fors etiam nostris invidit questibus aures.

Juppiter omnipotens, utinam ne tempore primo
Gnosia Cecropiae tetigissent litora puppes,
Indomito nec dira ferens stipendia tauro *tarente*
Perfidus in Creta religasset navita funem,   175
Nec malus hic, celans dulci crudelia forma
Consilia, in nostris requiesset sedibus hospes.
Nam quo me referam ? quali spe perdita nitor ?
Idomeneosne petam montes ? a ! gurgite lato
Discernens ponti truculentum dividit aequor.   180
An patris auxilium sperem ? quemne ipsa reliqui,
Respersum juvenem fraterna caede secuta ?
Conjugis an fido consoler memet amore ?
Quine fugit lentos incurvans gurgite remos ?
Praeterea nullo litus, sola insula, tecto ;   185
Nec patet egressus pelagi cingentibus undis :
Nulla fugae ratio, nulla spes : omnia muta,
Omnia sunt deserta, ostentant omnia letum.
Non tamen ante mihi languescent lumina morte,
Nec prius a fesso secedent corpore sensus,   190
vengeance Quam justam a divis exposcam prodita multam
Caelestumque fidem postrema comprecer hora.
Quare facta virum multantes vindice poena,
Eumenides, quibus anguino redimita capillo
Frons exspirantes praeportat pectoris iras,   195
Huc huc adventate, meas audite querellas,
Quas ego, vae misera, extremis proferre medullis
Cogor inops, ardens, amenti caeca furore.
Quae quoniam verae nascuntur pectore ab imo,
Vos nolite pati nostrum vanescere luctum,   200
Sed quali solam Theseus me mente reliquit,

Tali mente, deae, funestet seque suosque.' *bring death on*
　Has postquam maesto profudit pectore voces,
Supplicium saevis exposcens anxia factis,
Annuit invicto caelestum numine rector,　　　　205
Quo tunc et tellus atque horrida contremuere
Aequora concussitque micantia sidera mundus.
Ipse autem caeca mentem caligine Theseus
Consitus oblito dimisit pectore cuncta, *drenched*
Quae mandata prius constanti mente tenebat ; 210
Dulcia nec maesto sustollens signa parenti
Sospitem Erechtheum se ostendit visere portum.
Namque ferunt olim, classi cum moenia divae
Linquentem natum ventis concrederet Aegeus,
Talia complexum juveni mandata dedisse.　　215
　' Nate, mihi longa jucundior unice vita,
Nate, ego quem in dubios cogor dimittere casus,
Reddite in extrema nuper mihi fine senectae,
Quandoquidem fortuna mea ac tua fervida virtus
Eripit invito mihi te, cui languida nondum　　220
Lumina sunt nati cara saturata figura,
Non ego te gaudens laetanti pectore mittam
Nec te ferre sinam fortunae signa secundae,
Sed primum multas expromam mente querellas,
Canitiem terra atque infuso pulvere foedans ; 225
Inde infecta vago suspendam lintea malo, *dyed mast*
Nostros ut luctus nostraeque incendia mentis
Carbasus obscurata dicet ferrugine Hibera.
Quod tibi si sancti concesserit incola Itoni,
Quae nostrum genus et sedes defendere Erechthi 230
Annuit, ut tauri respergas sanguine dextram,

Tu vero facito ut memori tibi condita corde
Haec vigeant mandata, nec ulla oblitteret aetas:
Ut simul ac nostros invisent lumina colles
Funestam antennae deponant undique vestem, 235
Candidaque intorti sustollant vela rudentes,
Quam primum cernens ut laeta gaudia mente
Agnoscam, cum te reducem aetas prospera sistet.'

Haec mandata prius constanti mente tenentem
Thesea ceu pulsae ventorum flamine nubes 240
Aereum nivei montis liquere cacumen.
At pater, ut summa prospectum ex arce petebat,
Anxia in assiduos absumens lumina fletus,
Cum primum inflati conspexit lintea veli,
Praecipitem sese scopulorum e vertice jecit, 245
Amissum credens immiti Thesea fato.
Sic funesta domus ingressus tecta paterna
Morte ferox Theseus, qualem Minoidi luctum
Obtulerat mente immemori talem ipse recepit,
Quae tum prospectans cedentem maesta carinam 250
Multiplices animo volvebat saucia curas.

At parte ex alia florens volitabat Iacchus
Cum thiaso Satyrorum et Nysigenis Silenis,
Te quaerens, Ariadna, tuoque incensus amore.
Quicum alacres passim lymphata mente furebant, 255
Euhoe, Bacchantes, euhoe, caput inflectentes.
Harum pars tecta quatiebant cuspide thyrsos,
Pars e divulso jactabant membra juvenco,
Pars sese tortis serpentibus incingebant,
Pars obscura cavis celebrabant orgia cistis, 260
Orgia, quae frustra cupiunt audire profani;

Plangebant aliae proceris tympana palmis, *upraised*
Aut tereti tenues tinnitus aere ciebant ;
Multis raucisonos efflabant cornua bombos
Barbaraque horribili stridebat tibia cantu.   265
  Talibus amplifice vestis decorata figuris
Pulvinar complexa suo velabat amictu.
Quae postquam cupide spectando Thessala pubes
Expleta est, sanctis coepit decedere divis.
Hic, qualis flatu placidum mare matutino   270
Horrificans Zephyrus proclivas incitat undas,
Aurora exoriente, vagi sub lumina solis,   *limine OCT.*
Quae tarde primum clementi flamine pulsae
Procedunt leviterque sonant plangore cachinni,
Post vento crescente magis magis increbrescunt, 275
Purpureaque procul nantes a luce refulgent ;
Sic tum vestibuli linquentes regia tecta
Ad se quisque vago passim pede discedebant.
Quorum post abitum princeps e vertice Peli
Advenit Chiron portans silvestria dona :   280
Nam quodcumque ferunt campi, quos Thessala
     magnis
Montibus ora creat, quos propter fluminis undas *region*
Aura parit flores tepidi fecunda Favoni,
Hos in distinctis plexos tulit ipse corollis,
Quo permulsa domus jucundo risit odore.   285
Confestim Peneus adest, viridantia Tempe,
Tempe, quæ silvae cingunt super impendentes,
Minosim linquens Doris celebranda choreis,
Non vacuus ; namque ille tulit radicitus altas
Fagos ac recto proceras stipite laurus,   290

Non sine nutanti platano lentaque sorore
Flammati Phaethontis et aerea cupressu.
Haec circum sedes late contexta locavit,
Vestibulum ut molli velatum fronde vireret.
Post hunc consequitur sollerti corde Prometheus, 295
Extenuata gerens veteris vestigia poenae,
Quam quondam silici restrictus membra catena
Persolvit pendens e verticibus praeruptis.
Inde pater divum sancta cum conjuge natisque
Advenit caelo, te solum, Phoebe, relinquens 300
Unigenamque simul cultricem montibus Idri :
Pelea nam tecum pariter soror aspernata est,
Nec Thetidis taedas voluit celebrare jugales.

Qui postquam niveis flexerunt sedibus artus,
Large multiplici constructae sunt dape mensae, 305
Cum interea infirmo quatientes corpora motu
Veridicos Parcae coeperunt edere cantus.
His corpus tremulum complectens undique vestis
Candida purpurea talos incinxerat ora,
At roseo niveae residebant vertice vittae, 310
Aeternumque manus carpebant rite laborem.
Laeva colum molli lana retinebat amictum,
Dextera tum leviter deducens fila supinis
Formabat digitis, tum prono in pollice torquens
Libratum tereti versabat turbine fusum ; 315
Atque ita decerpens aequabat semper opus dens,
Laneaque aridulis haerebant morsa labellis
Quae prius in levi fuerant exstantia filo.
Ante pedes autem candentis mollia lanae
Vellera virgati custodibant calathisci. 320

Haec tum clarisona pellentes vellera voce *striking*
Talia divino fuderunt carmine fata,
Carmine, perfidiae quod post nulla arguet aetas.

O decus eximium magnis virtutibus augens,
Emathiae tutamen opis, clarissime nato,   325
Accipe quod laeta pandunt tibi luce sorores, *reveal*
Veridicum oraclum : sed vos, quae fata sequuntur,
Currite ducentes subtegmina, currite, fusi. *threads*

Adveniet tibi jam portans optata maritis
Hesperus, adveniet fausto cum sidere conjux,   330
Quae tibi flexo animo mentis perfundat amorem,
Languidulosque paret tecum conjungere somnos,
Levia substernens robusto bracchia collo.
Currite ducentes subtegmina, currite, fusi.

Nulla domus tales unquam contexit amores,   335
Nullus amor tali conjunxit foedere amantes,
Qualis adest Thetidi, qualis concordia Peleo.
Currite ducentes subtegmina, currite, fusi.

Nascetur vobis expers terroris Achilles,
Hostibus haud tergo sed forti pectore notus.   340
Qui persaepe vago victor certamine cursus
Flammea praevertet celeris vestigia cervae. *outstrip*
Currite ducentes subtegmina, currite, fusi.

Non illi quisquam bello se conferet heros,
Cum Phrygii Teucro manabunt sanguine *campi* 345
Troicaque obsidens longinquo moenia bello
Perjuri Pelopis vastabit tertius heres.
Currite ducentes subtegmina, currite, fusi.

Illius egregias virtutes claraque facta
Saepe fatebuntur natorum in funere matres   35
Cum in *cinere*m canos solvent a vertice crines
Putridaque infirmis variabunt pectora palmis.
Currite ducentes subtegmina, currite, fusi.

Namque velut densas prosternens cultor aristas
Sole sub ardenti flaventia demetit arva,   35
Trojugenum infesto prosternet corpora ferro.
Currite ducentes subtegmina, currite, fusi.

Testis erit magnis virtutibus unda Scamandri,
Quae passim rapido diffunditur Hellesponto,
Cujus iter caesis angustans corporum acervis   36
Alta tepefaciet permixta flumina caede.
Currite ducentes subtegmina, currite, fusi.

Denique testis erit morti quoque reddita praeda,
Cum teres excelso coacervatum aggere bustum
Excipiet niveos percussae virginis artus.   36
Currite ducentes subtegmina, currite, fusi.

Nam simul ac fessis dederit fors copiam Achivis
Urbis Dardaniae Neptunia solvere vincla,
Alta Polyxenia madefient caede sepulcra,
Quae, velut ancipiti succumbens victima ferro,   37
Projiciet truncum submisso poplite corpus.
Currite ducentes subtegmina, currite, fusi.

Quare agite optatos animi conjungite amores.
Accipiat conjux felici foedere divam,
Dedatur cupido jam dudum nupta marito.   37
Currite ducentes subtegmina, currite, fusi.

om. nonnulli

Talia praefantes quondam felicia Pelei
Carmina divino cecinerunt pectore Parcae.
Praesentes namque ante domos invisere castas 385
Heroum et sese mortali ostendere coetu
Caelicolae, nondum spreta pietate, solebant.
Saepe pater divum templo in fulgente revisens,
Annua cum festis venissent sacra diebus,
Conspexit terra centum procumbere tauros : 390
Saepe vagus Liber Parnasi vertice summo
Thyiadas effusis evantes crinibus egit,
Cum Delphi tota certatim ex urbe tuentes   ruentes OCT
Acciperent laeti divum fumantibus aris :
Saepe in letifero belli certamine Mavors 395
Aut rapidi Tritonis era aut Rhamnusia virgo
Armatas hominum est praesens hortata catervas.
Sed postquam tellus scelere est imbuta nefando
Iustitiamque omnes cupida de mente fugarunt,
Perfudere manus fraterno sanguine fratres, 400
Destitit extinctos natus lugere parentes,
Optavit genitor primaevi funera nati
Liber ut innuptae poteretur flore novercae,
Ignaro mater substernens se impia nato,
Impia, non verita est divos scelerare parentes, 405
Omnia fanda nefanda malo permixta furore
Iustificam nobis mentem avertere deorum.
Quare nec tales dignantur visere coetus,
Nec se contingi patiuntur lumine claro.

LXV.

Etsi me assiduo confectum cura dolore
   Sevocat· a doctis, Ortale, virginibus,
Nec potis est dulces Musarum expromere fetus
   Mens animi : tantis fluctuat ipsa malis—
Namque mei nuper Lethaeo gurgite fratris
   Pallidulum manans alluit unda pedem,
Troia Rhaeteo quem subter litore tellus
   Ereptum nostris obterit ex oculis.
Alloquar, audiero nunquam tua *facta* loquentem ?
   Nunquam ego te, vita frater amabilior,
Aspiciam posthac ? At certe semper amabo,
   Semper maesta tua carmina morte canam,
Qualia sub densis ramorum concinit umbris
   Daulias, absumpti fata gemens Ityli—
Sed tamen in tantis maeroribus, Ortale, mitto
   Haec expressa tibi carmina Battiadae,
Ne tua dicta vagis nequiquam credita ventis
   Effluxisse meo forte putes animo,
Ut missum sponsi furtivo munere malum
   Procurrit casto virginis e gremio,
Quod miserae, oblitae molli sub veste locatum,
   Dum adventu matris prosilit, excutitur,
Atque illud prono praeceps agitur decursu,
   Huic manat tristi conscius ore rubor.

LXVI.

Omnia qui magni dispexit lumina mundi,
  Qui stellarum ortus comperit atque obitus,
Flammeus ut rapidi solis nitor obscuretur,
  Ut cedant certis sidera temporibus,
Ut Triviam furtim sub Latmia saxa relegans   5
  Dulcis amor gyro devocet aereo,
Idem me ille Conon caelesti numine vidit
  E Bereniceo vertice caesariem
Fulgentem clare, quam multis illa dearum
  Levia protendens brachia pollicita est,   10
Qua rex tempestate novo auctus hymenaeo
  Vastatum fines iverat Assyrios,
Dulcia nocturnae portans vestigia rixae
  Quam de virgineis gesserat exuviis.
Estne novis nuptis odio Venus, atque parentum 15
  Frustrantur falsis gaudia lacrimulis,
Ubertim thalami quas intra limina fundunt?
  Non—ita me divi—vera gemunt—juerint.
Id mea me multis docuit regina querellis,
  Invisente novo praelia torva viro.   20
At tu non orbum luxti deserta cubile,
  Sed fratris cari flebile discidium,
Cum penitus maestas exedit cura medullas?
  Ut tibi tunc toto pectore sollicitae
Sensibus ereptis mens excidit! at te ego certe 25
  Cognoram a parva virgine magnanimam.
Anne bonum oblita es facinus, quo regium adepta es
  Conjugium, quod non fortior ausit alis?

D

Sed tum maesta virum mittens quae verba
    locuta es !
  Juppiter, ut tristi lumina saepe manu !   30
Quis te mutavit tantus deus ? An quod amantes
    Non longe a caro corpore abesse volunt ?
Atque ibi me cunctis pro dulci conjuge divis
    Non sine taurino sanguine pollicita es,
Si reditum tetulisset. Is haud in tempore longo 35
    Captam Asiam Aegypti finibus addiderat.
Queis ego pro factis caelesti reddita coetu
    Pristina vota novo munere dissoluo.
Invita o regina tuo de vertice cessi,
    Invita—adjuro teque tuumque caput,   40
Digna ferat, quod siquis inaniter adjurarit—
    Sed qui se ferro postulet esse parem ?
Ille quoque eversus mons est, quem maximum
    in oris
    Progenies Thiae clara supervehitur,
Cum Medi peperere novum mare cumque juventus 45
    Per medium classi barbara navit Athon.
Quid facient crines, cum ferro talia cedant ?
    Juppiter, ut Chalybum omne genus pereat,
Et qui principio sub terra quaerere venas
    Institit ac ferri stringere duritiem !   50
Abjunctae paulo ante comae mea fata sorores
    Lugebant, cum se Memnonis Aethiopis
Unigena impellens nutantibus aera pennis
    Obtulit, Arsinoes Locridos ales equus,
Isque per aetherias me tollens advolat umbras 55
    Et Veneris casto collocat in gremio.

psa suum Zephyritis eo famulum legarat,
  Graia Canopeis incola litoribus.
Hi dii uen ibi variofne solium in limine caeli *Hic inveni timavio OCT*
  Ex Ariadneis aurea temporibus *templis*   60
Fixa corona foret, sed nos quoque fulgeremus
  Devotae flavi verticis exuviae,
Uvidulum a fluctu cedentem ad templa deum me
  Sidus in antiquis diva novum posuit ;
Virginis et saevi contingens namque Leonis   65
  Lumina, Callisto juxta Lycaoniam,
Vertor in occasum, tardum dux ante Booten
  Qui vix sero alto mergitur Oceano. *late at night*
Sed quanquam me nocte premunt vestigia divum,
  Lux autem canae Tethyi restituit—   70
Pace tua fari hic liceat, Rhamnusia virgo,
  Namque ego non ullo vera timore tegam,
Nec si me infestis discerpent sidera dictis *rend*
  Condita qui veri pectoris evoluo— *quin OCT*
Non his tam laetor rebus, quam me afore semper, 75
  Afore me a dominae vertice discrucior,
Quicum ego dum virgo quondam fuit omnibus expers
  Unguentis una milia multa bibi.
Nunc vos, optato quas junxit lumine taeda,
  Non post unanimis corpora conjugibus   80
Tradite, nudantes rejecta veste papillas,
  Quin jucunda mihi munera libet onyx, *onyx-box*
Vester onyx, casto petitis quae jura cubili.
  Sed, quae se impuro dedit adulterio,
Illius a ! mala dona levis bibat irrita pulvis, 85
  Namque ego ab indignis praemia nulla peto

CATULLUS.

52

Sed magis, o nuptae, semper concordia vestras
  Semper amor sedes accolat assiduus.
Tu vero, regina, tuens cùm sidera divam
  Placabis festis luminibus Venerem,   90
Sanguinis expertem non vestris esse tuum me ;
  Sed potius largis effice muneribus
⌐ Sidera cur iterent :† ‘ utinam†coma regia fiam,
  Proximus Hydrochoi fulgeret Oarion.’

offering

Sidera corruerint utinam! Oct

LXVIIIA.

Quod mihi fortuna casuque oppressus acerbo
  Conscriptum hoc lacrimis mittis epistolium,
Naufragum ut ejectum spumantibus aequoris undis
  Sublevem et a mortis limine restituam,—
‘ Quem neque sancta Venus molli requiescere somno 5
  Desertum in lecto caelibe perpetitur ;
Nec veterum dulci scriptorum carmine Musae
  Oblectant, cum mens anxia pervigilat,’—
Id gratum est mihi, me quoniam tibi dicis amicum,
  Muneraque et Musarum hinc petis et Veneris : 10
Sed tibi ne mea sint ignota incommoda, Manli,
  Neu me odisse putes hospitis officium,
Accipe queis merser fortunae fluctibus ipse
  Ne amplius a misero dona beata petas.
Tempore quo primum vestis mihi tradita pura est, 15
  Jucundum cum aetas florida ver ageret,
Multa satis lusi : non est dea nescia nostri
  Quae dulcem curis miscet amaritiem.
Sed totum hoc studium luctu fraterna mihi mors
  Abstulit. O misero frater adempte mihi,   20

Tu mea tu moriens fregisti commoda, frater,
 Tecum una tota est nostra sepulta domus ;
Omnia tecum una perierunt gaudia nostra,
 Quae tuus in vita dulcis alebat amor.
Cujus ego interitu tota de mente fugavi   25
 Haec studia atque omnes delicias animi.
Ignosces igitur si, quae mihi luctus ademit,
 Haec tibi non tribuo munera, cum nequeo.
Nam quod scriptorum non magna est copia apud me,
 Hoc fit quod Romae vivimus : illa domus,
Illa mihi sedes, illic mea carpitur aetas ;   35
 Huc una ex multis capsula me sequitur.
Quod cum ita sit, nolim statuas nos mente maligna
 Id facere aut animo non satis ingenuo,
Quod tibi non utriusque petenti copia posta est :
 Ultro ego deferrem, copia siqua foret.   40

LXVIIIв.

Non possum reticere, deae, qua me Allius in re
 Juverit aut quantis juverit officiis,
Ne fugiens saeclis obliviscentibus aetas
 Illius hoc caeca nocte tegat studium :
Sed dicam vobis, vos porro dicite multis   5 (45)
 Milibus et facite haec carta loquatur anus.
  .   .   .   .
 Notescatque magis mortuus atque magis,

Nec tenuem texens sublimis aranea telam
  In deserto Alli nomine opus faciat.   10 (
Nam mihi quam dederit duplex Amathusia curam
  Scitis, et in quo me corruerit genere,
Cum tantum arderem quantum Trinacria rupes
  Lymphaque in Oetaeis Malia Thermopylis,
Maesta nec assiduo tabescere lumina fletu   15 (
  Cessarent tristique imbre madere genae,
Qualis in aerei perlucens vertice montis
  Rivus muscoso prosilit e lapide,
Qui, cum de prona praeceps est valle volutus,
  Per medium densi transit iter populi,   20 (
Dulce viatori lasso in sudore levamen
  Cum gravis exustos aestus hiulcat agros :
Hic, velut in nigro jactatis turbine nautis
  Levius aspirans aura secunda venit,
Jam prece Pollucis, jam Castoris implorata : 25 (
  Tale fuit nobis Allius auxilium.
Is clausum lato patefecit limite campum,
  Isque domum nobis, isque dedit dominam,
Ad quam communes exerceremus amores.
  Quo mea se molli candida diva pede   30 (
Intulit et trito fulgentem in limine plantam
  Innixa arguta constituit solea,
Conjugis ut quondam flagrans advenit amore
  Protesilaeam Laodamia domum,
Inceptam frustra, nondum quum sanguine sacro 35 (
  Hostia caelestes pacificasset eros.
Nil mihi tam valde placeat, Rhamnusia virgo,
  Quod temere invitis suscipiatur eris.

Quam jejuna pium desideret ara cruorem
   Docta est amisso Laodamia viro,   40 (80)
Conjugis ante coacta novi dimittere collum,
   Quam veniens una atque altera rursus hiems
Noctibus in longis avidum saturasset amorem,
   Posset ut abrupto vivere conjugio,
Quod scibant Parcae non longo tempore abesse 45 (85)
   Si miles muros isset ad Iliacos.
Nam tum Helenae raptu primores Argivorum
   Coeperat ad sese Troja ciere viros,
Troja, nefas, commune sepulcrum Asiae Europaeque,
   Troja, virum et virtutum omnium acerba
     cinis.   50 (90)
Quae ve*l* et id nostro letum miserabile fratri
   Attulit. Ei misero frater adempte mihi,
Ei misero fratri jucundum lumen ademptum,
   Tecum una tota est nostra sepulta domus,
Omnia tecum una perierunt gaudia nostra, 55 (95)
   Quae tuus in vita dulcis alebat amor.
Quem nunc tam longe, non inter nota sepulcra
   Nec prope cognatos compositum cineres,
Sed Troja obscena, Troja infelice sepultum
   Detinet extremo terra aliena solo.   60 (100)
Ad quam tum properans fertur *simul* undique pubes
   Graeca penetrales deseruisse focos,
Ne Paris abducta gavisus libera moecha
   Otia pacato degeret in thalamo.
Quo tibi tum casu, pulcherrima Laodamia, 65 (105)
   Ereptum est vita dulcius atque anima
Conjugium. Tanto te absorbens vertice amoris

Aestus in abruptum detulerat barathrum,
Quale ferunt Grai Pheneum prope Cylleneum
    Siccare emulsa pingue palude solum,   70 (110)
Quod quondam caesis montis fodisse medullis
    Audit falsiparens Amphitryoniades,
Tempore quo certa Stymphalia monstra sagitta
    Perculit imperio deterioris eri,
Pluribus ut caeli tereretur janua divis,   75 (115)
    Hebe nec longa virginitate foret.
Sed tuus altus amor barathro fuit altior illo
    Qui tuum domitum ferre jugum docuit.
Nam neque tam carum confecto aetate parenti
    Una caput seri nata nepotis alit,   80 (120)
Qui, cum divitiis vix tandem inventus avitis
    Nomen testatas intulit in tabulas,
Impia derisi gentilis gaudia tollens,
    Suscitat a cano volturium capiti :
Nec tantum niveo gavisa est ulla columbo 85 (125)
    Compar, quae multo dicitur improbius
Oscula mordenti semper decerpere rostro,
    Quam quae praecipue multivola est mulier :
Sed tu horum magnos vicisti sola furores
    Ut semel es flavo conciliata viro.   90 (130)
Aut nihil aut paulo cui tum concedere digna
    Lux mea se nostrum contulit in gremium,
Quam circumcursans hinc illinc saepe Cupido
    Fulgebat crocina candidus in tunica.
Quae tamen etsi uno non est contenta Catullo, 95 (135)
    Rara verecundae furta feremus erae,
Ne nimium simus stultorum more molesti.

Saepe etiam Juno, maxima caelicolum,
Conjugis in culpa flagrantem contudit iram,
　Noscens omnivoli plurima furta Jovis.　100 (140)
At, quia nec divis homines componier aequum est,
　Ingratum tremuli tolle parentis onus.
Nec tamen illa mihi dextra deducta paterna
　Fragrantem Assyrio venit odore domum.
Quare illud satis est, si nobis is datur unus,
　Quem lapide illa, dies, candidiore notat.
Hoc tibi, quod potui, confectum carmine munus
　Pro multis, Alli, redditur officiis,　110 (150)
Ne vestrum scabra tangat robigine nomen
　Haec atque illa dies atque alia atque alia.
Huc addent divi quam plurima, quae Themis olim
　Antiquis solita est munera ferre piis.
Sitis felices et tu simul et tua vita　115 (155)
　Et domus *ipsa*, in qua lusimus, et domina,
Et qui principio nobis terram dedit aufert
　A quo sunt primo *mi* omnia nata bona,
Et longe ante omnes, mihi quae me carior ipso est,
　Lux mea, qua viva vivere dulce mihi est. 120 (160)

LXX.

Nulli se dicit mulier mea nubere malle
　Quam mihi, non si se Juppiter ipse petat.
Dicit : sed mulier cupido quod dicit amanti
　In vento et rapida scribere oportet aqua.

LXXII.

Dicebas quondam solum te nosse Catullum,
    Lesbia, nec prae me velle tenere Jovem.
Dilexi tum te, non tantum ut vulgus amicam,
    Sed pater ut natos diligit et generos.
Nunc te cognovi : quare, etsi impensius uror,
    Multo mi tamen es vilior et levior.
Qui potis est ? inquis. Quod amantem injuria ta
    Cogit amare magis sed bene velle minus.

LXXIII.

cease anyone Desine de quoquam quisquam bene velle mereri
    Aut aliquem fieri posse putare pium.
Omnia sunt ingrata, nihil fecisse benigne
prodest oct   *Jam juvat* : immo etiam taedet obestque mag
Ut mihi, quem nemo gravius nec acerbius urget
    Quam modo qui me unum atque unicum amic
    habuit.

LXXV.

Huc est mens deducta tua mea, Lesbia, culpa,
    Atque ita se officio perdidit ipsa suo,
Ut jam nec bene velle queat tibi, si optima fias,
    Nec desistere amare, omnia si facias.

LXXVI.

Si qua recordanti benefacta priora voluptas
    Est homini, cum se cogitat esse pium,
Nec sanctam violasse fidem nec foedere in ullo
    Divum ad fallendos numine abusum homines,

Multa parata manent in longa aetate, Catulle,   5
   Ex hoc ingrato gaudia amore tibi.
Nam quaecumque homines bene cuiquam aut dicere
     possunt
   Aut facere, haec a te dictaque factaque sunt.
Omnia quae ingratae perierunt credita menti.
   Quare jam te cur amplius excrucies ?   10
Quin tu animo offirmas atque istinc teque reducis
   Et diis invitis desinis esse miser ?
Difficile est longum subito deponere amorem :
   Difficile est, verum hoc qualibet efficias.
Una salus haec est, hoc est tibi pervincendum ; 15
   Hoc facias, sive id non pote, sive pote.
O dii, si vestrum est misereri, aut si quibus
     unquam
   Extrema jam ipsa in morte tulistis opem,
Me miserum aspicite, et, si vitam puriter egi,
   Eripite hanc pestem perniciemque mihi,   20
Quae mihi subrepens imos, ut torpor, in artus
   Expulit ex omni pectore laetitias.
Non jam illud quaero, contra ut me diligat illa,
   Aut, quod non potis est, esse pudica velit :
Ipse valere opto et taetrum hunc deponere mor-
     bum.   25
   O dii, reddite mi hoc pro pietate mea.

LXXVII.

Rufe, mihi frustra ac nequiquam credite amico—
   Frustra ? immo magno cum pretio atque malo—

Sicine subrepsti mi atque intestina perurens
  Mi misero eripuisti omnia nostra bona,
Eripuisti, heu heu nostrae crudele venenum   5
  Vitae, heu heu nostrae pectus amicitiae.

LXXXII.

Quinti, si tibi vis oculos debere Catullum,
  Aut aliud si quid carius est oculis,
Eripere ei noli, multo quod carius illi
  Est oculis seu quid carius est oculis.

LXXXIII.

Lesbia mi praesente viro mala plurima dicit :
  Haec illi fatuo maxima laetitia est.
Mule, nihil sentis : si nostri oblita taceret,
  Sana esset : nunc quod gannit et obloquitur,
Non solum meminit, sed, quae multo acrior est res, 5
  Irata est. Hoc est, uritur et loquitur.

LXXXIV.

Chommoda dicebat, si quando commoda vellet
  Dicere, et insidias Arrius hinsidias ;
Et tum mirifice sperabat se esse locutum
  Cum quantum poterat dixerat hinsidias.
Credo : sic mater, sic Liber avunculus ejus,   5
  Sic maternus avus dixerat atque avia.
Hoc misso in Syriam requierant omnibus aures :
  Audibant eadem haec leniter et leviter,
Nec sibi postilla metuebant talia verba.
  Cum subito affertur nuntius horribilis,   10

Ionios fluctus, postquam illic Arrius isset,
  Jam non Ionios esse, sed Hionios.

LXXXV.

Odi et amo : quare id faciam, fortasse requiris.
  Nescio, sed fieri sentio et excrucior.

LXXXVI.

Quintia formosa est multis : mihi candida, longa,
  Recta est—haec ego sic singula confiteor.
Totum illud ' formosa ' nego ; nam nulla venustas,
  Nulla in tam magno est corpore mica salis.
Lesbia formosa est, quae cum pulcerrima tota est, 5
  Tum omnibus una omnes surripuit Veneres.

LXXXVII.

Nulla potest mulier tantum se dicere amatam
  Vere, quantum a me, Lesbia, amata, mea, es.
Nulla fides ullo fuit unquam foedere tanta,
  Quanta in amore tuo ex parte reperta mea est.

XCII.

Lesbia mi dicit semper male nec tacet unquam
  De me : Lesbia me dispeream nisi amat.
Quo signo ? quia sunt totidem mea : deprecor illam
  Assidue, verum dispeream nisi amo.

XCIII.

Nil nimium studeo, Caesar, tibi velle placere,
  Nec scire utrum sis albus an ater homo.

XCV.

Zmyrna mei Cinnae, nonam post denique messem
Quam coepta est nonamque edita post hiemem,
Milia cum interea quingenta Hortensius uno

.   .   .   .

Zmyrna cavas Satrachi penitus mittetur ad undas,   5
    Zmyrnam cana diu saecula pervoluent.
At Volusi annales Paduam morientur ad ipsam
    Et laxas scombris saepe dabunt tunicas.
Parva mei mihi sint cordi monumenta . . . .
    At populus tumido gaudeat Antimacho.   10

XCVI.

Si quicquam mutis gratum acceptumve sepulcris
    Accidere a nostro, Calve, dolore potest,
Cum desiderio veteres renovamus amores
    Atque olim missas flemus amicitias,
Certe non tanto mors immatura dolori est   5
    Quintiliae, quantum gaudet amore tuo.

XCIX.

Surripui tibi, dum ludis, mellite Juventi,
    Saviolum dulci dulcius ambrosia.
Verum id non impune tuli ; namque amplius horam
    Suffixum in summa me memini esse cruce,
Dum tibi me purgo nec possum fletibus ullis   5
    Tantillum vestrae demere saevitiae.
Nam simul id factum est, multis diluta labella
    Guttis abstersisti omnibus articulis.

[T]e quicquam nostro contractum ex ore maneret,
  Tamquam commictae spurca saliva lupae.   10
[P]raeterea infesto miserum me tradere amori
  Non cessasti omnique excruciare modo,
[U]t mi ex ambrosia mutatum jam foret illud
  Saviolum tristi tristius elleboro.
[Q]uam quoniam poenam misero proponis amori, 15
  Nunquam jam posthac basia surripiam.

CI.

[M]ultas per gentes et multa per aequora vectus
  Advenio has miseras, frater, ad inferias
[U]t te postremo donarem munere mortis
  Et mutam nequiquam alloquerer cinerem.
[Q]uandoquidem fortuna mihi tete abstulit ipsum, 5
  Heu miser indigne frater adempte mihi,
[N]unc tamen interea haec, prisco quae more parentum
  Tradita sunt _tristi_ munere ad inferias,   *by way of sad tribute*
[A]ccipe fraterno multum _manantia_ fletu,   *flowing with*
  Atque in perpetuum, frater, ave atque vale.   10

CII.

[S]i quicquam tacito commissum est fido ab amico,
  Cujus sit penitus nota fides animi,
[M]eque esse invenies illorum jure sacratum.
  Corneli, et factum me esse puta Harpocratem.

CVII.

[S]i cui quid cupidoque optantique obtigit unquam
  Insperanti, hoc est gratum animo proprie.

Quare hoc est gratum, nobis quoque carius auro,
　Quod te restituis, Lesbia, mi cupido.
Restituis cupido atque insperanti ? ipsa refers te 5
　Nobis ? o lucem candidiore nota.
Quis me uno vivit felicior, aut magis hac me est
　Optandus vita ? dicere quis poterit ?

CVIII.

Si, Comini, populi arbitrio tua cana senectus
　Spurcata impuris moribus intereat,
Non equidem dubito quin primum inimica bonorum
　Lingua exsecta avido sit data volturio,
Effossos oculos voret atro gutture corvus,　　　5
　Intestina canes, cetera membra lupi.

CIX.

Jucundum, mea vita, mihi proponis amorem
　Hunc nostrum inter nos perpetuumque fore.
Dii magni, facite ut vere promittere possit
　Atque id sincere dicat et ex animo,
Ut liceat nobis tota perducere vita　　　5
　Aeternum hoc sanctae foedus amicitiae.

CXIV.

Firmano saltu non falso Mentula dives
　Fertur, qui tot res in se habet egregias,
Aucupia omne genus, pisces, prata, arva, ferasque.
　Nequiquam : fructus sumptibus exsuperat.
Quare concedo sit dives, dum omnia desint :　　　5
　Saltum laudemus, dum modo ipse egeat.

CXVI.

Saepe tibi studioso animo venante requirens
   Carmina uti possem mittere Battiadae,
Qui te lenirem nobis, neu conarere
   Telis infeste mittere in usque caput, *infestum oct*
Hunc video mihi nunc frustra sumptum esse laborem,
   Gelli, nec nostras hic valuisse preces.
Contra, nos tela ista tua evitamus amictu, *amictu oct*
   At fixus nostris tu dabis supplicium. *wrapped close*

NOTES.

NOTES.

I.

P. 1. 1. ' To whom am I to give my dainty, new-born little volume ? ' The present indicative is constantly used in Latin with a deliberative force ; cf. LXIII. 55. The words *lepidum* and *novum* mean both that the book is bright and new from the publisher's hands, and that it contains delicate wit presented in a form new to Latin literature.

2. **pumice.** For the use of pumice stone in the preparation of books, see XXII. 6 note.

3. **Corneli.** Corn. Nepos, compatriot of Catullus and about eight years his senior, chiefly known as biographer of illustrious men, but also writer of love poems now lost. The ' Chronica ' here referred to are also lost.

4. **aliquid** in opposition to *nugas*. Catullus calls his light poems ' nothings,' but his friend always considered them ' of serious value,' ' a something of importance.' *Si vis esse aliquis* = if you would be a *somebody*. Translate ' would set upon my trifles no trifling value.'

6. **explicare,** to unfold and show as a whole, as a robe-maker exhibits his wares (*explicat vestem*), or as a general deploys his troops (*explicat ordines*), so that all may be comprehended at a glance ; cf. LIII. 3. Here the word almost = ' tabulate.'

7. **laboriosis** is said to mean ' on which labour has been spent,' according to A. Gellius, who (N. A. IX. 12) quotes a line from Catullus' friend, Calvus,

' *Durum rus fugis et laboriosum,*'

and explains the last word as ' *in quo laboratur.*' But Calvus means ' the hard, work-a-day country,' employing the simple personification which is also used here. If *carta* (a sheet) can

be called *docta* (learned), it may also be called *laboriosa* (dil
gent) : and in LXVIII B. 6 (46), we find ' *carta loquatur anus*
The whole of Gellius' article is confused and unfortunate.

8. quicquid hoc libelli, ' Therefore take to yourself all this
of a little book : whatever its worth may perhaps be, yet ma
it, O guardian maiden, endure without fading more than on
generation.' The best MSS. read *Qualecumque quod,* for whic
quidem is the earliest and perhaps best correction. Ellis reads

> ' *Quare habe tibi quicquid hoc libelli*
> *Qualecunque : quod o patrona virgo* '

= ' Take this slight book, such as it is, and may it,' &c. Th
virgo may be Minerva, or the Muse. Cf. LXVIII B. 1-6 (40-46
Munro thinks neither appropriate, and, after Bergk, reads :

> ' *Qualecumque quidem patronei ut ergo* '

= ' that, poor as it perhaps may be, yet for its patron's sak
it may endure.' This makes capital sense, but there is n
evidence that Catullus wrote it.

With *quicquid hoc libelli* compare Verg. Aen. I. 78, ' *quod
cumque hoc regni* ' = ' this empire, be it great or small,' on whic
see Dr. Henry's ' Aeneidea.''

On the Hendecasyllabic metre of this poem see Appendix I. A

II.

1. deliciae, ' my lady's pet ' : so ' *amores* ' = ' mistress
' favourite.'

3. primum digitum, ' finger tip,' not ' first finger,' which i
called *index.*

appetenti, ' reaching forward to catch.' Translate ' t
whose sallies she will offer her finger tip.'

5. desiderio, ' my heart's desire.' Cicero (Fam. XIV. 2 fin.
writes to his wife, ' *mea lux, mea desideria, valete.*' For th
" Lover's vocabulary " in Catullus see Appendix II. 3.

nitenti, ' bright-eyed.'

6. Carum nescio quid, like *solaciolum,* is accusative afte
jocari. On the ' cognate ' acc. see VII. 9 note. Translat
' is pleased to play I know not what dear frolic and sof
diversion of her pain.'

credo. And well she may . would that I, like your mis

tress and mine, when the oppressive intensity of my passion shall be assuaged, could make merry with you ! ' *Credo* as usual (cf. LXXXIV. 6) is isolated and abrupt : it implies that Lesbia is sure to find solace in so sweet a bird.

gravis ardor : cf. *gravis aestus*, LXVIII B. 22.   Ellis reads :

> ' *Et solaciolum sui doloris,*
> *Credo, et cum gravis acquiescit ardor :* '

= ' either as a gentle assuagement of her pain or when,' &c. *Solaciolum* he puts in ' apposition with the clause *nescio quid libet jocari*,' or perhaps would regard it, with Lachmann, as a second nominative to *libet*.   But *libet* cannot have a substantive for subject ; for only neuter pronouns can stand as nominatives to impersonal verbs.   Munro suggests with confidence :

> 8. ' *Credo ut, cum gravis acquiescet ardor,*
> 7.   *Sit solaciolum sui doloris,*'

and distinguishes *dolor* as the pain felt by Lesbia when her lover is away, *ardor* as her fevered excitement in his presence.

Baehrens alters *et* to *in* before *solaciolum*, and reads the next verse :

> ' *(Credo, tum gravis acquiescet ardor).*'

All these alterations are uncertain and antagonistic.

P. 2. 10. **curas** is specially used of the pains of love.   So Hor. A. P. 85 :

> ' *Et juvenum curas et libera vina referri.*'

Cf. LXIV. 96, LXVIII. 18.

11-13. **tam gratum est.** Ellis would translate, ' To play with you *would* be as welcome,' &c.   But these lines are more probably a fragment of another piece accidentally attached to the already complete poem on account of the similarity of metre.   This may also have occurred XIV. 24-26, LI. 13-16, LXV. 19-24, LXVIII (41 ad fin.).

puellae, Atalanta, who would only ' loose her girdle ' (part of the marriage ceremonial) to one who surpassed her in speed of foot.   Milanion entered the contest, and, as they ran, flung on the course a golden apple.   This she was tempted to pick up, and by doing so checked her speed and lost the race.

aureolum, ' daintily gilded,' or ' delicate golden.'

soluit is a trisyllable. Cf. LXI. 53, *zonula soluunt sinus* ;
LXVI. 38, *dissoluo* ; 74, *evoluo.*

III.

1. ' Goddesses of beauty, gods of passion, and all there are
among men of finer feeling, come and mourn.'

This poem has been often imitated, often translated. It is
a characteristic specimen of Catullus' style, showing the
natural symmetry of his thought, the simple directness of his
expression. After the invocation, half the poem tells the
preciousness and the graces of the bird, half the sadness of its
lot and the bereavement of its mistress. The words are so
unaffected, and their order seems so spontaneous,

> ' ut sibi quivis
> Speret idem, sudet multum frustraque laboret
> Ausus idem.'

2. quantum, &c. See Appendix II. 1. a. on Catullus'
phraseology.

7. ipsam Ellis bids us take with *matrem*, ' as well as the
child knows her very mother.' But *suam* is thus left incomplete ; and it is awkward and unCatullian to say *ipsam tam
bene quam* for *tam bene quam ipsam.* Lachmann would read
' *ipsa.*' *Suam ipsam* = ' his own mistress.'

8. sese is emphatic : ' nor would he dislodge himself.'

13. at used in sudden imprecation : cf. XXVIII. 14 :

> ' At vobis mala multa di deaeque
> Dent, opprobria Romuli Remique.'

' Out ! shame upon you, shameful shades of Orcus, that swallow
in your depths all pretty things ! '

17. tua opera, ' by your doing,' ' you are to blame that.'
The phrase, in usage, conveys an idea of reproach : compare
Cic. Phil. II. § 23, where ' *opera mea* ' is coupled with ' *culpa
mea.*'

18. My mistress' sweet eyes are sadly swollen and red with
tears.' *Flendo :* so *fando* = ' with words ' (Verg. Aen. II. 6).

turgiduli. Catullus uses diminutive nouns, proper names,
adjectives, and even verbs ; see Appendix II. 2.

IV. '

1. Catullus points out to some guests his old yacht. Made at Cytorus or Amastris (the first the name of the hill, the second of the town) in Paphlagonia (at this time part of the province of Bithynia), it had received him on board at its 'birthplace' (or, according to Munro, at some port on the Propontis), and had carried him, by Rhodes and the Cyclades, along the Adriatic coast, and by the rivers Po and Mincio, into the lake Benacus (now Lago di Garda), on the island or peninsula of which, Sirmio (see XXXI.), the poet had a country seat. Here the vessel now lay, beached or docked, in honourable superannuation.

It seems probable that in many of Catullus' poems, however they present to us the freshness of originality, he freely imitated a Greek model. See on LI., LXI., LXII., LXIII., LXIV., XVI. The Grecisms in this poem are the gender of *phaselus* (generally feminine in Latin), the construction *ait fuisse celerrimus*[1] (an enlargement in the Greek spirit of existing Latin idiom, not peculiar to Catullus ; see Hor. Ep. I. vii. 22, *it esse paratus*, and cf. Verg. II. 377, &c.), together with the attraction of the gender of the adjective (cf. Hor. Sat. I. ix. , *dulcissime rerum*, &c.), the construction *iste post phaselus* (cf. XXXI. 1 note), the case-ending and lengthening of *Proponti-da*, the lengthening of the final syllable of *impotentia*, the vocative form *Amastri*, and the sudden change to direct address, together with the position of *Tibi*. The metre is pure Iambic : see Appendix I. B.

3. 3. impetum. 'No timber floated whose dash she failed to lead, whether called to wing her way with light blade or with canvas.' The oars were the ship's wings (πτέρα νηός, Homer). as well as the sails.

6. Adriatici. The journey is traced backwards, from the Italian coast to the Euxine.

8. nobilem, 'renowned in story.'

Thraciam, adjective agreeing with Propontida.

10. 'Where that, the yacht of after-time, was earlier a leafy wood ; for many a day, on Cytorus' ridge, she sent forth whispers from her prattling leafage.'

15. ultima, 'from the remotest spring of her life,' or 'from the primal germ of her race.'

---

[1] It is to be remarked that the MSS. read *celerrimum*, which would be parallel to XXXI. 5, XXXVI. 7, XLII. 4.

17. **imbuisse** combines the notions of dipping into water 𝑎
of initiation, like our 'baptise.'

18. **inde,** 'thence' (Ellis) or 'next' (Munro).

impotentia, 'ungoverned.' *Impotens* = without self-cont
Comp. Hor. Od. I. xxxvii. 10, '*quid libet impotens sperare*
'ungoverned enough to hope for anything.' Contrast ' pot
sui ' = ' lord of himself.'

19. ' Whether the breeze whistled to larboard or to s𝑡
board, or the bright weather, following fair, had taken w
one leap both sheets.'

Jupp. secundus = a fair following wind (*Juppiter* by it
expresses *bright weather*). *Simul . . . pedem* = lay on the sai
as to pull both sheets (the sail being a square sail) equally ta
while the vessel ran before the wind; in the former wo
(' *laeva . . . aura* ') she is represented as tacking right or l

22. **litoralibus diis :** *Glauco et Panopeae et Inoo Melicer*
Verg. G. I. 436.

23. **sibi,** 'for her.' Possibly ' by her '; but *sibi* = a se m
commonly in later Latinity.

esse facta = '*had been* made.'

24. **novissime** = ' last of all,' *a mari* = on leaving the sea
the rivers.
Many editors would emend to *a marei novissimo* = ' from
farthest part of the sea,' but without occasion.

ad usque = ' on and on until reaching,' ' right up to.'
CXVI. 4 :

> *Telis infeste mittere in usque caput.*

25. ' But these are bygones : now in sequestered rest
spends her age, consecrating herself to thee, O Castor, broth
twin, and to thee, twin-brother of Castor.'

fuere, ' belong to the past.' Cf. Verg. Aen. II. 325 :

> ' *Fuimus Troes, fuit Ilium et ingens*
> *Gloria Teucrorum.*'

senet = ' *is* old,' not ' grows old,' which would requ
senescit.

V.

1. This poem contains the creed of all passionate lovers, since lovers began. To translate without spoiling it has been the ambition of many, but no one has yet succeeded:

' *Multi illam agricolae, multi coluere juvenci.*'

Compare in this respect the dialogue of the coquetting lovers, Hor. Od. III. ix.

On Lesbia, see General Introduction I.

vivamus = make the best of life. Comp. '*vixi*,' Hor. Od. III. xxix. 43.

2. Valuing all the gossip of over-serious sages at a poor pennyworth.'

P. 4. 5. ' But for us, once our little day has reached its setting, waits a sheer night of sleep, never to be broken.'

6. **perpetua** = continuous.

8. **mille altera**, ' another thousand,' *mille* and *centum* are regarded as neuters plural : so '*altera*' (*decem*), Virg. Ec. III. 71.

9. **usque**, continuative, = ' yet again.'

10. **conturbabimus.** *Conturbare rationes* or *tabulas* = to ' wreck the accounts,' as by the addition of confusing figures, said of fraudulent bankrupts ; see Mayor's Juvenal, VII. 129 note, for the usage of the word. Catullus' plan, to obscure the total of kisses, is to kiss without counting.

ne sciamus. It is an ancient superstition that you should never know the exact number of your blessings, lest calamity follow. The knowledge in possession of another person gives him a dangerous power over you. Compare the last two lines of VII.

12. ' Or any miscreant have power to blight with envy.'

13. **sciet** (Bücheler) for MSS. *sciat*, which would convey a notion of indefinite frequency not appropriate here.

VII.

1. In v. Catullus is kissed by Lesbia, here he kisses her— a difference purely grammatical.

2. **tuae**, ' of you,' not ' of yours ' see 9.

superque. The conjunctive particles *et, que, τε, καί,* are often used where we should employ the disjunctive ' or.'

3. **numerus,** often = ' quantity.' See Mayor's Second Philippic, xxvii. § 66. Here it is better, however, to translate *numerus* as ' multitude,' taking *harenae* as a collective noun = ' grains of sand.' Compare LXI. 206 :

> ' *Ille pulveris Africi*
> *Siderumque micantium*
> *Subducat numerum prius.*'

and Hor. ' *numeroque carentis arenae.*'

4. **laserpic.** = σιλφιοφόρος, Strabo 133. The plant *silphium* or *laserpicium,* from which *laser* (assa foetida) was drawn, grew in the *district* called *Cyrenae,* and was an emblem of the *city* Cyrene, whose founder, Battus, was honoured as a god after death.

5. **Jovis** = ' of Juppiter Ammon,' whose oracular temple, in the oasis called Ammonium, was visited by Alexander.

7. **tacet** = ' tells no tales.' It might possibly mean ' when the night is *moonless.*' Cf. Verg. Aen. II. 255 :

> ' *tacitae per amica silentia lunae.*'

Cato uses ' *luna silens* ' = *interlunia.*

9. Literally ' to kiss you so many kisses,' *te* being accusative of object, *basia* cognate accusative.

The ' cognate ' accusative is of two kinds : (*a*) it expresses by a substantive the material result of the action signified by the verb, as οἰκοδομῶ δόμον, *aedes aedifico ;* ' *sternere approbationem* ' (XLV.) ; (*b*) or merely reiterates the action of the verb in a nominal form, generally for the convenience of modifying the action by an epithet in the shape of an adjective (as *multa* here).

10. **Vesano.** Cf. *vesaniente vento* (XXV. 13), *furorque vecors* (XV. 14, XL. 4), *vemens* (L. ad fin.). In these words the prefix seems privative in force. But *repallida* (Hor. Sat. I. ii. 129) and *vegrandis* (Pers. I. 97) seem to mean ' very pale,' ' very great.'

11. **curiosi** = ' busy bodies.'

12. **fascinare** = βασκαίνειν (root βα = φα = fa. Cf. βάζειν,

φημί, *fari*) originally meant ' to use words about a person,'
hence ' cast a spell over ' : *fascinum*, like βασκάνιον, signifies
an amulet worn to repel witchcraft.

IX.

1. **Verani.** Veranius, as we learn from XII., went to Spain
with Fabullus, another friend of Catullus ; and they were probably together again in Macedonia, on the staff of the pro-
consul L. Piso Caesoninus (57 B.C.), while Catullus was in
Bithynia. They shared the poet's pleasures and poverty at
Rome (XIII., XXVIII., XLVII.), but are otherwise unknown.

2. **antistans,** ' worth more to me than.'

mil. trecentis = any great number. Cf. XLVII. 3 :

' *Usque ad milia basiem trecenta.*'

P. 5. 7. **loca . . . . nationes,** ' scenes and feats and peoples.'

8. **ut mos est tuus** = in your own interesting manner, ' as
you alone can tell.'

applicansque collum, ' and drawing your neck towards me,
will seal your genial face and eyes with lovers' kisses.' Not
' laying my neck on yours,' but clasping my hands behind your
neck and drawing you towards me.

10. **quantum . . . beatiorum,** ' O all ye favourites of fortune, what is gladder or more fortunate than I ? '
Ellis would make this, not an appeal to happy men, but an
indefinite relative phrase = ' out of all fortune's favourites
what is,' &c. The similar phrase, however, III. 2, ' *quantum
est hominum venustiorum,*' is a direct address, and the sudden
turning to the vocative is in Catullus' manner.

X.

1. ' As I idled in the square, my friend Varus carried me
away to call upon his mistress, a little naught—I was at once
convinced—confessedly as full of wit as she was charming.'

6. **quid esset,** &c., ' what were the present state and prospects of Bithynia, and how much money had it been worth to
me ? '

9-11. 'I answered, with simple truth, that there was nothing for natives, governors, or staff. Why, then, I asked, should any one of us return with larded locks?'

ipsis = the provincials, and **quisquam** = any of the members of the staff.

I adopt without hesitation the reading of 11 proposed in Munro's 'Elucidations,' where he demonstrates the regularity of the imperfect subjunctive, introduced by *cur*, in reported interrogations.

14. quod . . . . esse, *i.e.,* the '*lectica octophorus*' first came into use in Bithynia.

15. comparasti, 'levied' or 'collected and trained.'

16-23. 'Adopting the tone of a man of means in the presence of the lady, "No," said I, "I was not so pinched, although a poor province had been my misfortune, as not to set up my eight straight-backed fellows." That was a bounce —I had not a creature, at home or abroad, fit to shoulder the broken leg of an old truckle-bed.'

17. facerem, 'make myself out to be.' Munro compares XCVII. 9, 'et se facit esse venustum.'

unum beatiorem. The comparative seems throughout this piece to be used in the colloquial sense of a modified positive, no *special* contrast being meant; so also '*quantum est hominum beatiorum*,' IX. 10, III. 2, XII. 3, XXXIII. 3, 4, which suggest that here *unum beatiorum* may = *unum e beatioribus.* Ellis similarly would render 'a particularly lucky fellow,' comparing XXXVII. 17. It is to be admitted that the use of *unus* with a comparative of this kind requires illustration. Perhaps therefore we must understand *quam ceteram cohortem* (Munro), and translate 'wishing to make myself out the happy exception.'

P. 6. 24. ut . . . . cinaediorem, 'playing her impudent part to perfection.'

26. commoda seems to be the imperative of *commodare,* 'to lend.' But there is no other example of the shortening of the final vowel in a polysyllabic imperative.

[M]any emendations have been suggested ; as Hand's

> ' *Istos. commodum enim volo ad Sarapim*,'

[whe]re *da* is understood before *Istos*, and *commodum* = just in
[tim]e ; or Munro's ' *commode enim* ' = comfortably ; or Ellis'
[*co*]*mmoneam. Volo* ' (com. = ' give an order to ').

[T]he worship of *Serapis* came from Sinope to Alexandria ;
[hen]ce, with other Egyptian cults, to Rome, in the last
[year]s of the Republic.

[27]. **mane me** = ' not so fast.'

[T]he shortening of *manĕ* (cf. *cavĕ*, L. 18) has cast a doubt on
[the] line. Emendations are : ' *mane* ' *inquii* (Ellis) ; *minime*
[m]*ii* (Lachmann, &c.) ; *mi anime* (Bergk) ; and ' *memini*
[*ser*]*io* (Munro).

[28]. **istud** = *octo homines rectos*, cf. 14, *quod illic natum
[dic]ur esse*, and is directly governed by *paravit* 30, the inter-
[ven]ing clauses, expressive of the poet's haste and perturbation,
[for a] moment interrupting the construction, which is resumed
[in 30]*s*.

[M]unro makes *quod* a conjunction : ' when I said just now
[that] I had them.' Ellis makes *istud* and *quod* refer to the
[wor]ds *me habere :* ' as for what I happened to say, *i.e.* that I
[had] them.'

[29]. ' A dear friend of mine is Cinna, I mean Gaius Cinna,
[i]t was bought them for himself. But whether things are
[hi]s or mine, is all one to me—I use them as freely as if I have
[bou]ght for myself.' *Quam* seems to = *quam si*, of which there
[is n]o other example. Even if it were possible, Munro, who,
[afte]r Achilles Statius, emends to *paratis* (neut. abl. plu. of
[part]iciple), objects that the proper tense after *si* (expressed
[or o]mitted) would be *parassem*. This would undoubtedly be
[the] common and conventional form. But if we had (or could
[und]erstand) the *si*, the thought would be rather different, and
[wou]ld be, ' I use his property as freely as whatever I may
[hav]e bought for myself,' where *pararim* would be the regular
[tens]e. And this suggests the reading *quae* for *quam* [as in
[LX]II. B., 88 (128) *quam quae* must be read for *quam quam*,
[q.v.] ; in which case the sense would be, ' I use no more
[freel]y my own property.'

Cinna—est Gaius = ' Cinna, I mean Gaius Cinna,' as disti
guished from some other Cinna (cf. XCV.). This punctuati
follows a suggestion of Mr. Munro. The common readin
Cinna est Gaius, is very harsh. For although the transpositi
of *praenomen* and *nomen* is found often in Lucilius (
' *Cornelius Lucius Scipio Barbatus* ' Inscr. Scip.), and occ
sionally but rarely in later poets, and although the tran
position of *nomen* and *cognomen* (cf. XII. 1) is common, ev
in prose, when only these two names are used, yet an inve
sion of *praenomen* and *cognomen* seems unexampled.

33. ' But you are excessively stupid and tiresome, f
refusing to admit a slip of the tongue.'   *Male* sometimes
' very,' with words of negative meaning : see Horace's *ma
dispari*, Od. I. xvii. 25 ; *male parvus*, Sat. I. iii. 45, &
With words of positive meaning *male = parum*, as *digito ma
pertinaci*, Hor. Od. I. xi. 24 ; *male fida*, Verg. Aen. II. 2
male sanus, &c.

XI.

1. Catullus begs his acquaintance, Furius and Aureli
(XV., XVI., XXI., XXIII., XXVI.), who have sworn etern
inseparable friendship with him, to do him a little servic
and carry to Lesbia his final repudiation of her. He is e
bittered by her infidelity, and this explains the half ironic
tone of his address to his friends, which suggests a dou
of their faith too. This is evidently, from its allusio
one of Catullus' latest poems ; for Caesar did not go
Britain till 55 B.C. The difference between the treatme
of the Sapphic metre by Catullus and Horace is shown
Appendix I. D.

comites C., ' pledged to be Catullus' comrades.'

3. ' Where, waking far-off echoes, the oriental wave buff
the shore.'

ut = ' where,' a rare but undoubted usage. Cf. XVII. 10 :

' *Verum totius ut lacus putidaeque paludis
    Lividissima maximeque est profunda vorago.*'

So Verg. Aen. XII. 270 (cf. v. 329) :

> ' *Hasta volans ut forte novem pulcerrima fratrum*
> *Corpora constiterant contra.*'

ὥς, identical in origin and form with *ut*, has in later Doric the same meaning : Theocr. I. 13, v. 101.

5. **Hyrcanos**, living S.E. of the Caspian, called also *mare Hyrcanum.*

6. **Sacas** = Scythians of the East.

7. **colorat aequora** = covers the plains with his dark slime, ' floods and darkens the plains.' Or, perhaps better, *aequora* = the spreading waters of the Nile, ' dyes his broad floods.'

9. **gradietur**, *i.e.*, on foot, ' march.'

10. ' Viewing the scenes that bear the impress of great Caesar.'

11. **horribiles**, ' inhuman.'

ultimos, ' world's end.'

As this verse seems unmetrical (*quĕ ulti-* being a rather startling hiatus), various emendations have been offered, the best of which perhaps is ' *horribilem insulam ulti-*' (Ellis), which *in MS.* involves curiously little alteration. At the same time Munro's ' *horribile aequor* ' is very attractive.

P. 7, 15. ' Carry to my lady a little message, couched in no pleasant terms.'

21. **respectet**, ' look back to find my love, as once she might,' *i.e.*, when tired of her other lovers. Ellis renders, ' look fondly back upon,' but this ignores the point of *ut ante.*

22. **culpa**, ' frailty,' like *peccare*, a special term in the Lover's Vocabulary : see Appendix II. 3.
Catullus' bitterness is intensified by a delicacy of imagination and feeling, in strange combination with the fierce loathing coarseness of expression, by which it is accompanied.

24. **ultimi prati** = ' the skirt of the meadow.'

E

XII.

1. Asinius Marrucinus' only claim to immortality is his pilfering habit here stigmatised, for he is nowhere else mentioned. He was probably elder brother of G. Asinius Pollio, who justified Catullus' praise by becoming friend of Virgil and Horace, and eminent as soldier, senator, advocate, historian, and tragic dramatist : see Hor. Od. II. i.

Compare, on these petty thefts, XXV., Mart. XII. xxix.

Marr. Asini. Compare Hor. Od. I. vi. 1, *Crispe Sallusti* &c., and see X. 30 note.

sinistra = the *thieving* hand. Cf. XLVII. 1 :

> ' *Porci et Socration, duae sinistrae*
> *Pisonis.*'

= the *two left* hands of (*i.e.*, pilferers for) Piso. Compare Plaut. Pers. ' *furtifica laeva.*'

2. **in joco,** ' while we are deep in frolic and wine.'

3. ' You think this brilliant ! Blunderer, you are off the scent : it is an arrant shabby and unlovely action.' *Quamvis* goes with *sordida :* cf. CIII. 2, ' *Deinde esto quamvis saevus et indomitus.*'

7-9. ' Who would sink a whole talent to have your felonies compounded ; for he is a boy of fluent wit and humour.'

leporum disertus puer, a rare usage.

A genitive of quality may be used when the substantive expressing the quality is accompanied by an adjective. Thus we can say *munus maximi risus* (XVII. 7), *centum puer artium* (Hor. Od. IV. i. 15), *litus amoeni secessus* (Juv. III. 4). But we may not say *munus risus, puer artium, litus secessus*. It seems, however, that if a substantive be attended by an adjective (as *puer* by *disertus* here) a simple genitive of quality is allowable, though very uncommon. Thus in Verg. Ecl. IV. 24, we have ' *fallax herba veneni.*' The whole phrase may then be said to weld itself together, as ' treacherously poisonous herb,' ' fluently witty boy.' The same rules apply to the ablative as to the genitive of description ; and in the same way we have an exception in Cat. LXIV. 50 (see note), and another from Virgil.

Ellis, however, makes *leporum* directly follow *disertus* = ' fluent,' or perhaps ' discerning, in matters of wit and fun '— apparently a kind of genitive of respect. There is no other such example. Munro would read *Ducentum puer.*

14. Saetaba, ' of Saetabus ' (Alcoy), in Hispania Tarra-conensis, famous in Roman times for flax.

Hibere, MSS. abl. of *Hiber* ='Iβηρ, the river Ebro. See Ellis' note on text. The common, but perhaps unnecessary, correction is *Hiberis,* in support of which Munro compares Mart. IV. 55. 8, x. 65. 3.

XIII.

P. 8. 2. ' In the course, if the gods befriend you, of a few days.'

5. ' Sunny maiden and wine and wit and funds of laughter.'

6. **venuste noster** = ' as you are our model of taste.'

9. **meros amores,** ' the essence of delight.' Cf. Mart. XIV. ccvi.,

> ' *Collo necte puer meros amores*
> *Ceston de Veneris sinu calentem.*'

10. **seu quid,** ' or a something, if there be such, still more fragrant and exquisite.' Cf. XXII. 13, LXXXII :

> ' *Quinti, si tibi vis oculos debere Catullum*
> *Aut aliud si quid carius est oculis,*
> *Eripere ei noli, multo quod carius illi*
> *Est oculis seu quid carius est oculis.*'

11. ' I will give you a balsam, vouchsafed to my lady by the Loves and Joys : once you smell it, you will pray the gods to turn you wholly into nose.'

totum agrees with *te,* but is adverbial in sense, a common Latin construction. Cf. Cic. ad Fam. XV. 7, ' *sum totus vester,*' and Hor. Sat. I. ix. 2 :

> ' *Nescio quid meditam nugarum, totus in illis.*'

XIV.

Gaius Licinius Macer Calvus was born 82 B.C., and, like Catullus, in company with whom he is often mentioned by Augustan writers as an epigrammatist and erotic poet, died young. He was, according to Cicero and Quintilian, an orator of great promise, his impeachment of Vatinius being especially famous. His vehemence was so striking ' *ut in media ejus actione surgeret Vatinius reus et exclamaret* " *rogo vos, judices, num, si iste disertus est, ideo me damnari oportet ?* " ' (Seneca, Controv. VII. 19). Compare LIII. L. and XCVI. are addressed to him, and perhaps LV.

1. **jucundissime,** ' most genial.' Cf. L. 16, IX. 9.

munere isto, ' for your wicked present.' If at the Saturnalia, the Roman equivalent (if not the origin) of our Christmas festivity, you received a book as a present, you were bound by etiquette to read it.

3. **odio Vatiniano** = ' as Vatinius hates you,' ' with all the spleen of Vatinius.' Ellis prefers an allusion to Vatinius' notorious unpopularity ; if this is meant, render ' as Vatinius is hated.' But, as Vatinius had such special reason to hate Calvus, the former interpretation seems preferable.

5. ' that you should wilfully poison me with such a dose of poets.'

7. **impiorum,** ' this heap of outcasts ' who write *dis invitis*.

8. ' But if, as I shrewdly guess, this original and exquisite offering is a gift to you from the pedant Sulla.'

dat = *dedit*. Cf. Verg. Aen. IX. 266 :

> ' *Cratera antiquum, quem dat Sidonia Dido.*

10. **est mi male . . . . beate.** Cf. X. 18, XXIII. 5, XXXVIII.

12. ' portentous and predestinate volume.'

P. 9. 13. **tu scilicet,** ' you *of course felt bound* to send,' or (less well) ' you *of all men* sent.'

14. **misti,** so *promisti* CX. 3, *luxti* LXVI. 21, *duxti* XCI. 9, *subrepsti* LXXVII. 3, *abstersti* XCIX. 8. 1. Compare *accestis*, Verg. Aen. I. 201 : cf. IV. 606, 682, V. 786, VI. 57, XI. 118. Remark *tristi*, LXVI. 30, where however the syllable contracted is *-vis* not *-sis*.

continuo, ' forthwith.' Ellis compares, however, Ov. Fasti V. 734, VI. 720, where ' *continua die,*' *continua nocte,*' = ' next day,' ' next night.' If *continuo die* be taken in the same way here, the present must have come on the eve of the Saturnalia, and this would certainly agree with v. 17, *si luxerit*. Mr. Munro now thinks *continuo* is the adjective.

16. **non hoc . . . . sic abibit** = ' this shall not pass without consequences,' ' shall not end where it stands.' Cf. ' *mirabar hoc si sic abiret,*' Ter. And. II. i. 4. ' *Nisi facient quae illos aequum est, haud sic auferent,*' Adelphi III. iv. 8. Cf. Cic. Att. XIV. i. 1, de Fin. V. iii. 7.

17. **si luxerit**, 'with the first streak of dawn.' *Si* with 2nd Fut. =*simul atque.* Cf. Verg. Aen. v. 64 :

> ' *Praeterea si nona diem mortalibus almum*
> *Aurora extulerit radiisque retexerit orbem*,'

and Cic. Phil. XIV. ii. 6, '*Ad literas veniam si pauca ante, quae ad ipsas litteras pertineant, dixero*.' The original meaning of *si* in this usage was probably ' as surely as,' ' if it be allowed that '; but in Cicero's time this conditional sense had faded into a merely temporal force.

librariorum scrinia, 'the copyists' (or publishers') book-cases.'

18. **Aquinos** =probably the poetaster of Cicero, Tusc. v. xxii., '*Adhuc neminem cognovi poetam (et mihi fuit cum Aquinio amicitia) qui sibi non optimus videretur*.'

19. **Suffenum**. XXII. Munro says this is genitive plural, after *omnia venena* ; but these words are better taken as a summary, 'every literary drug.' A bad book was 'poison' to Catullus. Cf. XLIV. 10 to end.

20. **remunerabor**, ' return your present in kind.'

21. Cf. XXVII. 5, XXXVI. 18.

22. ' Away to the regions whence you brought your bad feet.' *Malum pedem* alludes to the faulty measure of the poems, as well as their unwelcome appearance.

Three verses, the fragment of another poem (cf. II. 11-13 note) here follow in the MSS. :

> ' *Si qui forte mearum ineptiarum*
> *Lectores eritis manusque vestras*
> *Non horrebitis admovere nobis*.'

XVII.

1. The metre is Priapean. See Appendix I. c. (i.).

ludere, ' celebrate your games.' We hear of annual celebrations at Rome on the pons Sublicius, from which figures of men, made of rushes, were thrown down. Hence the appropriateness of the boon which the poet begs of the municipality in 8, 9.

2. **paratum habes**. Cf. LX. 5, *contemptam haberes*, the beginning of the analytic perfect, used also by Cicero, but always, as yet, specially emphatic.

sed, &c., ' but in dread of the crazy shanks of that miserable structure, propped on its poor posts that have done other service, lest it turn on its back and find a bed in the depths of the swamp.'

3. **axulis**, diminutive of *axis* = round post. The vulgate *assulis* = laths.

redivivis, used especially of old building material that is employed again, 'resurrected.' Cf. Cic. Ver. I. 56, *lapide redivivo.*

5. **sic**, see Hor. Od. I. iii. 1. 'On one condition may you get a bridge good enough to satisfy your wildest longings, on which the orgies of the leaping god himself may be solemnised.'

6. **Salisubsali**, said to be a name of Mars, who was served by dancing priests (*Salii*). Hercules had also *Salii.*

7. **munus maximi risus**, see XII. 11 note.

10. **Verum**, '*only*,' 'only let it be where the whole fen and pool of corruption provides the bluest and deepest slough,' the strong smell of which is intended to wake him from his torpor. For *ut* = where, cf. XI. 3 note.

12. **nec sapit**, 'has not as much sense as a babe of two years, rocked asleep on its father's elbow.'

14. **viridissimo flore**, 'in her spring's freshest green.'

15. **et** = 'what is more,' is commonly so used with a repeated word ; but may be used without such repetition. Cf. '*timeo Danaos et dona ferentes*' = 'I fear the Greeks, and, still more, when they bring gifts.'

17. **uni** = *unius* : see Ellis' note.

P. 10. 18. 'Never rousing himself to his duty, he lies as an alder lies in a ditch, hamstrung by the Ligurian axe, just as little awake to everything as if the world did not contain it.'

Nulla sit, 'as if it did not exist at all,' said of the alder. This agrees better with *Talis*, which resumes *velut*. It might, however, refer to *puella*, 'as if he had no wife at all.'

21. 'No better than that, yonder dullard of mine.'

24. 'In the hope that he may startle his blank lethargy by the shock, and cast his sluggish spirit in the clogging mire.'

soleam, 'sock,' made of leather, but with an iron sole—the part left behind in the mud.

pote = *possit*. Cf. XLV. 5, LXVII. 11, LXXVI. 16. For the lengthening before a double consonant, cf. XXII. 12, XLIV. 18, LXIII. 53, and Appendix I. J.

XXII.

The metre is Choliambic or Scazon, Appendix I. B. 3.

1. **probe** = ' well enough.'

2. **venustus, dicax, urbanus,** ' of taste and wit, and with the tone of town.'

4. **aut decem aut plura** = ' if not ten thousand, then more.'

5. **perscripta** = fairly copied out.

palimpsesto relata, ' not vulgarly entered on twice-scoured parchment (or paper).'

palimpsesto. The ordinary construction is with the accusative, and Baehrens emends to *palimpsestos.*

6. ' Royal sheets, virgin volumes and virgin finials, scarlet leathers, parchment wrappers, and everything pencil-ruled and pumice-planed.'
Sheets (*cartae*) were made of strips of papyrus rind pressed together, and of course were of more than one quality. Several sheets were united to form a long narrow ' *liber*,' which was provided with a wooden cylinder, round which it was rolled for convenience of stowage and carriage, and from which it was gradually unrolled by the reader. This roller (*umbilicus*) had projecting ends (also called *umbilici*), shaped like horns or bosses. The *lora* were strips of leather hanging from the rolled volumes, and containing the titles of the books ; or, more probably, they were bands employed to tie up the rolls. *Membranae* were envelopes of skin in which the books were kept, and were often coloured, answering to our leather bindings. Lines were ruled in lead to direct the writer, and pumice-stone was employed to remove all blots, errors, or irregularities in the writing, as well as to smooth all roughnesses, and finish the edges, both of the paper and of the parchment covering. Part of the *membrana* overlapped the top of the paper, and on it was sometimes written the title of the work. This may explain why any part of the *membrana* should have been ruled with lines, which Munro thinks was

never the case. Compare the third and fourth lines of the
following passage in *Tibullus*, a *locus classicus :*

> ' *Lutea sed niveum involvat membrana libellum,*
> *Pumex*[1] *cui canas tondeat ante comas,*
> *Summaque praetexat tenuis vestigia cartae,*
> *Indicet ut nomen littera facta tuum,*
> *Atque inter geminas pingantur cornua frontes.*'

Here the *frontes* are the ends of the roll. Cf. also Mart. III
10, Ovid. Trist. II. 1.

Ellis and other editors alter without occasion to *membrana*,
but 8 refers summarily to all portions of the book before
mentioned. Munro would punctuate after *membranae*, and
connect 8 with what follows, finding otherwise no meaning in
the verse. But *haec* more naturally begins the sentence ; and
8 summarises the elaborate perfection of the external ' get-up '
of these unfortunate poems.

9. **haec cum legas,** ' as often as you read these verses.'

Bellus, &c., ' fine and city-bred gentleman.' *Urbanus*
signifies the polished manners and lively talk of Rome, in
contrast to the heaviness and dulness of the country.

10. **unus,** ' ordinary,' ' mere,' as *unus e multis :* cf. *unus
paterfamilias,* Cic. de Or. I. 132, *unus manipularis,* ad Att.
IX. X.

11. **rursus** = *reversus :* ' drops to an ordinary ditcher : so
unlike himself, so changed does he become.'

Abhorret, sc. *a se* = ' so inconsistent with himself is he.'
But of this use there are no other instances, and therefore
Munro would take the word generally = ' so absurd is he.'

mutat, intransitive.

12. **scurra** = ' a practised wit,' much like *urbanus*, with
which it is combined, Plaut. Most. I. i. 14 :

> ' *Tu urbanus vero scurra, deliciae popli,*
> *Rus mihi tu objectas.*'

---

[1] Al. *Pumicet et.*

modō before *sc-*, see Appendix I. J.

13. **tritius**, ' of finer grain '; or ' more dexterous ' (cf.
ριβων),—a rare and doubtful use. The MSS. read *tristius*, for
which Ellis suggests ' *strictius = acutius* vel *argutius* ' ; Munro
tersius or *tertius* = ' more polished.'

aut si quid. Cf. XIII. 10 note.

15. ' Yet, strange to say, he is never so near heaven as when
he writes a poem.'

P. 11. 18.   ' Of course we all deceive ourselves in the same
way, and there is no man whom you may not see to be in
some one point a Suffenus. We have all been given our
private delusions ; but we do not see what is in the back of the
wallet.'

21. **manticae** = two bags tied together, and slung over the
shoulder. In the first part we carry our neighbours' vices,
our own in the half that hangs behind us. Cf. Phaedrus IV.
0.[1]   A possible translation is, ' that which is in the back of
the wallet,' i.e., ' *proprium vitium*.' But Munro strongly
supports the other rendering, ' the half of the wallet which is
on his back,' by comparing Verg. Aen. IX. 274, *campi quod
ex habet*, Lucr. IV. 372, *quod liquimus ejus*, etc.

XXVI.

1. **nostra.** Many editors, on the authority of one good MS.,
read *vestra*.
   ' Due on my little homestead falls, Furius, not the blast
of the south wind, ... but a bill of 15,200 HS.'

2. **opposita est** = ' is mortgaged for ' and ' faces towards.'
   The point of the piece lies in the pun on these two meanings
of *opponere*. Cf. Juvenal XI. 18, ' *lancibus oppositis* ' ; Ter.
Phorm. 161, ' *ager oppositust pignori decem ob minas*.'

[1] *Peras imposuit Juppiter nobis duas ;
Propriis repletam vitiis post tergum dedit,
Alienis ante pectus suspendit gravem.
Hac re videre nostra mala non possumus ;
Alii simul delinquunt, censores sumus.*

3. **Apheliotae,** ' east wind,' Latin *subsolanus* (Seneca Q. N.
v. 16), *Favonio contrarius* (Pliny H. N. II. 122).

horridum, ' shrivelling.'

XXVII.

1. ' Young steward of old Falernian wine.'

2. **inger** = *ingere*, ' pour in.'   Ellis quotes Mart. VIII. xliv.
9, *conger*.

calices amariores, ' more acrid,' ' of sharper flavour.'

3. ' As the law of our sovereign, Postumia, bids.'

magistrae.   At a Roman wine-party one of the company
was chosen *magister bibendi*, or lord of the revels, and his
ruling on all points was absolute.   Cf. Hor. Od. I. iv. 18 :

> ' *Nec regna vini sortiere talis,*'

and Sat. II. vi. 67, where a president was dispensed with :

> ' *prout cuique libido est,*
> *Siccat inaequales calices conviva solutus*
> *Legibus insanis.*'

4. **acino,** ' grape-berry.'

5. **quod jubet,** ' for so sne orders.'   Others emend to *quolubet*.

6. ' Water, wine's undoing ; and seek a home with melancholy.   Here is the pure draught of the enthusiastic god.'

7. **Thyonianus.**   Bacchus is said to be called Thyoneus
from *Thyone*, a name of his mother or his nurse.   But the
word has more probably a reference to the orgies of the god
(θύω).

The original, which suggested this poem, is a fragment of
Diphilus :

> ἔγχεον σὺ δὴ πιεῖν.
> Εὐζωρότερόν γε νὴ Δί', ὦ παῖ, δός·   τὸ γὰρ
> ὕδαρες ἅπαν τοῦτ' ἐστὶ τῇ ψυχῇ κακόν

XXX.

The metre is Choriambic, much used by Sappho and Alcaeus; see Appendix I. E. Alfenus is unknown, if he be not the Varus of X. Cf. LXIV. 133-150, for the matter.

1. **Immemor**, 'treacherous.' Such negatives have more force than a mere negation of the simple adjectives: so *inutilis* = positively 'harmful,' &c.

2. 'Has your hard heart so soon lost pity for your once cherished friend ?'

3. **dubitas**, 'tremble.'

4. 'although treachery is irreligion, and finds no favour with the gods.' Hom. Od. XIV. 83:

οὐ μὲν σχέτλια ἔργα θεοὶ μάκαρες φιλέουσι.

nec = *non*. See Munro, Lucret. II. 23 note. Or *nec* = 'yet . . . . not,' 'although . . . . not.' Cf. Verg. Aen. I. 130, and infra, LXII. 29, LXIV. 84.

5. **Quae**, 'this truth.' Munro would read *Quom*, and connect this with the succeeding verse.

P. 12. 7. animam tradere, 'surrender my soul to you, cruel heart, luring me into love's perilous land by promises of perfect security.'

8. **inducens** = 'inveigle': cf. Cicero, Phil. II. xxxii. 79, '*nihil queror de Dolabella, qui tum est impulsus, inductus, elusus*;' ad Att. III. xv. 7, '*proditus, inductus, conjectus in fraudem.*'

9. **Idem**, 'in spite of the past.'

retrahis te = 'break faith,' 'shirk your duty': cf. Hor. Epist. I. xviii. 58, '*ne te retrahas et inexcusabilis absis.*'

10. 'suffering wind and airy rack to sweep into nothingness all you have said and done.' Cf. LXIV. 60, 143, &c.

11. **at** = 'nevertheless,' after *si*. Cf. Aen. I. 542, &c.

12. **postmodo,** 'yet a little while and she will overwhelm
you with remorse.' *Modo* in these compounds has the force
of 'just.'

XXXI.

1. **Sirmio** (Sermione) is a peninsula connected with the
southern shore of the Lago di Garda by a narrow strip of land,
which at times is covered by water.

paene insularum. This adjectival use of the abverb with
a substantive, so common in Greek, when preceded by an
article, is very rare in Latin, owing probably to the Latin
want of the article. We have, indeed, a use, similar to the
Greek, when the adverb is preceded by a demonstrative, in
'*iste post phaselus*,' IV. 10, or by an adjective qualifying the
same substantive, '*omnes circa populi*,' Livy XXIV. iii., '*duabus
circa portis*,' Id. XXIII. xvi., or a possessive genitive dependent
on the same substantive '*eri semper lenitas*,' Ter. Andr. 175 (Pl.
Pers. 385, quoted by Wagner, is not necessarily parallel).
But the only other exact parallel to *paene insula* is quoted by
Munro from Caesar B. G. VI. xxxvi. 2, '*paene obsessionem*'

insularumque, 'or islands.' Cf. VII. 2 note.

2. **Ocelle,** L. 19. Cf. the use of ὄμμα (Æschyl. Eum. 1025),
ὀφθαλμὸς (Pind. O. II. 18, VI. 27), and Cic. Attic. XIV. 6,
'*ocellos Italiae meas villulas*.'

quascunque, 'upborne (or, begotten) in pellucid meres, or on
the illimitable ocean, by either water-god'; *i.e.*, the god of
fresh water or of the sea.

5. **Thyniam.** Cf. Claud. in Eutrop. 247,

'*Thyni Thraces erant, quae nunc Bithynia fertur.*'

credens liquisse. See IV. 2 and foot-note.

7 *sqq.* 'Can there be a greater blessing than when the cords
of care are snapped, and the mind lets slip its burden; when,
spent with toil in far-off places, we come to our sanctuary at
home, and find rest on the long-dreamed-of couch? This
single moment repays all our pains.'

13. **vosque.** The *que* is placed with the pronominal subject, although that is not the first word in the clause, by a license found in Propert., III. 21, 16, quoted by Ellis, but very rare. Compare the Greek formula of address—title, pronoun, enclitic particle. Cf. LXXVI. 11 note.

Lydiae. The Etruscans, anciently believed to be of Lydian origin, had settlements in early times in the neighbourhood of the Po.

We should rather expect *Lydii lacus*, but the hypallage is not uncommon when the adjective denotes a proper name. Compare Hor. Od. I. xxxi. 9, III. vi. 38 ; Proper. I. xx. 9 ; Verg. Aen. VIII. 526 ; Lucret. II. 501, v. 24. Many conjectures (such as *vividae*, by Munro) have been proposed in place of *Lydiae*, but needlessly.

14. ' Let every merry sound with which home is haunted break into laughing.'

quicquid est cachinnorum. See Appendix II. I. a.

XXXIV.

The metre is composed of three Glyconic verses, and one Pherecratean. See Appendix I. C. (ii).

1. **Dianae sumus in fide,** ' Diana is our guardian, maidens and boys without blemish.'

The boys and maidens employed in religious ceremonies must be free from bodily or moral blemish, and must be *patrimi matrimique*, that is, have both father and mother still living. Cf. LXI. 36.

In fidem populi Romani venire (Caesar B. G. II. 13) = ' to come under Roman protection ; ' ' *municipia in fide mea essent* ' (Cic. Planc. XLI. 97) = ' I am patron of the country towns.'

P. 13. 5. ' Child of Latona, cradled by thy mother near the Delian olive,' which rose to assist Latona in her travail.

deposivit. For archaic forms in Catullus see Appendix II. 5.

11. **saltuumque reconditorum,** ' sequestered forest-lawns.'

12. **sonantum,** but *micantium*, LXI. 207 (198).

13. 'Thou art invoked as Juno Lucina when young mothers are in pain; thou art invoked as the Magic Power of Meeting Ways, and as the Moon when thou shinest with counterfeit light.'

Compare Hor. Od. III. xxii.; and, for the whole poem, Hor. Od. I. xxi.

'Triple Hecate' is invoked in all her functions. It was a matter of moment to call a god by the title most pleasing to him. Cf. 21, and Aesch. Ag. 160:

$$Ζεύς, ὅστις ποτ' ἐστίν, εἰ τόδ' αὐ-$$
$$τῷ φίλον κεκλημένῳ.$$

Hence often, as a safeguard, all the titles were given.

15. **Trivia,** the goddess of three meeting roads ($τριοδῖτις$).

potens = 'possessed of mysterious influence,' was specially used of magic power, Ov. Her. XII. 168, Verg. Aen. VI. 247 (quoted by Ellis). Compare '*efficax scientia,*' Hor. Ep. XVII. 1, in the sense of the 'black art.'

notho. The moon's light is called 'bastard,' as not produced by herself, but reflected from the sun. Cf. Lucr. v. 575, '*Lunaque sive notho fertur loca lumine lustrans.*'

17. **cursu,** 'measuring thy yearly path by monthly progress.'

21. 'Hallowed be thou, by whatever name thou wilt.'

23. **antique . . . es,** 'as thou wert wont in the good old times.'

XXXV.

1. **tenero,** 'the poet of passion.'

3. **novi.** Comum in 59 B.C. received, under Caesar's conduct, a large accession of colonists.

4. **Larium litus,** 'the shore of Lake Larius.' *Larius* is used as an adjective. Cf. in Horace, '*Dardanae genti,*' '*Metaurum flumen,*' &c., and in Virgil (Aen. iv. 552), '*cineri Sychaeo.*'

5. 'For I wish him to hear and welcome some premeditations of his friend and mine.' The *amicus sui meique* may be a common friend of Catullus and Caecilius, or, perhaps, may mean Catullus himself.

7. si . . . vorabit, 'as sure as he is wise, he will press on his journey hotly.' Comp. 2nd Henry IV. act i. sc. 1, 'He seem'd in running to devour the way,' and '*corripuere viam*,' Verg. Aen. I. 418, v. 145, 316.

P. 14. 11. si . . . . nuntiantur, 'if the news I hear be true,' *vera* being the true predicate.

12. deperit = 'dies of love for him.' Cf. XLV. 5.

impotente = 'that cannot restrain itself.' Cf. IV. 18, VIII. 9.

13. incohatam, 'his inauguration of the queen of Dindymus,' *i.e.*, a poem begun upon the subject.

Dindymi dominam = Cybele, see LXIII. 1.

14. misella, 'love-sick.' Cf. XLV. 31.

15. medullam. Cf. XLV. 16. The marrow was thought to be the seat of the passion of love.

16. 'I pardon you, maiden, who prove yourself more poetical than the muse of Sappho.' *Doctus* at this time meant not learned generally, but possessed of *poetical taste and culture*, and was the title specially given to Catullus himself by later poets.

XXXVI.

1. 'Chronicles of Volusius, polluted sheet, I call you to discharge a vow in my lady's name.'

Volusius may stand for Tanusius Geminus of Padua, known to have written a history. Cf. XCV. 7.

4. 'Should I be won back to her, and silence my volleys of scathing epigrams.'

5. iambos. Cf. Hor. Od. I. XVI. 2, '*criminosis iambis*.'

7. **tardipedi deo** = Vulcan, 'the halting deity' (ἀμφιγυήεις) = fire.

Daturam without *se :* see foot-note to *celerrimum* IV. 2.

8. **infelicibus**, 'faggots from an accursed tree.' Cf. Cic. Mil. 13, '*infelicibus lignis semiustulatus.*'

9. 'And by this my lady saw that she, with merry wit, offered the worst of all things to the gods.' Nothing to Catullus was so vile as a bad poet's worst writings. The wit of Lesbia was shown, not merely in sacrificing the worst things to the gods, but in valuing so contemptuously a reconciliation with Catullus.

Other translations might be given : (*a*), 'the sweet sinner (*pessima puella*) saw that this (i.e., *Annales Volusi*) was the sacrifice she promised, in her flash of frolic, to the gods '; (*β*), 'this vow to the gods my wicked lady knew to be merry and witty.' But (*a*) would require *haec ;* and both (*a*) and (*β*) would harshly give to *pessimi* and *pessima* different meanings.

Mr. Munro writes : "*Hoc*, I feel sure, is an accusative—*hoc jocose* **vovere** = *hoc jocosum votum vovere. Pessima*, I believe, goes with *puella.* I have a strong persuasion that Baehrens, in his Analecta Catull., is right, and that the poem has no proper point, unless we suppose that the poet is jocularly perverting Lesbia's proposal. *She* meant that, in order to her being reconciled to Catullus, first of all, the poems ' *pessimi poetae,*' i.e., the poems which Catullus himself, the ' *pessimus poeta,*' naughtiest of poets, had written against herself, should be burnt. The poet chooses to take ' *pessimus poeta*' in the sense of ' worst of poets ' and turns it against poor Volusius." The objections to this are, that the *purpose* of Lesbia's vow was to cause Catullus to *cease* his lampoons (5), which could hardly be done by burning the old ones ; and, secondly, that this interpretation gives no force to the emphatic ' *electissima,*' which surely means ' the most carefully picked,' i.e., the very worst specimens of the worst poet. These Catullus decides to be the ' *Annales Volusi.*'

11. 'Therefore hear now, thou fruit of dark ocean, whose spirit haunts hallowed Idalium ' (a grove in Cyprus) ' and Urii, wide of prospect ' (near Brundisium), ' and Ancon ' (in Picenum), ' and reedy Cnidos ' (a city of Caria), ' and Amathus and Golgi ' (cities of Cyprus), ' and Dyrrhachium ' (formerly Epidamnus), ' the hostel of the Adriatic ; grant an acceptance

and quittance of the vow, as surely as it is neither dull nor in bad grace.'

18. interea, ' while my prayer rises.'

P. 15. 19. pleni ruris, 'full of rusticity and plentifully lacking wit.' Cf. xxii. 14, '*infaceto infacetior rure.*'

XXXVIII.

1. ' Your friend, Cornificius, is ill, heaven knows how ill, and in what pain, and growing daily, hourly worse.' Cornificius is probably the contemporary erotic poet of that name.

2. herculĕ et. This hiatus seems inadmissible ; '*et est*' or '*et a !*' has been suggested.

4. ' Yet, least and easiest duty, with what word of sympathy have you comforted him ? '

6. Sic meos amores. ' To think that you, the object of my love, should act thus ! ' ' My dear friend act so ! ' Ellis would render, ' to treat my passion thus ! ' But there is nothing here to show that Catullus' sickness arose from his passion for Lesbia, and *meos amores* must mean the ' object of my love.' The accusative is the regular construction with the indignant infinitive, as in Cicero's ' *Senatumne servire populo,*' &c.

7. paulum quidlibet. ' Send me any morsel of sympathy, and let it be sadder than the tears of Simonides,' the master of pathos. *Quidlibet* must be taken with *paulum*, ' a little word, as little or as much as you please.' Cf. Hor. A. P. 9 :

' *pictoribus atque poetis*
Quidlibet audendi semper fuit aequa potestas.'

For the omission of the verb (*da*, or an equivalent) cf. LV. 10 :

' *Camerium mihi, pessimae puellae.*'

XXXIX.

2. usque quaque, ' he breaks into smiles at every step.' Cf. Cic. Phil. II. xliii. 110.

4. si ad pii, &c. ' Visit the benches round a prisoner, when the advocate is drawing tears ; visit a scene of mourning, by the pyre of a dutiful son, a lone mother weeping the loss of her sole hope ; let the occasion, the place or his business be what it may, he grins, and has this habit to a disease.'

9. monendum te est mihi, ' I must have a word with you.' This construction, the nominative of the verbal noun retaining its power of governing a case, is rare. It occurs in Lucr. I. iii. :

  ' *Aeternas quoniam poenas in morte timendum est*,'

and in six other passages of the same author ; Verg. Aen. II. 230 (according to the best MSS.), ' *pacem Trojano ab rege petendum* ' ; Cic. de Sen. II., ' *viam quam nobis quoque ingredi- endum sit.*' Compare Plaut. Am. I. iii. 21, ' *tibi hanc curatio est rem.*' Munro would incline to keep the old correction, *monendus es*, for the *monendum est* of the MSS., which con- stantly interchange *m* and *s* final.

10. urbanus, ' Roman bred.'

13. ut . . . attingam, ' to lay a finger on my own folk.'

14. puriter, ' who uses a clean dentifrice.' Cf. *miseriter* LXIII. 49. We have in Lucr. III. 676, &c., *longiter ;* Id. III. 839, *uniter ;* and *naviter*, Cic., Lucr., Liv. See Appendix II. 6.

P. 16. 17. Celtiber = Κελτίβηρ.

XL.

1. ' Pray, lovesick Ravidus, what infatuation drives you headlong upon my epigrams ? ' *Ravide* may have been pro- nounced *Raude*, or the verse is hypermetrical, or the *e* is elided before the initial vowel of v. 2.

miselle. Cf. xlv. 31.

3. ' What god, better left uninvoked by you, makes haste to fire the frantic duel ? '   Or *non bene advocatus* might possibly = ' whom you have neglected to worship aright.'   Cf. Hom. Il. i. 65 :

εἴτ' ἄρ' ὅ γ' εὐχωλῆς ἐπιμέμφεται.

If this be so, then 4 will resemble in form and sequence of thought Il. i. 8—

τίς τ' ἄρ σφωε θεῶν ἔριδι ξυνέηκε μάχεσθαι.

5. **pervenias in ora,** ' force your way to the lips of men,' ' become a subject of common talk.'   Cf. Ennius' ' *volitare per ora virum.*'

6. **qualibet,** ' at any cost.'

8. **cum longa poena,** ' since you have chosen to love my love and be gibbeted for ever.'

XLIII.

1. **salve,** ' my service to you.'

puella = Ameana, ' *Ista turpiculo puella naso,*' xli. 3.

3. **longis,** ' tapering.'

4. ' Nor (to deal plainly) too refined a tongue.'

5. ' Mistress of the fraudulent bankrupt of Formiae,' that is, Mamurra, Caesar's *praefectus fabrum* in Gaul, and the object of Catullus' especial hatred.   Cf. xxix. and cxiv. note.

decoctoris. So Cic. Phil. ii. 18, *decoxisse* = ' to run through one's property and become bankrupt.'

6. **provincia,** ' Provence.'

8. ' O tasteless, lackwit generation.'

XLIV.

P. 17. 1. seu **Sabine** seu **Tiburs,** ' whether your title be Sabine or **Tiburtine.'**   *Sabine* is an instance of very rare attraction, that of a predicative adjective to the voc. case, made perhaps easier here by the omission of the substantive verb.   Cf. Verg. Aen. IX. 641, *macte nova virtute puer* ; Tib. I. vii. 58, *sic venias hodierne* ; Aesch. Supp. 535, γενοῦ πολυμνήστωρ ἔφαπτορ Ἰοῦς ; Theoc. XVII. 66, ὄλβιε κῶρε γένοιο.   Such passages as Verg. Aen. II. 282, '*Quibus Hector ab oris Expectate venis ?* ' (and add X. 811, XII. 947, Pers. III. 29) are not parallel, as the vocative does not contain the main predication.

Tibur, twenty miles from Rome, was a fashionable locality at this time, much more esteemed than the neighbouring Sabine district, and praised by Horace, Od. I. vii. 13, I. xviii. 2, II. vi. 5, IV. iii. 10.   There the great, such as Maecenas, Sallust, Quintilius Varus, had their villas ; and Catullus confesses his desire for the vanity of a fashionable address.

2. ' Tiburtine they swear you, who have no heart to hurt my feelings, but those who have the heart protest under any forfeit that you are Sabine.'

3. **cordi,** a locative, ' at heart.'

7. ' And cleared my chest of a villainous cough, which— serve me right—my belly made me catch, while I was hankering after profuse dinners.'

expuli is nearer the MSS. *expulsus sum* than *expui*.

9. **dedit** comes before its time, as *gemunt* in LXVI. 18, ' *non, ita me divi, vera gemunt, juerint.*' Cf. LXVIII. B. 28, 108. This is said to be an Alexandrine trick ; but see Munro on Lucr. III. 843.

10. **Sestianus** . . . . **conviva,** ' to dine with Sestius.'   Cicero speaks of the absurdities of ' *dicta Sestiana* ' (ad D. VII. 32), and uses his name as a term of literary condemnation (ad Att. VII. 17, ' *nihil unquam legi scriptum* σηστιωδέστερον ').

11. **petitorem,** ' prosecutor ' in a suit, or ' candidate ' at an election.

12. **veneni.** Cf. XIV. 19.

13. **gravedo . . . . tussis,** 'a freezing catarrh and fits of coughing convulsed me.'

15. 'nursed myself well with rest and infusion of nettles.'

17. **ulta.** Catullus is now addressing the *villa.* Compare for change of gender LXVI. 63 note.

18. **deprecor,** 'cry mercy,' 'plead.'

nefariā. For metre see Appendix I. J.

19. **recepso,** 'shall find house-room for.' For the form, answering to the Greek sigmatic future, see Roby L. G. § 619.

20. **frigus,** the 'icy breath' of bad style.

21. 'Who only invites me when I have read a villainous book.'

XLV.

P. 18. See General Introduction II. p. xxi.

3. **perdite amo,** 'lost in love of you,' 'love consumedly.'

amare porro, 'love on.'

4. **assidue,** 'devotedly,' 'unchangeably.'

5. **quantum qui pote plurimum perire** = ὅσον τις οἷός τε ἐστι τὰ μάλιστα φιλῆσαι, 'as deeply as the deepest devotion possible,' if *qui = quis,* as it has been said to do in Verg. Aen. VI. 140 ;

> ' Sed non ante datur telluris operta subire
> Auricomos quam qui decerpserit arbore fetus.'

But no such indefinite use of *qui* is known, and it is better to supply *is pote* before *qui* (relative), ' as much as he can love who can love the most.' Cf. Cic. Fam. v. 2, ' *tam sum amicus reipublicae quam qui maxime.*'

perire, ' to love to distraction ' = *perdite amare*, and is found with a simple accusative in Plautus Truc. :

> ' *Tres unam pereunt adolescentes mulierem.*'

So Poen. IV. 2, 135, and cf. *deperit* in Catullus XXXV. 12, c. 2. The common construction is with the ablative, as in Prop. III. 6, 13 :

> ' *Ipse Paris nuda fertur periisse Lacaena.*'

6. **Indiaque**, ' or in parched India.'   Cf. VII. 2 note.

7. **caesio**, ' green-eyed.'

8-9. **sinistra**, ' Love, standing on the left, as before, sneezed towards the right his blessing.'   The words *ut ante*, while appropriate in 17, seem awkward here, and are perhaps corrupt.   Indeed the MSS. vary much in the reading of the whole sentence.   Many commentators take *sinistra ut ante* together, ' as he had done before on the left ' ; supposing the passion of the lovers to have hitherto wanted the god's full approval.   Sneezing has been regarded as ominous from the earliest times, and the omen so given variously interpreted. The difficulty of the present passage is increased by our ignorance of the Roman interpretations.   Was a sneeze absolutely lucky, or only when occurring on a particular side ?   On what side, then ?   Or was a sneeze, heard first on the left and then on the right, the best sign ?   The last seems the case from the present poem.   Perhaps, however, *dextram* means no more than ' favourable ' (as in Verg. Aen. IV. 294), the left side being the lucky side in Roman superstition, and the play on the word being characteristic of popular adages and mysterious maxims.

For the cognate accusative *approbationem*, cf. Prop. II. 3, 23 :

> ' *Aureus argutum sternuit omen Amor.*'

10. **reflectens** = bending back her head, so as to lift her face from his bosom.

11. **ebrios**, ' brimming,' ' love-laden.'   Cf. Anacr. μεθύων ἔρωτι.

13. **Sic.**   Cf. XVII. 5.   ' So surely may we be constant

slaves of this our one Sovereign Lord, as it is sure that in my molten marrow glows a far greater and far fiercer fire.'

mea vita. Cf. LXVIII. B. 115.

20. **mutuis,** ' their souls respond, with love for love.'

21. **misellus,** XXXV. 14.

22. **Syrias.** The plural generalizes, ' than all your Syrias ' or ' than any Syria,' without meaning that more than one Syria (though that would be true) exists. Cf. Hor. Od. I. xiv. 7 :

> ' *Vix durare carinae*
> *Possint imperiosius*
> *Aequor* '

=' scarce could any keel endure the tyranny of that sea.'

For the thought compare Hor. Od. III. ix. 1 :

> ' *Donec gratus eram tibi . . . .*
> *Persarum vigui rege beatior.*'

23. ' With Septimius alone loyal Acme yields to pleasure and to passion.'

26. **auspicatiorem,** ' more happily heralded,' ' born under a brighter star.'

XLVI.

P. 19. 1. **egelidos tepores,** ' unfrozen warmths.' In Verg. Aen. VIII. 610 :

> ' *Natumque in valle reducta*
> *Ut procul egelido secretum flumine vidit.*'

egelidus is said to mean ' very cold ' (cf. *edurus*) ; there is, however, a variant ' *et gelido.*' Ovid uses the word like Catullus (Amor. II. xi. 10) :

> ' *Et gelidum Borean egelidumque Notum.*'

2. ' At last heaven's aequinoctial roar sinks into stillness before the genial breezes of the west.'

4. **campi,** ' table-lands.' Cf. XXXI. 6.

5. ' Sultry Nicaea's teeming tilth.'

7. 'Surprised by joy, my soul is impatient to be free, my feet quicken with glad enthusiasm.'

8. **coetus**, 'unions.'

9. 'Who have travelled far from home together, but must return by widely parted, widely different ways.'

longe with *profectos*.

10. **diversae** = 'taking different directions;' *variae* = some wholly by sea, some partly by land, &c.

XLVII.

Catullus' friends, Veranius and Fabullus (IX., XII., XIII.), served together in Spain, and afterwards in Macedonia under L. Piso Caesoninus, whom Cicero prosecuted. They returned with empty pockets (XXVIII.), while creatures like Porcius and Socration were allowed by the governor to come back with fortunes, collected by rapine.

1. **sinistrae**, XII. 1 note.

2. **scabies famesque mundi**, 'murrain and lean kine of the world.' Catullus calls Aurelius '*pater esuritionum*,' XXI.

5. **lauta**, 'fashionable.'

6. **de die**, 'before the business day was over.'
To begin festivities so early was a sign of prodigality; and also of debauchery, as they might thus be of longer duration. Cf. Terence Adelph. v. 9, '*apparare de die convivium;*' Hor. Od. I. i., '*partem solido demere de die.*'

7. 'Stand at the crossways to catch invitations.'

XLIX.

To discover the secret meanings of this little poem, it has been broken by the critics like a butterfly on the wheel. Cicero on some occasion, now quite unknown, has used his legal eloquence to Catullus' satisfaction; is thanked by him in a playful address; and that is all. To find here sarcasm, and an imitation of Cicero's style, and a logical sophism, is an occupation 'λίαν δεινοῦ καὶ ἐπιπόνου καὶ οὐ πάνυ εὐτυχοῦς ἀνδρός.'

1. **disert.,** 'most eloquent.'

2. **quot sunt,** &c. Variations of this phrase are found in XXI. 2, XXIV. 2.

7. **patronus,** 'advocate.' Cicero was especially sought as counsel for the defence (Epis. ad **Fam.** VII. 1).

L.

P. 20. 1. **Licini,** XIV. 1 note.

otiosi, 'in an idle mood.'

2. **lusimus,** 'we toyed with verse.' *Ludere* = to compose light poems, especially love poems : cf. LXVIII. 17, *multa satis lusi,* LXI. 228 ; so Hor. Od. I. xxxii. :

> '*Poscimur ; si quid vacui sub umbra*
> *Lusimus tecum.*'

3. **ut convenerat esse delicatos,** 'since we had sworn our-selves to frolic.' *Convenerat* = ' a compact had been arranged between us ': in this impersonal construction *inter* is generally used with the names of the contracting parties or pronouns. *Delicatus* is used of light, frivolous conversation : cf. Cic. de Off. I. 40, '*turpe est in re severa delicatum inferre sermonem.*'

5. **numero,** 'measure.'

6. **reddens mutua,** lit. 'paying our debts to one another,' ' retaliating,' ' giving and taking.'

per jocum atque vinum = making our answers '*while* we jested and drank,' or ' *in the shape of* a jest or a challenge to drink.'

8. **incensus,** 'fired by your brilliance and humour.'

9. ' Food failed to give pleasure to my poor body, and the peace of sleep to lap my eyes,'

11. ' Ungovernable in my delirium, I tossed over the whole bed.'

14. **labore,** ' torment.'

15. **lectulo,** ' my poor bed.'

16. **jucunde.** Cf. xiv. 2.

18. **cave.** Cf. x. 27, *manĕ.* Servius on *fervĕre* (Verg. Aen. iv. 409) says there existed *cavĕre* as well as *cavēre. Cave* in ordinary conversation was pronounced in such a manner, that *Caunias* could be mistaken for *cave ne eas ;* but here it must be dissyllabic. See Appendix I. ' *Cautum,* i.e. *cauitum,*' is no evidence for the existence of *cavēre* (as Ellis seems to say), unless *monitum* proves a *monēre* to have existed.

19. **despuas,** ' void your rheum against ' = ' scornfully reject,' or ' turn from.'

ocelle, xxxi. 2, ' my star.'

21. **vemens,** ' impetuous,' for the form cf. *vecors.*   Cf. vii. 10 note.

LI.

This is a translation, or adaptation, probably fragmentary, of a poem of Sappho, which is confessedly incomplete as we now have it.   The original is as follows :

φαίνεταί μοι κῆνος ἴσος θεοῖσιν
ἔμμεν ὤνηρ, ὅστις ἐναντίος τοι
ἰζάνει καὶ πλασίον ἀδὺ φωνείσας ὑπακούει
καὶ γελαίσας ἱμερόεν· τό μοι μάν
καρδίαν ἐν στήθεσιν ἐπτόασεν.
ὡς γὰρ σ’ ἴδω βροχέως με φώνας οὐδὲν ἔτ’ εἴκει.
ἀλλὰ καμ μὲν γλῶσσα ἔαγε, λέπτον δ’
αὔτικα χρῶ πῦρ ὑποδεδρόμακεν
ὀππάτεσσι δ’ οὐδὲν ὄρημ’, ἐπιρρόμβεισι δ’ ἄκουαι,
ἀ δὲ ἴδρως κακχέεται, τρόμος δέ
πᾶσαν ἄγρει, χλωροτέρα δὲ ποίας
ἔμμι, τεθνάκην δ’ ὀλίγῳ ’πιδεύην φαίνομαι,

As a translation Catullus' poem has been much overpraised. Even his simplicity seems elaborate beside the Greek : for instance, *gemina*[1] *teguntur lumina nocte* is artificial compared with ὀππάτεσσι δ' οὐδὲν ὄρημα. The whole of 2, *identidem, spectat, misero, sonitu suopte* are superfluous. There is an omission of ἀδὺ φωνείσας and of αὔτικα, both important. *Omnes eripit sensus, torpet* and *sub artus* are inadequate renderings.

On the versification, see Appendix I. D.

2. **si fas est,** ' if religion allow.'

divos, ' the great gods.'

3. **identidem,** ' again and again.'

5. **dulce ridentem,** ' the music of your laughter.' For the construction, see LXI. 8 note, 219, LXIII. 24. Compare Hor. Od. I. xxii. 24 :

> ' *Dulce ridentem Lalagen amabo*
> *Dulce loquentem.*'

misero, &c. ' Oh ! it ravishes all my senses from me. Let me but look on you, Lesbia, nothing of me survives. My tongue is frozen ; films of fire filter to the depths of my frame ; sounds, not of the air, chime in my ears ; and a double night closes over my eyes.'

P. 21. 7. **Nihil est super mi.** The last feet of the stanza are wanting, and are variously supplied from conjecture, in accordance with the Greek. As the text stands, it must be translated in some such way as the above, *est super* being taken as *superest.*

9. **torpet.** Compare Hor. Od. IV. i. 35 :

> ' *Cur parum decoro*
> *Inter verba cadit lingua silentio ?* '

10. **suopte** (' suo-p-te ' = ' quite their own ') is an archaic form.

11. **tintinant.** This verb and its derivatives elsewhere have the second syllable long.

13-16. This stanza is probably, although thoroughly Sapphic in form, a fragment of another poem, accidentally attached to the preceding. See note on II. 11-13. The sentiment is in

---

[1] The reading " *geminae* " (Munro) would certainly be simpler, but still the phrase would remain rather artificial.

strong contrast to that of the previous verses ; resembling rather Ovid. Rem. Am. 143 :

> ' *Tam Venus otia amat.   Qui finem quaeris amori—*
>   *Cedit amor rebus—res age : tutus eris.*'

otium, ' excess of ease is your bane.'

14. **exultas .... gestis,** ' throb and start.' or ' run riot and are restive.'

15. **beatas,** ' rich.'

LII.

1. **Quid est ?**   ' What question is there ? ' ' what more would you wait for ? '

emori = ' to die and be done,' ' why delay the end-all, death ? '

2. **struma,** ' scrofulous.   Nonius is unknown.

3. **per consulatum.** ' Vatinius swears false oaths by his consulship.' Vatinius was not consul till 47 B.C., and it is probable that Catullus died about 54 B.C.   Cicero, however, tells us, as early as 56 B.C., that Vatinius was always bragging of his coming consulate ; and it must therefore be to this confident anticipation of office by Vatinius that Catullus refers.

LIII.

1. ' A fellow in the crowd made me laugh the other day ; for after,' &c.

corona = the ring, or crowd of hearers.   Compare Hor. Epp. I. xviii. 53, A. P. 381, Cic. Phil. II. xliv. 112, ' *cur armatorum corona senatus saeptus est ?* ' Virgil uses the verb in the sense of forming a cordon of troops (Aen. IX. 380) :

> ' *Omnemque abitum custode coronant.*'

3. **crimina explicasset,** ' had unfolded to a miracle his denunciations of Vatinius.' Cf. XIV. 2 note, and for *explicare*, I. 6 note.

5. **salaputium** probably refers both to the tiny stature and the amatory propensity of Calvus : ' Good God, little Cupid is an orator ! '

LX.

This is an imitation of the commonplace in Eur. Med. 134 et seq. ; cf. LXIV. 154 et seq.

2. **latrans**, &c., ' whose belly ends in barking dogs.'

3. **taetra**, ' unnatural,' ' revolting,' ' inhuman.'

4. **in novissimo casu**, ' at the last extremity of misfortune,' ' in his last anguish.'

5. **contemptam haberes** = ' held in fixed scorn.' Cf. XVII. 2 note.

LXI.

P. 22. This song is written for the celebration of the marriage of Catullus' friend, Manlius Torquatus, with Vinia Aurunculeia. See General Introduction I. p. xii.

The Roman marriage rites took place in the evening. A lucky [1] day was chosen both with reference to the calendar, that it might not be a day marked there as black, nor the eve of a black day, and also after consultation of the auspices.[2] When the happy day had arrived, and drew near its close, a feast was prepared in the house of the bridegroom, who awaited [3] there the arrival of his bride. His doors were hung with garlands of flowers, and before them stood a quire of virgins,[4] and of boys carrying torches.[5] While they sang an invocation to the god and praises of the estate of marriage, the bride (who might be a child scarcely more than twelve years of age) [6] had been dressed in the wedding raiment at her own home. She wore a long white robe with a purple fringe, bound round the waist by a girdle (which was to be formally untied by the husband),[7] a bright yellow veil,[8] and shoes of the same colour.[9] Her hair was parted with a spear point, and she was then taken from her mother's arms with a little show of force.[10] Preceded by a boy dressed in the praetexta, carrying a torch, her arms held by other two boys, who wore similar robes,[11]

[1] v. 11, *hilari die.* [2] v. 20, *bona alite.* [3] v. 171. [4] v. 36, [5] v. 98, 121.
[6] v. 56, *puellulam.* [7] v. 53. [8] *flammeum*, 8, 122. [9] v. 10, 167.
[10] v. 3, *rapis*, 58. [11] v. 132.

she was led in procession to her future home. As she approached she was welcomed by the chorus,[1] and lifted over the threshold [2]—having previously anointed the posts, and wound them round with wool—by the *pronubi*, who were men that were ' husbands of one woman.' She was received by her husband, solemnly touched fire and water, saluted her lord with the words, *ubi tu Caius ego Caia*, and then took the keys of the house, of which she was now the mistress.[3] After the banquet, the bride was conducted towards the nuptial couch by the *praetextatus*, who, loosing her arm, delivered her to the *pronubae* (women but once married, or *univirae*), and they laid her in the bed.[4] The husband [5] then passed into the chamber, attended by the congratulations and good wishes of the chorus. They closed the door, sang an adieu, and the ceremonial was complete.

Though this Epithalamium is Greek in form and in metre (see Appendix I.), we have seen that it presents a marriage scene distinctively Roman. In this respect it differs from the following poem, which might be a literal translation from a Greek original.

The bridegroom, Manlius Torquatus, to whom LXVIII A. is addressed, was probably the friend of Cicero, L. Manlius Torquatus, who is made to take part in the dialogue *De Finibus*. From LXVIII A. 5, it would seem,[6] ' that the bride, Vinia Aurunculeia, died soon after her marriage, and left her husband to inconsolable grief. He fell in battle in Africa, 46 B.C.

For the metre see Appendix I. C. iii.

1. ' Haunter of mount Helicon,' as the son (*genus*) of Urania. She was the most solemn of the Muses, and Hymen is therefore invoked in his most serious and sacred character.

2. **cultor.** Cf. *colens*, v. 17, *colis*, XXXVI. 14, *silvicultrix*, LXIII. 72.

3. **rapis,** ' halest.' Marriage was traditionally regarded as a more or less violent abduction.

5. **O Hymen Hymenaee.** The Greek form of invocation : cf. Ὑμὴν ὦ Ὑμέναιε, Theocr. XVIII. 57, and below LXII. 5 : ' O Hymen Hymeneal.'

7. **Suave olens.** Cf. *grave olens* Verg. G. IV. 270, *suave rubens* Ecl. III. 63, *dulce ridentem* LI. 4, *turpe incedere* XLII. 8, *canit grave* LXIII. 25.

amaraci, ' sweet-breathing marjoram.'

----

[1] v. 76-165.   [2] v. 166.   [3] v. 31, *dominam*.   [4] v. 181-190.
[5] v. 196-229.   [6] But see Note.

8. flammeum, ' the bright veil.' Hymen is attired in the bride's costume, excepting the girdle.   See the account of the marriage ceremonial above.

11. ' Awake, for it is a happy day : let thy silvery voice swell our wedding songs.'

14. Pelle humum, ' beat the ground,' in the dance.   Cf. Hor. Od. III. xviii. 15 :

> ' *Gaudet invisam pepulisse fossor*
> *Ter pede terram.*'

16. Vinia Manlio.   Ellis reads *Junia Mallio*.

17. ' In all the beauty in which our Lady of Idalium, Beauty's Queen, came before the Phrygian arbiter,' Paris, ' a gracious maiden harbingered by a bird of grace,' *i.e.* by favourable auspices.

colens.   For this use of the participle in description, cf. LXIV. 8 :

> ' *Diva quibus retinens in summis urbibus arces.*'

19. bona cum bona alite.   Cf. Hor. Epod. I. :

> ' *Mala soluta navis exit alite,*'

and Hor. Od. I. xv. 5 :

> ' *Mala ducis avi domum.*'

For the repetition, cf. 186-7, 232-3.

21. ' She shall shine out, as the myrtle of the Asian meadow shines out with her blossoming sprays, which the Hamadryad queens love to feed with dew-drops as their playthings.'

22. Asia, ' of the Asian meadow,' near the Cayster.
Asia in the sense of ' Asiatic ' has the first syllable short.

26. aditum ferens, ' speed hither thy coming ' : cf. 79, LXIII. 47.

27. Thespiae rupis = Helicon, near which lay the city Thespia.

P. 23. **29.** ' Which are washed by the falling waters of the nymph, cool Aganippe.'

super irrigat.   Cf. *super impendentes*, LXIV. 287.

30. **frigerans**, a very rare word : cf. *fulgeret*, LXVI. 94.

Aganippe, Verg. Ecl. x. 12.

31. ' Call home home's mistress.'

33. ' Capture her thought in love's meshes, as a tree is entwined in the grasp of the gadding ivy.' Catullus' mastery of the language of flowers has been spoken of in the General Introduction I.

36. **integrae.** Cf. XXXIV. 2 note.

38. **par dies**, ' for whom as high a day is on the wing.'

in modum, ' to our rhythm ' ; or, ' to my beat ' : cf. Hor. Od. IV. vi. 33-36, 41-44.

> ' *Deliae tutela deae, fugaces*
> *Lyncas et cervos cohibentis arcu*
> *Lesbium servate pedem meique*
>   *Pollicis ictum. . . . . .*
> *Nupta jam dices : ego dis amicum*
> *Saeculo festas referente luces*
> *Reddidi carmen, docilis modorum*
>   *Vatis Horati.*'

43. **munus**, ' prerogative.'

44. ' forerunner of gracious passion, uniter of gracious love.'

conjugator only occurs here.

46. **anxiis**, ' heart-sick lovers.' So Ellis reads for MSS. *amatis*.

53. **zonula soluunt sinus**, ' free the folds of their robe from the soft girdle.' Cf. II. 13 note.

54. **timens cupida**, ' with ears where hope belies fear.' Remark the collocation.

56. **fero**, ' passionate.'

in manus refers to the *conventio uxoris in manum viri*, by which the husband acquired supreme authority over the wife.

57. floridam, ' in her bloom.'

P. 24. 61. ' Passion can find no fruit, fit to be sanctioned by good report, without thy aid ; but is enabled by thy grace. What god can be likened unto our god ? '

65. compararier. For the archaic forms in Catullus see Appendix II. 5 (i.).

68. stirpe vincier, ' be outstripped by his children,' *i.e.*, be blest with a constantly improving posterity. This is not a common Roman sentiment. Compare, however, Statius Sat. IV. 4, 74 :

 ' *Surge agedum juvenemque puer deprende parentem* '

quoted by Ellis, and the boast of Diomede :

 ἡμεῖς τοι πατέρων μέγ' ἀμείνονες εὐχόμεθ' εἶναι.

Avantius read *nitier*, ' rest on a new stock of children.' The ordinary reading is *jungier =* ' be continued by posterity.'

71. ' Did a land lack thy rites, she could not put forth defenders for her borders.'

quae = *si qua.*

78. ' Mark you how the torches toss their tresses of fire ? ' Cf. 98. For *coma* (κομή), used of fire, compare *cometa* (κομήτης). Add Aesch. Prom. 1,044, πυρὸς ἀμφήκης βόστρυχος (from Ellis).

81. ' True-born shame ' (or ' modesty ') ' tarries long ' (or ' hangs back ') ; ' and more attentive to its counsels, despite of all (*tamen*), than to any other (*magis*), she weeps because she needs must go.'

tardet. ἅπαξ λεγόμενον, if from *tardere.* Possibly, however, the construction of the lost portion of the stanza required a subjunctive here ; in that case *tardet* would be *active*, ' hold her back,' and comes from the common *tardare.*

P. 25. 91. Talis. ' In your likeness the hyacinth ever stands forth pre-eminent in a rich master's many-coloured garden of flowers.' Observe that the poet compares, not the bride to the flower, but the flower to the bride.

92. hortulo, ' pleasure-garden.'

93. stare. Cf. Hor. Od. I. ix. 1 :

  ' *Vides ut alta stet nive candidum*
   Soracte.'

where *stet =* ' stands out.'

F

95. **prodeas**, ' we *pray you* to come forth, young bride.
This line is omitted in the MSS.

97. **videtur**, ' if at length it is your pleasure.'

98. ' Mark how the torches toss their tresses of gold.'

156. ' Behold in what power and splendour your lord's
house stands ready for you. Accept its constant service unto
you for ever, until white age, shaking a palsied brow, nod
" ay " to all in all things.'

163. **annuat**. The MSS. read *annuit*, as they read *servit*,
158.

166. **transfer**. ' Lift—and be the omen full of grace—lift
across the threshold your softly golden feet, and enter the
polished doorway.'

P. 26. 181. Before 181 is a pause in the song, during which
the feast takes place : unless the feast precedes the arrival of
the bride, as in LXII. 3, which is probable.

182. ' Purple-robed page loose the little maiden's fair round
arm.'

183. **adeant**, *i.e.* the bride and the *pronubae*. Ellis reads
adeat.

186. ' Gracious matrons, who have lived in grace, each with
one venerable lord.' Cf. CXI. :

> ' *Viro contentam vivere solo*
> *Nympharum laus e laudibus eximiis,*'

and Hor. Od. III. xiv. 5 :

> ' *Unico gaudens mulier marito.*'

188. collocate, ' bed.'

193. ore floridulo, ' bright with a tender bloom upon her face, like the pale convolvulus.'

197. nihilo minus, ' no less beautiful than she.'

199. neglegit, ' does not pass you by.'   Hom. Il. IV. 127.

203. juverit, ' may Venus' grace attend you.'

204. quae cupis capis, ' win your will,' ' harvest your hopes.'

207. micantium, but *sonantum*, XXXIV. 12.

208. subducat numerum, ' let him first cast up the sum.' Cf. VII. 3 note.

P. 27. 210. ludi, ' toyings.'   *Ludi* is used collectively, like *pulveris*, ' particles of dust.'   See Ellis' note.

212. non decet. ' A name so time-honoured should not want for heirs, but be continued by new births from the same stock for ever.'

216. Torquatus parvulus. Cf. Verg. Aen. IV. 320 :

> ' *si quis mihi parvulus aula*
> *Luderet Aeneas qui te tantum ore referret.*'

218. porrigens. Other compounds of *por* are *polliceor*, *polluo*, *porricio*, *possideo*, and, rarer and more antique, *polluceo*, *pollingo*, *porcio*, *portendo*.   See Roby's Latin Grammar, § 2042.

219. **Dulce rideat.**   Cf. LI. 5 ; Verg. Ec. IV. 60 :

> ' *Incipe parve puer risu cognoscere matrem.*'

' My prayer is that a baby Torquatus, on his mother's lap, may stretch out tiny hands to its father, and smile sweetly upon him with little lips half-parted : that he may bear the features of his father Manlius, and easily announce himself to all men though they know him not, his face a witness to his mother's chastity : that he may have honour reflected from his gracious mother, to seal his descent, as high as the peerless glory that rests, reflected from that most gracious mother, on Telemachus, born of Penelope.'

223. **omnibūs.**   Archaic lengthening ; or erroneous reading corrupted from *obviis ;* or a transposition of *insciis* and *omnibus.*

231. **ostia,** ' door.'   Cf. Verg. Ec. III. 111.

232. **lusimus satis,** ' enough of our merry song.'   Cf. L. 2.

234. **munere,** ' gracious pair, may you live in grace ; and constantly employ in your high duties a prime of health and strength.'

LXII.

This marriage-song has no special occasion.   At least it contains no names, and no ideas peculiarly Roman.   It is probably modelled upon, if not translated from, some Alexandrine Epithalamium, or perhaps a Sapphic original.   The form is that of a dialogue between the two parts of a double chorus. The young men invoke, the maidens reproach, the Evening Star ; the latter sing the beauty of virginity, the former the praises of the married state.   The victory lies, of course, with the advocates of marriage, who continue with a final persuasion of the bride to be reconciled to her happier lot, and conclude the hymn.

On the Catullian Hexameter, see Appendix I. G.

1. **Vesper.**   The planet Venus is at one time the evening, at another the morning star.   As the first it is called *Vesper*

Hesperus (ἕσπερος) *Hesperius*, (ἑσπέριος) *Vesperugo*, *noctifer*,
&c. ; as the second *Lucifer* (φώσφορος), *Eous*, *jubar*. Compare
" *In Memoriam* " :

> ' Sweet Hesper-Phosphor, double name
>   For what is one, the first, the last,
>   Thou like my present and my past,
> Thy place is changed : thou art the same.'

Add Meleager :

> Ἠοῦς ἄγγελε χαῖρε, Φαέσφορε, καὶ ταχὺς ἔλθοις
> Ἕσπερος ἣν ἀπάγεις λάθριος αὖθις ἄγων

Plato :

> Ἀστήρ πρὶν μὲν ἔλαμπες ἐνὶ ζωοῖσιν Ἑῷος,
> νῦν δὲ θανὼν λάμπεις Ἕσπερος ἐν φθιμένοις.

Verg. Ciris 348-51 :

> ' *Postera lux ubi laeta diem mortalibus almum*
> *Praegelida veniens miseris quatiebat ab Oeta,*
> *Quem pavidae alternis fugitant optantque puellae :*
> *Hesperium vitant, optant ardescere Eoum.*'

The last is an obvious imitation of 38 sqq., and suggests
strongly the reading *Eous* instead of the MSS. *eosdem.*[1]

Olympo. Cf. Verg. Ec. VI. 86, ' *processit Vesper Olympo.*'

P. 28. 2. ' late in time, at last flings on the air his long-
awaited beacon.'

3. **pingues**, ' though laden with rich meats.'

4. **dicetūr.** Cf. LXIV. 20, LXVI. 11. ; Verg. Ec. VI. 53, ' *fultŭs
hyacintho.*' See Appendix I. J.

5. **Hymen.** LXI. 5 note.

7. **Nimirum.** ' We may be sure that the herald of night
flaunts his fires on the crest of Oeta.' Cf. Verg. Ec. VIII. 30 :

> ' *tibi deserit Hesperus Oetam.*'

Servius says ' *Oeta mons Thessaliae . . . . in eodem monte
Hesperus coli dicitur, qui Hymenaeum, speciosum puerum,
amasse dicitur.*'

---

[1] Compare the lines of Caius Cinna, Catullus' friend, whom he may
have wished to flatter most sincerely by imitation :
> ' *Te matutinus, flentem conspexit Eous,*
> *Et flentem paulo vidit post Hesperus idem.*'

9. non temere. 'And yet not thoughtlessly: they will sing what we must in duty regard.'

visere. So the best MSS. An obvious emendation is *vincere*, 'what it is our task to surpass.'

11. 'We have no easy palm, brothers, already won.'

aequales i.e., *aetate*, ἥλικες.

12. secum requirunt, 'silently recall their studied lays. They do not study in vain: they bring with them something fit to live. How should they not, for they labour in the deep mines of thought?'

15. 'We have parted our thoughts to one side, our ears to another.' Cf. Verg. Aen. VIII. 20:

> '*animum nunc huc celerem nunc dividit illuc.*'

16. jure, 'deservedly.'

amat, 'for victory is the friend of diligence.' Cf. Eurip. Phoen.: τὸ νικᾶν ἐστὶ πᾶν εὐβουλία.

17. saltem, 'fling your courage, at least, into the contest.'

20. fertur, 'what more pitiless fire rides in Heaven than thine?'

22. retinentem, 'pluck the clinging child from,' &c.

23. ardenti, 'to a burning lover surrender,' &c.

P. 29. 27. qui desponsa, 'who shinest to ratify covenants of marriage, long plighted by husband and by father, yet un- joined (not made into union), until thy gleam has gone up on high.'

29. nec, 'and yet not.' Cf. xxx. 4 note.

32. The sequence of thought may have been: 'Hesperus is a robber, for he brings night, when watchers wake and robbers lurk.' To which the answer is returned (37): 'True, robbers lurk by night; but Hesper returns as Phosphor, and arrests them.' Thus 32-35 would have run something like the following:

> '*Hesperus e nobis, aequales, abstulit unam:*
> *Ecqua tuum virgo non oderit, Hespere, nomen?*
> *Namque tuo adventu vigilat custodia semper:*
> *Nocte latent fures: tu noctem furibus affers.*'

37. fures, 'thieves of love.' Cf. VII. 8, '*furtivos hominum amores.*'

idem .... eosdem, 'whom thou returnest, changed not in person but in title, to arrest still in their trespass.' For *Eosdem*, Schrader reads *Eous*. Cf. v. 1 note.

40. quid tum, 'what shall be said?' Cf. Verg. Ec. x. 38 :
'*quid tum, si fuscus Amyntas?*'

42. secretus, 'a flower, growing in a nook, within garden walls.'

44. 'To which the breezes give sweetness, and the sun strength, and the rains stature.'

mulcent, 'sweeten.' Ellis renders 'stroke.'

47. 'Once that flower is nipt with the thin nail, and its blossom shed.'

49. 'So it is with the maiden so long as she remains untainted, endeared to her kindred; but, the flower of pure maidenhood once fallen from her soiled form, she impassions youths and she is dear to maidens no more for ever.'

P. 30. 53. vidua, 'unwedded.' So of the elm, reversely, Hor. Od. IV. v. 30 :
'*Et vitem viduas ducit ad arbores.*'

nudo, 'on an unsheltered soil.'

55. 'But ever, as she bends her uninvigorated frame in drooping heaviness, about to brush topmost tendril with root.'

56. jam jam, 'about to.' Verg. Aen. II. 530.

flagellum. Verg. Geor. II. 279.

58. marito, 'her husband, the elm.' Cf. Hor. II. xv. 4 :
'*platanus coelebs*
Evincet ulmos.'

60. inculta, 'uncherished,' 'falls untended into years.'

61. par, 'when in fulness of time she has won an espousal in her own station.' Cf. Ov. Her. IX. 32 :
'*Si qua voles apte nubere, nube pari.*'

Or, perhaps better, *par conubium = conubium quod adipisci*

par est, 'which it befits her to win'; just as *invisa parenti*
suggests that it is a daughter's duty to get married : or, less
likely, *par =* 'a marriage like this,' cf. LXI. 38, '*virgines,
quibus advenit par dies.*'

65. 'It is rebellious to resist one to whom you have been
surrendered.'

LXIII.

For a complete account of the worship of Cybele see Ellis'
introduction to this poem, a fine example of his vast erudition.
For the Galliambic metre see Appendix I. F.

The worship of the 'Great Mother' (whom Lucretius iden-
tifies with *Tellus*, giving an explanation of the allegorical
elements of her procession, II. 600) was introduced into Rome
from Phrygia, in obedience to a command of the Sibylline
books, 203 B.C. Her image, a small black stone, was brought
from *Pessinus*, a town on the slope of Dindymus ; in her
honour a temple was built, and the games called *Megalesia*
established.

There is nothing, however, that is specially Roman in the
treatment of her *cultus* in the present poem. Every allusion
is essentially Greek ; and all internal evidence would allow, if
indeed it does not suggest, that we have here a translation of
a lost Greek model. The ἅπαξ λεγόμενα, such as *hederigerae
properipedem, silvicultrix, nemorivagus, erifugae*, would then
be attempts to render the Greek compounds of the original ;
so *foro*, v. 60, is used in the sense of ἀγόρα, the associations
of which word (and not at all those of the Latin *forum*) are
intended to be presented. Roman literature on the subject
of the *magna mater*, it is also to be remarked, contains no
allusion to Attis, down to the date of the present poem ; of
which we may at least affirm, that in versification, phraseology,
and conception, it is essentially Greek.

The distinctive features of the worship of Cybele were an
enthusiastic excitement, amounting to madness (μαίνεσθαι τῇ
θεῷ), fasting, and self-castration. Attis, here a Greek youth,
not a god, is represented as leaving his home under an irresistible impulse which had seized him as a devotee of the Idaean
Mother ; as crossing the Aegean ; as landing near the Phrygian
Ida : and as penetrating the forests, that clothe the mountain
to its summit, the sacred abode of the goddess, whence he is
suffered to return no more.

Catullus' friend, Caecilius, seems to have begun a poem on this subject ; xxxv. 14.

1. **super,** ' on the crest.'

P. 31. 2. **citato cupide pede,** ' with restless foot and hot desire.'

3. **opaca . . . . loca,** ' the dark forest-bound demesne.'

4. **vagus animis,** ' lost in passion.'

8. **niveis,** like *teneris,* 10, = womanish.

citata. Attis is henceforward spoken of indifferently as of either sex. Translate, ' the restless feminine shape.'

typanum is another form of *tympanum,* ' tambourine.'

9. **tubam.** As the trumpet is an instrument employed, not in Greek, but in Roman ritual, Ellis would render this word (very harshly) as in opposition to *typanum,* and somehow equivalent to ἀντὶ σάλπιγγος, the tambourine which is in the rites of Cybele what the trumpet is in the rites of other gods, ' the tambourine that is trumpet to Cybele.'

Munro reads ' *ac typum,*' signifying a medallion of Cybele worn by her worshippers. A simple, but rather weak, altera-tion is to *tuum Cybelle.* The name has various forms, Κυβήλη, Κύβελλα, Κυβέλη, Κυβήβη.

mater. Cf. *magna mater, Idaea mater, mater deorum.*

initia, ' ritual,' ' mystic instrument.'

12. **Gallae.** The emasculated priests of the Phrygian goddess were generally called *Galli.* Cf. Verg. Aen. ix. 617 :

> ' *O vere Phrygiae, nec enim Phryges, ite per alta*
> *Dindyma, ubi assuetis biforem dat tibia cantum.*
> *Tympana vos buxusque vocat Berecyntia matris*
> *Idaeae : sinite arma viris.*'

13. **vaga pecora,** ' wandering sheep.'

15. **sectam,** ' path.' Cf. Cic. Nat. Deor. ii. 22, ' *omnis natura habet quasi viam quandam et sectam quam sequatur.*' Ellis renders ' following my rule,' certainly adopting the commoner meaning of the word.

16. **truculentaque pelagi,** ' the savagery of ocean.' Cf.

Verg. Aen. IX. 81, '*pelagi petere alta.*' *Pelage* is read, unnecessarily, by many editors.

18. **aere**, ' with wanderings fired by the clang of brass.'
Munro rejects *aere* as violating the metre, and believes *omnia*
54 to be corrupt. If *erae* be read, it will depend on *animum*,
' the goddess's soul.'

21. **cymbalum**, if *vox* be read, is genitive ; if *nox* be read,
it will be accusative after *sonat*, like *hominem sonat*, Verg.
Aen. I. 328. But the evidence for the latter reading is very
slight.

reboant, ' reverberate.'

22. **curvo**, ' when the Phrygian piper sounds his deep note
on the horned reed,' *i.e.*, his pipe has a horn-shaped extremity.

canit grave. Cf. *dulce ridentem*, LI. 4, *turpe incedere*, XLII. 8,
LXI. 7, note.

24. **sacra sancta**, ' with shrill screams wake their inviolate
orgies.'

26. **nos celerare**, ' hasten our going with triple dancing
step.'

tripudiis = the dancing step of religious processions. Cf.
Liv. I. 20, '*Salios ancilia ferre ac per urbem ire canentes carmina cum tripudiis sollennique saltatu jussit.*'

27. **notha mulier**, ' counterfeiting womanhood.'

28. **thiasus**, ' rout.' LXIV. 253.

trepidantibus, ' tumultuous.'

29. **recrepant**, ' crash in answer.'

P. 32. 31. ' Feverish, panting, wandering waywardly, pouring
her soul in sighs, with nothing at her side but the tambourine, Attis leads through the dark woods.'

35 *sqq.* See General Introduction I. p. xi.

39. **oris aurei**. It is not necessary to take this as a descriptive genitive (' golden-visaged sun,' Ellis), as it may depend
on *oculis*.

40. **lustravit,** 'surveyed.' Perhaps 'brightened.' Cf. Verg. Aen. IV. 6 :

> ' *Postera Phoebea lustrabat lampade terras*
> *Humentemque Aurora polo dimoverat umbram.*'

41. **vegetis,** ' new risen.'

43. ' And found a haven in the fluttering bosom of Queen Pasithea.' Hom. Il. XIV. 250. A possible variant is *trepidantem.*

45. **ipse . . . . recoluit,** ' alone, within his soul, revived what he had done.'

46. **liquida mente,** ' with purged understanding saw what he lacked, and where he was.' *Sine queis,* cf. vv. 5, 6.

47. **animo aestuante,** ' in a surge of passion.' Cf. LXIV. 62, *fluctuat.*

48. **maria vasta,** ' the wilderness of wàters.'

49. **miseriter**   Cf. XXXIX. 14 note.

50. **creatrix . . . . genetrix,** ' that gave me being . . . . that gave me birth.'

51. **miser,** ' to my ruin.'

53. ' To be in the land of snow, where the wild beasts have their chilly stalls, and to visit all their ravening lairs.' Cf. Virg. Aen. VI. 179, ' *Stabula alta ferarum.*'

54. **omnia,** v. 18 note.

55. **locis,** ' quarter.'

reor, ' am I to think ? ' I. 1 note.

59. **abero,** ' shall I be lost to market-place, wrestling-school, race-course, and gymnasium ? '

P. 33. 61. **miser a miser . . . . anime,** ' twice unhappy soul ! again and again must I make my moan.'

62. **genus figurae,** ' what fashion of comely person have I not filled ? ' Another reading is *habuerim,* which is easier, and so far less likely to be original.

64. **olei,** ' the oiled ring.'

65. **tepida,** 'warm' with the feet of admirers.

68. **ministra, famula,** 'serving woman,' 'handmaid.'

69. **mei pars,** 'but half myself.'

70. **nive amicta,** 'snowy-mantled.'

71. **columinibus,** 'pinnacles,' peculiar pointed rocks of Phrygia. See Ellis' note.

73. **Jam jam.** Cf. LXII. 56.

dolet, 'pains me,' active. Cf. Prop. I. 16, 24:
  '*Frigida Eoo me dolet aura gelu.*'

Or, perhaps, impersonal. Cf. Plaut. Men. II. iii. 84:
  '*mihi dolebit non tibi si quid ego stulte fecero.*'

74. **hinc.** Ellis reads *huic* .... *abiit*, against the MSS. A word is wanting in the MSS.; and *celer*, supplied by Lachmann from a redundant *celeri* in 14, will not yield a proper construction without further change in the verse. Munro would read *hic* and *sonus excitus.* Bentley's *hic* .... *sonitus citus* affords a doubtful construction. For *hinc* cf. LXVIII. A. 10.

75. **Geminas deorum.** Cf. *deum*, 68. After Lachmann *matris* is read for *deorum*, which was thought to be an explanatory gloss. Munro suggests *deae tam.* It has been proposed to transpose vv. 75 and 76, and read *eorum=leonum ;* but this alteration, though attractive, is unjustified by any evidence not internal.

nuntia. Lucr. IV. 704, 1032, where, however, the word is not an undoubted substantive.

77. **laevum,** 'the lion to the left,' or less well, 'goading on the left side.'

pecoris hostem =ταυροκτόνον λέοντα.

78. **agitet,** 'drive.' Not in the MSS.

79. **ictu,** 'under the lash of frenzy.'

80. **libere nimis,** 'in presumptuous freedom.'

84. **religat,** 'binds up the loosened harness.'

85. ' Summoning all his might, the beast roused himself to speed in his soul.' See General Introduction I.

ferus, substantive. Cf. LXIV. 176 note.

P. 34. 93. rabidos. *rapidos* is found in almost all MSS., which however continually confuse the two words.

LXIV.

In this Epyllion Catullus has made extensive use of his wide knowledge of Greek literature : on the subject of his debts to the Greek poets, see *Quaestio* I. He has also been largely imitated by later Latin writers : see *Quaestio* II. For an account of the Catullian Hexameter, see Appendix I. G.

This poem has been much criticised for the ' inordinate disproportion of its parts,' and ' want of artistic finish at the junctures.' These are discoveries of the numbered tape and critical nail which cannot be grudged to the discoverers. They are made, however, by the same scholars who maintain, *alii alio modo*, the rigid mathematical symmetry of Catullus' other poems. These scholars will therefore be ready to admit that Catullus could not have committed these faults unconsciously. He must have intended the alleged ' disproportion of the parts,' he must have meant to be careless of ' artistic finish at the junctures.' In fairness, then, we should examine his purpose before condemning the means he took to work it out, and if the purpose be poetically good, then judge the means by their effect ; for there may, perhaps, be a higher unity than is attained by the observance of the unities, and its parts may be organically connected, requiring no ' callida junctura.'

The simple argument of the poem has been told in the General Introduction I. p. ix. The purpose of the poem is equally simple. It is to give a picture of the ' golden prime of the ages,' when man walked with gods. Man was frail indeed, even then ; but suffering followed close as the medicine of sin, and wronged innocence was exalted. An earthly hero was welcome to the gods, who honoured him with affinity to themselves, with gifts, and with their presence at his table. For men were then of pure, good birth ; and from the union of god and man sprang the brightest patterns of chivalry.

The general sentiment is similar to that of the Fourth Eclogue of Virgil. In one particular, the blessedness of family purity—a feeling much stronger and more predominant in Rome at the fall of the Republic than we can well understand now—appears in Catullus' address to the heroes (22-24)

and his closing lament (398 ad fin.) ; and the same feeling
also underlies the whole of Virgil's poem, breaking out more
clearly in the last lines, which end with a distinct echo[1] of
the ' Peleus and Thetis,'

' *Cui non risere parentes*
Nec deus hunc mensa dea nec dignata cubili est.'

Virgil hoped for the golden past to return. Catullus paints,
with the fondness of regret, two or three special scenes. Old-
world heroism, as without reproach, is portrayed in Peleus,
fit to consort with gods : as without fear, in Theseus. Theseus
should indeed have been in fear ' of his own soul ' ; but
the punishment of his sin is quick and heavy. More than this,
it is wrought through his filial love : contrast the heroic affection of Theseus and Aegeus, with the modern relation of father
and son shown in vv. 401-2. Ancient justice, moreover, not only
held the sword, to punish wrong ; but with her other hand
gave rich compensation to the wronged. From the lonely
shore Ariadne is raised to the stars, and her sobs are changed
into the wild mirth and music of Iacchus ' and his jolly crew.'
So, in a wedding mood, we are naturally brought back to the
marriage-hall. There, when the mortals retire, the scene
grows in grandeur and in solemnity, as the lesser gods and
then the great gods appear and take their places ; and as last
of all the most high Fates chant their annunciation of the
glorious issue of manhood and godhead united.

In this conception there is surely no gap or disproportion.
The subject is one ; all the parts are proper to its presentation,
and are arranged in a simple and graceful order. It is not the
arrangement of the Virgilian epic, still less of an eighteenth-
century épopée. It is the natural, effective arrangement of
his subject, chosen by one of the world's great poets, who do
not write by rule, although they are the true legislators in
literature.

1. **prognatae**, ' that grew to their stature on Pelion's crown.'

2. **liquidas**, ' clear-flowing.'

3. **Aeetaeos**, ' the frontiers of Aeetes,' father of Medea.

4. **lecti . . . . pubis**, ' chosen warriors, the staunchest
hearts of Argive chivalry.' Cf. 79.

5. **avertere** is specially used of carrying away spoil : cf.
Verg. Aen. x. 78, *avertere praedas*, and VIII. 208.

[1] Cf. also vv. 46, 47 of this Eclogue.

6. decurrere denotes smooth, rapid sailing. Cf. Verg. Aen. v. 212 :

> '*Prona petit maria et pelago decurrit aperto.*'

For the accusative, cf. Verg. Aen. III. 171 :

> '*Vastamque cava trabe currimus aequor.*'

8. Diva = Pallas πολιοῦχος. Compare Il. VI. 88 :

> '*νηὸν Ἀθηναίης γλαυκώπιδος ἐν πόλι ἄκρῃ.*'

For the descriptive use of the participle cf. LXI. 17, and infra, v. 193.

9. currum, ' with her own hand built a car to fly before the light breeze.' Cf. Aesch. Pr. 475, ναυτίλων ὀχημάτων.

10. texta, ' wedding a tissue of pine to the curved keel.'

11. rudem . . . . imbuit, ' initiated unschooled Amphitrite in voyaging.'

12. proscidit. Used by Virgil of *first* ploughing, Geor. I. 97 :

> '*proscisso quae suscitat aequore terga,*' &c.

13. tortaque remigio, ' the wave, swirling beneath the oars, turned into white foam.'

14. ' There arose wild faces out of the white eddy, the faces of Nereus' sea-daughters wondering at the portent.'

feri. Munro would read *freti*, and make *vultus* accusative after *emersere*, on the analogy of *emergere se*, and still more of '*emersere corpora,*' Dirae 57, where he believes the author to be imitating this passage.

16. illac haudque. The MSS. read *illa atque alia ;* Ellis, *illa atque haud alia ;* Munro, *illa (quaque alia ?)*.

18. Nutricum tenus, ' the bodies of the sea-nymphs, revealed breast high above the breakers.'

20. despexit hymenaeos. Cf. LXII. 4 note.

21. pater = Juppiter : cf. 26-7.

sensit, ' felt,' under the persuasion of prophecy.

P. 35. 22. nimis optato, ' born in the too happy prime of the ages.'

23. matrum. Ellis would read *mater* (meaning the Argo)

and would omit the next verse, which is quoted from the Veronese Scholia on Aen. v. 80. Munro most excellently continues v. 24, '*iterumque iterumque bonarum.*'

26. **eximie,** ' above all men.'

aucte, ' graced with a nuptial torch of happy promise.' Cf. LXVI. 11, '*novo auctus hymenaeo.*'

27. **columen,** 'pillar,' 'buttress.' Cf. **Hor.** Od. II. xvii. 4 :

> ' *Maecenas mearum*
> *Grande decus columenque rerum.*'

28. **concessit amores,** ' surrendered his own beloved.'

29. **Nereine** (cf. 15, Verg. Ecl. VII. 37) is perhaps as near to the corrupt readings of the MSS. as *Neptunine*, which is an unparalleled form (Neptunus being a pure Latin word), and may have arisen from the *neptem* in the next line. The MSS. of Catullus are peculiarly corrupt in proper names.

30. **neptem.** Thetis was daughter of Doris, who was daughter of Oceanus and Tethys.

31. **amplectitur,** ' whose stream encircles the whole round earth.'

32. **optato finito,** ' when the happy season came due and the days arrived.' This is an unusual sense of *finito*. *Optatae* is read = ' when the happy days arrived at their appointed season.' Other texts give *finitae* = ' the days determined by the approach of the welcome time ' (Ellis). Munro would read *optatae ;* but finds no meaning in *quae*.

33. **conventu,** ' in concourse.' *domum,* i.e. Pelei.

36. **Scyros.** An emendation is *Cieros*, a Thessalian town, like Cranno and Larissa, and certainly more appropriate than the distant island *Scyros*.

38. **Pharsalum.** Pharsalus was the chief town of Pharsālia,

the district in which the people were already living : hence
the sense of the passage, as well as metrical reasons, would
condemn the MSS. *Pharsaliam.*

frequentant, ' throng,' ' crowd.'

41. **prono,** ' the bull does not rend the sod with the deep-
sunk share.'

43. **squalida,** ' scales of rust steal over the forgotten
plough.'

44. **recessit,** ' far as the rich palace revealed its chambers '
—literally ' went back.'

46. ' The thrones are of white ivory, the tables bear glitter-
ing cups.' *Soliis* is said to be dative, like Verg. Aen. VI.
603, and so also *mensae* (Ellis). But the passage quoted is as
ambiguous as the present. It is therefore safer to translate,
' Ivory gleams on the thrones, and the vessels of the table
glitter together.' It is also just conceivable that *mensae* is
locative.

48. **pulvinar geniale,** ' the holy couch of consummation.'
Pulvinar is used only of the couch of a god.

49. **sedibus in mediis,** ' in the middle hall.'

Indo dente politum, ' made of polished Indian tusk.' Cf.
' *pictas abiete puppes,*' Verg. Aen. V. 633 (quoted by Munro) =
' poops of painted pine.' Cf. Id. I. 655. See XII. 9 note.

51. **variata,** ' pictured with antique shapes of men.' Cf.
160, *prisci praecepta parentis.* In both cases there seems a
kind of hypallage, for ' shapes of men of old,' ' antique injunc-
tions of thy sire.'

52. **virtutes** (LXVIII. B. 50 (90) ' *virum et virtutum omnium* '
Verg. Aen. I. 566 ' *virtutesque virosque* ') may be used here as
an equivalent of ἀρεταί in the sense of ' glories ' : compare
Euripides—so often imitated by Catullus—Herc. Fur. 357-8,
γενναίων δ' ἀρεταὶ πόνων τοῖς θανοῦσιν ἄγαλμα, said of heroes,
and cf. Hom. Il. I. 189, κλέα ἀνδρῶν. Or (but differently) it
may mean ' acts of virtue,' or ' valour,' like *audaciae* ' acts of
boldness,' Cic. pro Sulla, 27.

P. 36. 53. **fluentisono,** ' torrent-voiced.'

Diae, the old name of Naxos. Odys. XI. 321, Δίῃ ἐν
ἀμφιρύτῃ.

56. **sese quae visit visere credit** is Voss's magnificent correction of the MSS., ' *seseque sui tui se credit.*'

57. **Ut pote quae,** ' No wonder, since she then first waked
from the sleep that played her false.'

60. ' Bequeathing his void vows to the blustering gale.'
XXX. 10.

63. ' As she tossed in a great sea of troubles, she did not
hold fast on her golden head her fine-spun snood ; her bosom
was not sheltered by her mantle's thin covering ; her swelling
breasts were unbound from the shapely scarf. All these gar-
ments slipped idly down from her whole frame, and before their
mistress' feet were kissed by the salt breakers. Recking not
in such an hour, what came to floating snood or mantle, with
her whole feeling and her whole spirit and all her thought she
hung, love-lorn, on thee.'

70. **vicem.** Elsewhere this accusative is always used adverbially, with a genitive or possessive pronoun. So ' *tuam vicem,
Menedemi vicem, miseret me* ' = ' I am sorry for your sake, for
the sake of Menedemus.' Here it might be the direct object
of *curans,* ' caring about the lot of.'

72. **externavit,** ' dismayed,' ' confounded.' Cf. *conster-
nare.* Others have derived the word, somewhat strangely,
from *externus.* If that were possible, we should translate
' un-selfed,' ' put beside herself.' Cf. 166 and Ov. Met. I.
641.

74. ' In all that season, ever since Theseus in his pride.'

75. **curvis,** ' winding.' The shape of the Piraeus was compared to that of a mulberry or fig leaf.

76. **templa,** ' sanctuary.' Priam's palace is so called by
Ennius. Ellis (surely against the probabilities of MSS.) now
reads *tecta,* meaning perhaps the labyrinth, but suggests *septa.*
The common reading is *tecta.*

79. decus innuptarum, 'the glory of her maidenhood.'

P. 37. 83. projicere, 'hazard.'

84. funera . . . . nec funera, 'Cecropia's living deaths.'
Cf. Cic. Phil. i. 2, '*insepulta sepultura*.' The meaning is that
the vessel bore the victims, as it were in funeral procession,
to their end ; the difference being that their bodies were yet
alive, not dead. The expression is of course a Grecism
after τάφος ἄταφος, γάμος ἄγαμος, etc. *Nec* is either simply
the equivalent of *non* as in *fur nec-manifestus, res nec-mancipi* ;
or else is used correctively = ' although . . . . not,' ' and yet
. . . . not.' Cf. xxx. iv. and Ov. Met. viii. 231 :

> ' *At pater infelix, nec jam pater, " Icare " dixit,*'

quoted, however, by Munro in support of the former view.

91. distinctos, ' or the varied tints tempted forth by the
breath of spring.'

93. concepit, ' drained into the depths of her whole frame.'

95. immiti cordi, ' heartless exciter of the fevers of passion.'
Cf. Verg. Ecl. viii. 49.

> ' *Crudelis mater magis an puer improbus ille ?* '

The *furores* must, after what has just passed, be in the lover's
breast, not, as Ellis strangely takes it, in Love's.

96. curis . . . . misces. Cf. ii. 10, lxviii. 18 ; γλυκύπικρον
κέντρον ἐρώτων, Musaeus.

99. in flavo, ' sighing oft for the sake of the golden-haired
stranger.' Cf. Ovid. Fasti i. 417 :

> ' *Hanc cupit, hanc optat, sola suspirat in illa.*'

Hor. Od. i. xvii. 19 :

> ' *Dices laborantes in uno*
> *Penelopen vitreamque Circen,*'

and the use of *in* in the sense of ' devoted to,' ' for the sake
of,' with *ardere.*

101. **Quanto**, 'how much paler did she often grow than gold's pale brightness !' For ablative of amount in comparison see Roby, Lat. Gr. 1204.

104. 'Not without return, however, and not in vain were the warm vows breathed by her sweet silent lips as she offered to the great gods her girlish sacrifices.'

105. **succendit.** In Latin the metaphor is often contained in the verb, where we should express it in noun or adjective. The common emendation is *succepit* (*tritum pro novo atque elegante*). Munro, however, thinks *succendit* has no meaning.

107. **conigeram**, 'with its burden of cones and its resinous bark.'

108. **contorquens robur**, 'wrenching the strong timber.'

109. **exturbata**, 'dislodged by the roots, it falls far from its seat, crown downwards, and crushes all things round with its leaves in its death-agony.'

110. **comis obit omnia.** The MSS. give *cumeius obvia*, or *omnia* with alternative *obvia* above. Munro reads *comeis obit obvia* (=obstacles) ; Rossbach, *et cominus*. There are many other emendations more remote from the MSS.

P. 38. 116. **error**, 'lest he should be baulked by the structure's undistinguishable maze.' Cf. Verg. Aen. v. 591. VI. 27.

120. **laeta,** is the MSS. reading, for which Ellis adopts (*malgré soi*) Conington's feeble and inappropriate '*lamentata est*' instead of Lachmann's *laetabatur*, 'Who took in her daughter an ill-starred overmastering joy.'

122. **ratis.** Lachmann's *rati* is attractive : but we have *rate*, LXIII. 1.

123. **Venerit**, so Lachmann supplies the wanting verb.

124. **immemori.** Cf. xxx. 1 note.

128. 'That thence she might lengthen her gaze over the wild surges of ocean.'

129. **adversas**, 'that rose to meet her.'

130. 'Lifting high her bared ankles' soft draperies.'

132. 'Summoning from her tear-wet lips sad, chill sobs.'

135. **neglecto numine**, 'careless of the sanction of the gods, bearest home as thy freight the curse of perjury.'

138. **praesto**, 'Did never mercy stand beside thee to prompt thy cruel breast to pity me ? '

141. **voce**, 'in clear words.' *mihi jubebas* is unusual in verse.

P. 39. 142. **optatos**, 'long-dreamed-of nuptials.'

143. **discerpunt**, 'all these the winds of the air shred into nothingness.' Cf. XXX. and LX., which together reproduce much of this lament.

144. **Tum jam**, 'from the hour of my betrayal onwards.' See Ellis' note : but here we seem to require *nunc jam.*

145. **sermones**, 'look for loyalty in her lover's whispers.'

146. **Queis**, i.e. *nam viris.* Cf. for similar *ad sensum* construction Demosth. de Coron. 310, ἀνδρὶ καλῷ τε κἀγαθῷ, ἐν οἷς κ.τ.λ. ; Eurip. Orestes, 85, &c. 'For while their soul is restless to enjoy some desire,' &c.

150. **turbine**, 'whirled in death's innermost eddy.'

151. **germanum**, 'brother,' *i.e.*, the Minotaur.   *crevi* = 'resolved.'

152. **tibi fallaci**, 'thee, my betrayer.' Cf. 176. *supremo tempore*, 'last hour.'

154. **tumulabor**, 'nor, when I am dead, will a mound of earth be heaped above me.' Burial was all-important to the rest of the departed soul. Cf. Hor. Od. I. xxviii., Verg. Aen. III. 19 seq.

156. **conceptum exspuit**, 'conceived and spat out.'

160. Cf. 51 note.

Si . . . . at, 'if . . . . yet at least.' Cf. XXX. 11 note.

163. **vestigia**, 'softly laving thy white feet with water from the spring.' Cf. Verg. Aen. v. 566, '*vestigia primi alba pedis.*'

165. **ignaris**, 'brute breezes, that, endowed with no faculties, can neither hear spoken words, nor speak them back.'

167. **missas.** Cf. Hor. A.P. 390, '*nescit vox missa reverti.*'

170. **nimis insultans**, 'rioting in triumph in my hour of agony.'

P. 40. 172. **tempore primo**, 'in that first hour.'

174. **dira stipendia**, 'fatal tribute.'

176. **malus hic**, 'this evildoer, hiding cruel purposes under a mask of beauty.' For adjective used nearly as noun, when accompanied by a pronoun, cf. *tibi fallaci* v. 152, *ferus ipse* LXIII. 85, *tacito* CII. 1.

179. **Idomeneos**, 'Cretan.' Idomeneus was, however, nephew of Ariadne, so that the epithet seems to involve an anachronism.

181. **quemne**, 'What to him, whom,' &c. For relative with interrogative particle, cf. Verg. Acn. IV. 538, '*quiane,*' Plaut. Rudens 860, Ter. Phormio 922.

184. **lentos**, 'his springing oars.'

185. 'Worse than all, a homeless shore, an island of desolation !'

187. **ratio**, 'plan.'

nullā spes. Cf. XVII. 24, and contrast Verg. Aen. XI. 309, '*Ponĭte : spes.*'

191. **justam**, 'demand the full penalty for my betrayal.'

192. **fidem**, 'honour.'

193. **multantes.** For descriptive participle cf. 8 note.

194. 'Whose forehead, circled with snaky locks, heralds the exhaling passions of your breast.'

197. **vae misera.** The nominative is uncommon with *vae*, but cf. Verg. Ecl. IX. 28 :

> ' *Mantua vae miserae nimium vicina Cremonae,*'

and *vae demens*, quoted by Ellis from Ov. Am. III. vi. 101.

199. ' Since my plaints are just, and rise from my heart.'

201. **quali mente,** ' with the same thoughtless cruelty that made him leave me to my fate, may he bring death on himself and his.'

P. 41. 203. **profudit.** Mr. Munro informs me that one in Lucan and one in Claudian are the only other examples of *prōfundere*.

205. **numine,** ' bowed assent with his sovereign nod.'

206. **horrida,** ' ruffled.' Cf. 271. Observe the rare '*et....atque.*'

207. **mundus,** ' firmament.'

209. **consitus,** ' drenched in a cloud of darkness.'

211. **dulcia signa.** v. 235.

217. **dubios,** ' send far on perilous adventures.'

218. ' But a little ago restored to me in the last decline of my old age.' Aegeus left his mistress, Aethra, the princess of Troezen, pregnant with Theseus, bidding her tell her son, should she bear one, when he came to years, to lift his sword and sandals from beneath a rock under which he had placed them. This Theseus did, and so became known to his father.

221. **cara saturata figura,** ' whose wan eyes have not yet fed enough on my son's dear shape.'

224. **expromam,** used of taking from a treasury or store-house, LXV. 3 (cf. *promus* = house-steward). Hor. Epist. I. i. 12 :

> ' *Condo et compono qua mox depromere possum,*'

and Od. I. ix. 3.

225. ' Defiling my white hairs with sprinkled dust of the earth.'

226. **vago,** ' errant,' *i.e.*, going on long journeys. Ellis would render ' swaying,' a sense requiring more illustration.

infecta, ' darkly dyed.'

227. **dicet,** ' proclaim.' Lachmann alters to *decet.*

228. **ferrugo,** ' grain,' a deep red dye. Cf. Milton, Il Pens.,
' a robe of darkest grain.'

229. **Itoni,** near Mount Othrys in Phthiotis, where Pallas
had a temple.

P. 42. 233. **vigeant,** ' keep their freshness, undulled by any
lapse of time.'

236. **rudentes,** ' twisted halyards,' generally ' sheets.'

241. **liquere** has slipped into the dependent clause—a rare
occurrence in Catullus' direct style, suggesting the loss of a
verse after 241. ' Passed from Theseus' thought as clouds
compelled by the breath of the gales pass from a snowy mountain's airy crest.'

242. **prospectum,** ' sought a wide outlook from a pinnacle of
his citadel.' Aegeus leaped from the Acropolis, and fell on
the ground beneath, not into the sea, which is two or three
miles away.

243. ' Spending his love-strained eyes in endless weeping.'

244. **lintea,** ' the canvas of the bellying sail.'

247. **funesta.** A house containing a corpse was specially
called *funesta.* ' So, entering in his pride the roof of his home,
made a house of mourning by his father's death.'

251. **multiplices,** ' tossed a tangle of trouble in her wounded
soul.'

252. **parte,** *i.e.,* of the embroidered picture on the
coverlet.

253. **thiaso,** LXIII. 28.

Nysigenis. Nysa, in India, sometimes said to be birthplace
of Iacchus, and so of his aged attendants, the Sileni.

255. **quicum.** MSS. *quitum.*

lymphata. Verg. Aen. VII. 377, Hor. Od. I. xxxvii. 14—
literally, ' frenzied by the sight of a nymph ' = νυμφόληπτος.
Cf. *cerritus* (Hor. Sat. II. iii. 278) = maddened by the sight of
Ceres. Cf. *larvatus,* maddened by a ghost ; so πανικός,
lunaticus, &c.

256. Bacchantes. 'The Bacchantes, to cries of euhoe! euhoe! nodding their heads.' Cf. LXIII. 23. Ellis makes *bacchantes* a participle, like *inflectentes*, but *harum* would then be very difficult.

257. **thyrsos** = the wreathed spears of Iacchus.

259. Cf. Hor. Od. II. xix. 19:

> '*Nodo coerces viperino*
> *Bistonidum sine fraude crines.*'

260. **celebrabant,** 'carried in close procession the mysterious symbols in the deep recesses of the caskets—symbols whose form and meaning the uninitiated vainly long to know.' Cf Hor. Od. I. xviii. 11:

> '*Non ego te, candide Bassareu,*
> *Invitum quatiam nec variis obsita frondibus*
> *Sub divum rapiam.*'

celebrare = literally 'to crowd,' 'throng.' Cf. 288, 303.

261. **audire** = ' understand.'

P. 43. 262. proceris, 'some beat the tambourines with slender palms, or woke the thrilling ring of the rounded cymbal.'

263. **tenuis** = ' penetrating.'

264. 'Others made the trumpets blow freely their hoarse blare, or the oriental pipe shrill its piercing melody.'

bombos. Lucr. IV. 545, Pers. I. 97.

265. **barbara,** 'oriental,' 'Phrygian.' Cf. LXIII. 22, and so generally in Latin poets.

266. **amplifice,** 'royally.'

267. **complexa,** 'clasped and clothed the holy couch with a fit covering.'

suo probably refers to *pulvinar.* Cf. Verg. Ecl. VII. 54.

269. **decedere,** 'give place,' παραχωρῆσαι, ἐξιστάναι.

271. **horrificans,** 'ruffling.' Cf. v. 206.

proclivas, 'bowing.'

272. **lumina**, 'towards the glow of the traveller sun.' The MSS. give *sublimia*, hence a variant *limina*. There is the same variation Verg. Aen. VI. 255.

273. See General Introduction I.

275. **magis magis.** XXXVIII. 3, Virg. Geor. IV. 311.

276. **a**, 'over against.'

278. 'Each to his home, they depart and disperse with diverging footsteps.'

279. **princeps**, 'first of all,' as *confestim* (286), 'soon after him.'

284. **in distinctis**, 'in varied wreaths.' Cf. v. 90. Ellis joins *indistinctis*, 'unsorted.' But for the artistic arrangement of flowers, cf. Verg. Ecl. II. 46 seq.

285. 'Whose genial fragrance charmed the house into laughter.' Cf. Hym. Cer. 13, κηώδει δ' ὀδμῇ . . . . ἐγέλασσε.

287. **super impendentes.** Cf. *super irrigat*, LXI. 29.

288. **Minosim**, MSS. Scaliger, *Minyasin*; Ellis, *Magnessum* = Μαγνησσῶν = 'Magnesian women's Doric dances.' *Alii alia.*

289. **vacuus**, 'empty-handed.'

radicitus, 'with roots unbroken.'

290. **proceras**, 'tall laurels, straight of stem.'

P. 44. 291. **sorore Phaethontis** = poplar.

293. 'A broad screen of these he planted around the dwelling.'

296. 'Wearing faint traces of his ancient suffering.'

301. **unigenam**, 'his sister, the hauntress of the hills of Idrus.' Ellis prefers 'only-begotten,' and suggests *Irus* (in Trachis) for *Idrus* or *Idreus* (in Caria), the only known forms of the latter being *Idrieus* or *Idrias*.

cultricem montibus. Cf. LXVI. 58.

303. **celebrare**, 'grace with their presence.'

305. **constructae**, 'heaped up.'

308. 'Their palsied frames were clasped and covered with white robes, whose purple borders had fallen in folds about their ankles. On their heads, bright with the light of immortality, rested snowy fillets ; and their hands solemnly plied their never-ending task. The left hand held back the distaff, with its mantle of soft wool ; the right hand first drew the threads lightly down and gave them shape with upturned fingers, then twisted them along the down-turned thumb and twirled the spindle, poised by its rounded disc. And ever, as they span, the tooth nipped and smoothed the work ; and to their thin parched lips clung woolly flecks, that before had made a roughness on the even thread. At their feet osier baskets guarded soft balls of gleaming wool. At length, as they struck the balls, they poured forth in clear-toned accents such a heavenly and prophetic song as this, a song that no after-age shall convict of falsehood.'

310. **roseo**, so *purpureo ore*, of the deified Augustus, Hor. Od. III. iii. 12. The change to *Ambrosio* would be slight.

315. **turbine**. The *turbo* was a wooden disc (*verticillum*). fitted on the lower end of the spindle, and by its horizontal revolution steadied the motion of the spindle.

320. **custodibant**. Cf. LXVIII B. 45 note.

P. 45. 321. Haec, perhaps = *hae ?* see Munro, Lucretius VI. 456 note. *pellentes* = striking the masses of (unspun) wool to loosen the fibres. A less authenticated variant is *vellentes* = plucking the threads from the balls.

324. **decus**, 'the glory of thy parentage,' as Aeacides, or ' of thy marriage.'

325. **opis**, 'safeguard of the power of Emathia.'

327. **quae fata sequuntur**. *quae* (accusative after *sequuntur*) = *subtegmina*. 'Run, drawing the threads, to which the destinies are bound.' Or, *currite* governs the antecedent to *quae*, i.e., *fata*, ' Run out the following fates, O spindles, drawing forth the threads.' Cf. Verg. Ecl. IV. 46 :

> ' *Talia fata,*' *suis dixerunt,* ' *currite, fusi,*'
> *Concordes stabili fatorum numine Parcae ;*

Or, less well, with Ellis, *subtegmina* is in apposition with *quae fata*, ' drawing as threads the destinies that are to follow.'

331. **flexo animo**, MSS., ' to flood thee, thy soul subdued,

with heart's love, and to haste to share with thee soft
languors of sleep, pillowing thy manly neck on her smooth
arms.'   Ellis reads *flexanimo* = ' thee, soul-subdued ' (apparently).

mentis amorem.   Cf. 373.

335. **contextit**, 'sheltered love so deep, ... as is the
harmony between Peleus and Thetis.'   Lach. *conexit*, adopted
by Munro.

341. **vago . . . . cursus**, 'often conqueror in the wide-
ranging race ' = πόδας ὠκύς.

342. **flammea.**   Cf. Virg. Aen. XI. 718, *ignea*.

praevertet, ' outstrip.'

344. **se conferet**, ' match himself,'   Cf. Verg. Aen. I. 475,
' *impar congressus Achillei.*'

346. **longinquo**, ' distant ' ; or ' lengthy,' ' protracted,' the
latter sense being perfectly classical.

347. **heres** = Agamemnon, grandson of Pelops, whose perjury
consisted in violating his promise to give half his kingdom
should he win Hippodamia in the chariot race, to Myrtilus,
(charioteer of her father Oenomaus), whom he murdered.

P. 46. 351. **in cinerem**, ' when they bury their sons, and fling
upon their ashes their white hairs, and with weak palms
bruise their withered breasts.'   It was customary to fling
locks of hair on the funeral pyre.   Ellis reads *incurvo* =
' bowed heads,' for the MSS. *in civium*.   We might otherwise
translate, ' loose their white hair to receive the ashes,' *i.e.*,
sprinkle ashes on their heads.   But this is less probable.

354. **prosternens** (*praecerpens*, Ellis) = ' lopping.'   Cf. Shakspere, Troilus, v. v. :

'And then the strawy Greeks, ripe for his edge,
    Fell down before him like the mower's swathe.'

359. ' That spreads itself and is lost in the tides of Helles-
pont.'

360. **angustans**, ' choking its stream with stricken bodies
of the slain.'   Cf. Il. XXI. 218.

361. **tepefaciet.** These verbs are formed from two stems, consonantal and vowel, *tep-* and *tepe-*.   Cf. *tĕpĕfactat*, LXVIII. 29.

363. 'Lastly, they shall be attested by the sacrifice paid to death, when the smooth barrow, heaped into a high mound, shall receive as its due the snowy form of the stricken maiden.'

368. **solvere vincla**, 'to burst the belt of walls cast by Neptune round the city of Dardan.' Cf. Il. XVI. 100, Τροίης κρήδεμνα λύωμεν.

369. **madefient**. Rossbach, *mutescent, i.e.,* no more voices shall issue from Achilles' tomb. MSS., *madescent.*

370. **ancipiti** = ' two-edged.'

371. **truncum**, ' bent her knees and fell forwards, a headless corpse.'

375. **cupido jam dudum**, ' long expectant.'

dedatur, ' surrender.'

P. 47. 383. praefantes, 'dictating such strains of happiness to Peleus.' Pelei = Πηλεῖ: cf. *Achillei*, Verg. Aen. I. 475 ; but Peleo (dative) *supra*, 337. See Appendix II. 4 (ii.).

385. **praesentes**, ' in bodily form.'

386. **coetu**, dative, ' to the company of mortals.' Cf. LXVI. 37.

387. **pietate** = ' religion,' *i.e.*, duty to God and man.

388. **revisens** cannot be taken (by any archaism) with *templo in fulgente.* ' Returning ever when his yearly rites came round with their festal days, sat in his bright shrine, and saw,' &c.

393. **Delphi**, ' the men of Delphi.'

certatim, ' with rival eagerness watched and welcomed the god.'

ruentes is against the best MSS., and probably the altars were within the city.

396. **Tritonis**, ' the queen of streaming Trito,' (a river or lake) in Libya or Boeotia = Pallas. Cf. Τριτογένεια.

Rhamnusia, ' virgin of Rhamnus ' (in Attica) = Nemesis.

398. imbuta est, fugarunt, perfudere, destitit, optavit, non verita est, are all under the regimen of *postquam.*

403. liber, ' that he might be free to enjoy the beauty of his yet unwedded second bride.

405. divos scelerare parentes, ' cast a slur on the memory of her sainted parents.'

P. 48. 406. ' The medley of all things, fit and foul, brought about by sin and madness, has revolted the righteous heart of the gods, and turned it from us.'

409. contingi, ' to be bathed in the sunlight,' *i.e.*, appear on earthly scenes.

LXV.

The Ortalus of this poem may have been Cicero's rival ' *in regno forensi*,' Q. Hortensius Ortalus. Unable, under the grief caused by the news of his brother's death in the Troad, to fulfil a promise to send to Ortalus some original poems, Catullus is still able to send some translations from Callimachus, of which perhaps LXVI. was one. Catullus dwells on his brother's death with the utmost tenderness in LXVIII. 19-26, LXVIII. B. 91-98, CI.

1. ' Though I am worn out with grief that will not leave me, and called away by my distress from the virgin goddesses of poetry.' *Doctas*, cf. XXXV. 17.

3. fetus, ' fruits.' *expromere*, LXIV. 224.

4. mens animi, ' the imagination of my soul.' Cf. Lucr. III. 615, &c.

fluctuat, ' in such a tide of her own troubles is she tossed.'

6. pallidulum, ' for, but a little while ago, a rising wave from Lethe's stream washed up to my brother's poor pale foot.'

8. ereptum obterit, ' ravished, and crushes and hides from my eyes.'

9. This verse is omitted in almost all MSS. Munro would fill up the lacuna, ' *Nunquam ego te primae mihi ademptum in flore juventae,*' which Catullus might have written. If the text stand, the word lacking before *loquentem* may have been *facta* (Voss) ; *audiero* is irregular in tense (*audibo ?*). Cf. IX. 6 for sentiment.

12. **canam,** ' sings songs ever saddened by thy death.' The MSS. have *tegam,* ' veil in silence ' (Ellis). But it is hard to understand what this could mean, and Munro ingeniously explains the genesis of the corruption.

13. **concinit,** ' sings for ever.'

14. **Daulias.** Cf. Thuc. II. 29. Procne, wife of Tereus, who rules in Daulis of Phocis, slew, in a fit of resentment, her husband's son, Itys or Itylus. After the deed she was changed into a bird, the swallow or the nightingale, and doomed for ever to ' bewail the cruel end of lost Itylus.'

16. **expressa,** ' translated.'

Battiadae = of Callimachus, who called himself heir of Battus. Cf. VII. 4.

18-24. These lines have been thought to belong to another poem. Cf. II. 11-13 notes. Their connection, however, with the previous thought is much more natural than in the other cases there mentioned ; and, if they have fallen accidentally into this place, then fortune has ' shown herself a pretty poet.'
' Slipped from my mind, as the gift-apple, stealthily flung to a maiden by her lover, escapes from her innocent bosom. Laid in a fold of the poor thoughtless girl's soft robe, as she springs to greet her mother, it is shaken out. Heighho ! down to the ground drops the tell-tale in rolling descent, while the maiden's sad face is flooded with a guilty blush.'

23. **Atque.** Aul. Gellius (X. 29) says that *atque* has the un-usual sense of *statim* in the lines of Virgil (modelled on the present passage) occurring Geor. I. 201-3 :

' *Non aliter quam qui adverso vix flumine lembum*
Remigiis subigit, si bracchia forte remisit
Atque illum in praeceps prono rapit alveus amni.'

Conington there gives *atque* its usual connecting force, saying that here also it ' couples *agitur* with *excutitur*, or perhaps with *procurrit*.' But a particle that hesitates is lost ; and I am glad to receive the sanction of Ellis in taking *atque* as introducing ' in the form of an emphatic concluding clause a sudden and unexpected catastrophe.' Cf. *Atque*, LXVI. 33.

LXVI.

P. 49. This poem, generally called ' Coma Berenices,' is a version of the lost Βερενίκης πλόκαμος of Callimachus, and may have been one of the translations sent by Catullus to Ortalus, in lieu of original verses (LXV. 16).

Of Callimachus, Ovid in his critical catalogue of poets (Am. I. xv.) says :

> ' *Battiades semper toto cantabitur orbe :*
> *Quamvis ingenio non valet, arte valet.*'

This criticism is well borne out by the present translation. The poem contains little imagination of the higher kind, but considerable artistic fancy. It is written in the mock-heroic mood of Pope's ' Rape of the Lock,' and its commencement reminds us curiously of Keats' verses to the ' Mermaid's Tavern,' the resort of Shakspere and Jonson, where, in a similar spirit, he declares :

> ' I have heard that, on a day,
> Mine host's signboard flew away,
> Nobody knew whither ; till
> An astrologer's old quill
> To a sheepskin gave the story—
> Said he saw you in your glory
> Underneath a new-old sign
> Sipping beverage divine,
> And pledging with contented smack
> The Mermaid in the Zodiac.'

The same light ironical tone is visible in, and gives almost its only charm to, the present poem. The conception itself is mock-heroic. In detail, the great astronomer is introduced as knowing about all the luminaries of the firmament, the risings and obscurations of the stars, eclipses of the sun, and (mark the anti-climax) the love-affairs of the moon. The king goes out to mighty wars, a scarred veteran—of last night's love encounter. Note next the scepticism as to the genuineness of a bride's tears, and the playful *badinage* about the cause of

Berenice's grief. A weak sister may weep for the departure of a soldier-*brother*, but will her anguish be so terrible as that of Berenice ? Besides, Berenice was never weak, and the great instance of her strength of mind was shown in order to secure—her *husband*. Her grief, too, takes forms best expressed in the Lover's vocabulary. Then the Lock begins to exhibit its own vanity by the use of strong terms, mock-heroic, if words ever were so. It is vowed to the gods as the chief sacrifice—together with a hecatomb. The result of a great war is dismissed in a few words, our chief concern, of course, being to come to the fate of a ringlet. The Lock protests (swearing, too naturally, by the head it grew on) that it yielded only to irresistible force, and aids its grandiose phraseology *magnis componendo parva*, following with a general condemnation of steel, very pardonable in a victim—of the shears. The Lock's apotheosis is next described in a highly exalted tone, emphasized by an ample use of proper names, by a comparison of itself to (no less an one than) Ariadne, and by a bombastic account of its present sublime position. A strong protest is added to show its continued devotion to its mistress, a condescension so worded as to make us feel

> ' Methinks our lady doth protest too much.'

Lastly, its present majesty is marked by the demand for solemn oblations (to be accepted, too, from chaste votaries only), and then is degraded by the confession that the reason for demanding these sacrificial offerings is—to make the other stars jealous.

1. Cf. Callimachus, Frag. τῆδε Κόνων μ᾿ ἔβλεψεν ἐν ἠέρι τὸν Βερενίκης Βόστρυχον.

3. **rapidi**, ' how the fiery splendour of the scorching sun suffers eclipse.' Cf. Verg. Ecl. II. 10, ' *rapido fessis messoribus aestu* '; Georg. I. 92, ' *rapidive potentia solis.* '

4. **cedant**, ' are obscured at their appointed seasons.'

5. **Latmia.** Mount Latmos, in Caria, was the spot where the Moon met Endymion.

relegans. ' Sweet Love sent her, his exile, to the caves of the rocks of Latmos, calling her down from her orbit in mid-air.'

7. **Conon.** Cf. Verg. Ecl. III. 40,

> ' *Conon et quis fuit alter*
> *Descripsit radio totum qui gentibus orbem ?* '

caelesti numine is best taken with *fulgentem*, 'shining with heavenly influence.'

8. **Bereniceo.** Berenice, wife of Ptolemy III. (Euergetes), who began to reign 247 B.C.

11. **auctūs hymenaeo.** Cf. LXIV. 26. For quantity cf. LXII. 4.

14. **de**, ' wearing fond scars of last night's encounter, which he had waged to win the spoil of her virginity.'

vestigia. LXIV. 296.

15. **atque,** MSS. ' Can brides loathe the Lady of Love, or are the hopes of parents to be baulked by feigned tear-drops ? ' Rossbach and others alter to *Anne*—unnecessarily ; for *atque* = ' or.' Cf. LXI. 136, ' *hodie atque heri* ' = ' to-day or yesterday.'

parentum gaudia. Cf. LXIV. 380-1, LXVIII. B. 79 (119), LXII. 62, LXI. 51.
Munro, who rejects the above reading and explanation, would read *an quod auentum* (= husbands).

18. **gemunt** is out of place. Cf. 41, XLIV. 9.

jŭĕrint, MSS. **juverint.** Cf. Prop. III. xvii. 22, ' *Me jŭĕrint* ; ' and Ennius :

> ' *O Tite, siquid ego adjuero curamve levasso.*'

21. **At,** ironically introducing Berenice's poor shamefast plea, that it was as a brother, not as a husband, she would miss Ptolemy.
The Ptolemies, by Egyptian custom, married their sisters.

luxti. Cf. XIV. 14 note.

27. **facinus.** ' Have you forgotten the glorious deed, by which you gained your royal espousals—a deed which none other could more bravely dare ? ' The deed referred to here was probably the assassination, ordered by Berenice, of Demetrius, her suitor and the rival of Ptolemy, to punish his amour with her mother.

28. **alis** = *alius.* Cf. *alid*, XXIX. 15.

P. 50. 30. **tristi** = *trivisti.* Cf. XIV. 14 note.

31. tantus. ' What god had power to change you ? ' Cf. Verg. Aen. I. 605 :

> ' *Quae te tam laeta tulerunt*
> *Saecula ? qui tanti talem genuere parentes ? '*

an quod. ' Was it not because . . . . ? '

33. atque. Cf. LXV. 23 note.

ibi, ' then.'

me. The MSS. read *pro.*

37. coetu, dative. Cf. LXIV. 386.

38. pristina vota novo, ' pay an old-world vow with a novel sacrifice.' To make vows for the safe return of husbands was an ancient custom ; to pay them in the form of the sacrifice of a lock of hair was a new thing, at least in Egypt. Ellis renders, ' pay the vows of the past with an offering of to-day ' —a frigid antithesis, but perhaps possible in an Alexandrine poet.

dissolüo. Cf. II. 13, note.

41. quod = *caput.* ' By which head if any man have falsely sworn, may he reap fit reward ! ' Cf. 18.

42. qui = *quis.*

postulet = ' could claim.'

43. eversus, ' even that mountain was razed, which is the greatest in the world over which Thia's bright offspring rides.'

44. progenies Thiae = ἥλιος. Cf. Pind. Is. IV. μᾶτερ ἀελίου Θεία. Others read *Phthiae* (as nearer to the MSS., *Phitiae*), but *progenies* would be obscure (standing, perhaps, for ' Macedonians '), and *supervehitur* would be used in the unusual nautical sense of ' weathering a point,' the proper word for which is *superare,* as in Liv. XLII. 48 ; Verg. Ecl. VIII. 6, Aen. I. 244.

45. peperere (MSS., *propere*), ' created.' Rossbach, *propulere.*

46. barbara juventus, ' the Oriental chivalry.'

48. Chalybum. The Chalybes were mythical smiths. **For** the metre, cf. LXVII. 44 :

> ' *Speret nec linguam esse nec auriculam,*'

and XCVII. 2.   A fragment of the original survives :

> Χαλύβων ὡς ἀπόλοιτο γένος
> γειόθεν ἀντέλλοντα κακὸν φυτὸν οἵ μιν ἔφηναν.

ut, of strong wish or command. Cf. Hor. Sat. II. i. 43 :

> ' *Juppiter, ut pereat positum robigine telum.*'

50. stringere = ' make ductile,' ' draw into bars ' (*stricturae*).

51. abjunctae mea fata. Cf. Cicero, *meas absentis preces* ; Soph., τὰμὰ δυστήνου κακά—a common construction, especially with *ipse.*

comae sorores, ' my sister locks were moaning my ruin, who had just been severed from them.'
Ellis (less well) takes *abjunctae* with *comae sorores.*

52 et seq. ' When there suddenly bore down upon me, beating the air with waving pinions, Aethiopian Memnon's only begotten brother, Locrian Arsinoe's winged steed. He caught me up, and flew on his way through the shadows of the upper air, and laid me in Venus' holy lap. On this errand had our Lady of Zephyrium, the Greek denizen of Canopus' shores, despatched her own messenger ; that not only to thy honour, O god of wine, there should be fixed in heaven's spangled floor a golden crown from Ariadne's brows, but that I also should gleam there, the consecrated spoils of a princess's auburn head,—therefore, passing damp from ocean to the quarters of the gods, I was made by the goddess to take my place as a new constellation among the old.'

53. unigena, ' brother.' Cf. LXIV. 301. *Zephyrus* is thus the son of Eos, the mother of Memnon. The representation of a wind as a ' winged horse ' is found in Verg. Aen. II. 417, ' *Eois Eurus equis* ' (compare Aen. I. 52-63, where the winds are spoken of in terms applicable to horses), Val. Flacc. I. 608, ' *Thraces equi* ' (=winds from Thrace), Hor. Od. IV. iv. 44, ' *Eurus per Siculas equitavit undas,*' and especially Eurip. Phoen. 212, Ζεφύρου ἱππεύσαντος. That Zephyrus is meant is confirmed by 57, ' *suum Zephyritis famulum.*'

Another interpretation, which seems due to ‘too much learning,’ is given by Orelli. Arsinoe, wife of Ptolemy Philadelphus, is represented as riding on an ostrich, in a statue at Helicon. Probably there was a similar statue in the temple of Arsinoe-Venus, on the Libyan promontory of Zephyrium. Then *Unigena Memnonis* = the bird risen from the ashes of Memnon, and will be the *ostrich*. Ellis suggests another bird, a kind of hawk.

54. Arsinoe, wife of Ptolemy II., was deified as Arsinoe-*Aphrodite*. A temple was built to her on one of the promontories called Zephyrium : hence she is called *Zephyritis*, v. 57. There was a Zephyrium in the district of Cyrenae, anciently a Locrian settlement ; hence perhaps the epithet *Locridos* (*Elocridicos*, MSS.).

P. 51. 58. **Graia.** The Ptolemies were of Macedonian descent.

incola litoribus. For construction cf. LXIV. 301, *cultricem montibus Idri.* Arsinoe must had a temple near Canopus.

59. **Hii dii uen ibi,** MSS. The simplest emendation is ‘ *Dive, tibi,*’ &c., *i.e., Bacche,* who is spoken of simply as *deus* once or twice in Virgil (cf. ‘ *membra deo victus,*’ ‘ *Munera laetitiamque dei,*’ Aen. I. 636) ; and the context here would prevent any ambiguity. [Looking at *Hii dii* as one syllable reduplicated—a very common occurrence in all MSS.—this reading involves only the change of *n* to *t*.]
Ellis reads ‘ *Hic juveni Ismario* ’ = *Baccho,* but this loses us the undoubtedly sound and picturesque *vario*.

63. **uuidulum a fluctu.** Why the Lock had to be ‘ dipped in the wave ’ is not clear, unless it was as part of the ceremony of its transformation. Orelli reads *afflatu,* Baehrens *a luctu.*
In *uuidulum* remark the change of gender (cf. 37, 39), as also in *tuum me,* 91 ; compare XLIV. 17.

65. For the position of *namque* cf. Verg. Ecl. I. 14.

66. **juxta.** Ellis quotes *contrā* from Ennius in Varro L. L. VII. 12. *juncta Lycaonia* is suggested. Lycaon was father of Callisto.

71. **Rhamnusia virgo,** LXIV. 396.

pace tua, ‘ with thy pardon.’

73. **nec si,** ‘ not even if the stars rend me with cruel words,

for truthfully unfolding the secrets of my breast.' Rossbach
reads,

> '*Condita quin verei pectoris evoluam,*'

making *tegam* .... *quin* = ' hide .... so as not to.' In
this he is generally followed : but there seems no call for
correction of the text.

75. **rebus,** ' honours.'

77. If the text stand, there will be three ways of rendering
it, all open to objection :

(1) ' With which head, in the old time when our mistress
was a maiden, knowing no man, I drank many kinds of
unguent.' This leaves a difficulty in the *case* of *unguentis.*

(2) ' With whom, as I was a stranger to all unguents
while Berenice was in the former time of her virginity, so I
have since drained in her company unguents many a thousand ' (Ellis).   But there is no evidence that, even in the
exceptional country of Egypt, maidens avoided unguents,
which they certainly used in Greece.

(3) ' With whom, in the old days of her virginity, I—
deprived now of all unguents—drank many thousand kinds.'
This requires a *nunc* with *expers* to make it quite clear. [The
nunc might be found by an emendator who chose to read
nunc a for *una.*]
  Among emendations, Munro would read *explens unguentis se* ;
Conington, *expersa* (with hypermeter) ; Lachmann, *unguenti
si,* with apodosis *nunc vos,* &c., but otherwise as (1).

> ' *Grammatici certant et adhuc sub judice lis est.*'

80. **post,** ' henceforth.'

82. **quin,** for MSS. *quam,* Lachmann. ' Without your cup
of onyx pouring out to me the gifts I love.'

P. 52. 90. festis luminibus, ' with a festival of torches,'
λυχνοκαῖα.   A weaker rendering is ' on holidays.'

91. **Sanguinis.**   Bentley suggested *unguinis.*

non vestris, MSS.   The emendations *non siris, non jusseris* cannot stand : for Quintilian says, In. v. 50, ' *qui dicat, pro illo Ne Feceris, Non Feceris in idem incidat vitium*, and no certain example occurs, in classical writers, of this inaccuracy. Scaliger altered *non* to *ne*. We might possibly avoid the solecism and adhere to the MSS. by reading *non vestri est* (for *est esse* together, cf. LXXVI. 24) : ' It becomes you not that I, your own hair, should lack offering,' or (with Bentley) ' unguent.' Cf. LXVIII. B. 111 foot-note. On the gender *tuum me* see 63 note.

92. **effice.** ' Rather by your bounteous oblations give cause for the stars to exclaim again and again, "May I become a Royal Tress ! then let Orion flash next to Aquarius ! " '

Ellis alters to *affice muneribus*, which he admits to be ' an expression of prose.' Then, like most editors, he has to begin a new sentence at *sidera*, involving change of text, loss of rhythm, and difficulties of tense sequence. He reads,

> ' *Sidera corruerent utinam, coma regia fiam,*
> *Proximus Hydrochoi fulgeret Oarion,*'

where *fulgeret* is from *fulgĕre* : so Munro, who, however, prefers ' *corruerint*,' and then sees no irregularity, rendering ' though the stars shall all have to tumble down for it, I pray I may become again a royal lock. Orion, if he liked, might then shine next to Aquarius.' But none of the quotations to illustrate *fulgeret* (imperf. subj.) seem parallel, as they all refer the wish to a past time ; or, rather, the force of the tense is ' ought to,' ' ought to have.' It is much simpler to take *fulgeret* as imperative present from *fulgerare*.

94. **Hydrochoi** ='Υδροχοεῖ. See Appendix II. 4 ii. c. The meaning of the verse is, that each star, could it have its desire of becoming a royal lock gratified, would be indifferent to the confusion of the old abode, the heavens.

LXVIII A.

Much has been introduced into this poem by various commentators which seems hardly contained in the text ; some of it reflecting on the character of Manlius, some adding to the blackness of Lesbia's character. If vv. 5, 6 meant that Manlius has just lost his young wife Vinia, the bride of LXI., then it would be brutal of Manlius to ask for consolation in the shape of the lighter sort of love-poems. If vv. 28, 29 meant

that Lesbia was multiplying her immoralities, then Manlius
was hardly acting as a man of the world, or even as a friend,
in telling tales to Catullus in his absence from her. But both
these interpretations of the text are arbitrary.

Manlius is staying at or near *Verona*, where Catullus is
visiting his father's house, and is thus a sort of guest of
Catullus. He writes to the poet saying he is in great distress
(of what origin there is little to show, but probably in part
from ill-health [1]), and feels sadly the loss of his wife's society,
and asks for some light modern literature or love-poems of
Catullus' own to soothe his loneliness. Catullus replies that
he cannot send love-poems of his own, because his taste for
these has been checked and changed by his brother's recent
death. So, too, Manlius' hint, that Verona is not a becoming
place for a man of pleasure and of *ton*, is sadly answered. Nor
can the poet send books, because he has left his library behind
in Rome. Had he been able to grant, he would have antici-
pated, both requests of Manlius.

That Manlius was near Verona is shown by *hospitis officium*,
v. 12, by *hic*, v. 28, answering Catullus' own word *huc*, v. 36,
and by *ultro deferrem* ; for how was Catullus likely to have
taken books and poems to Manlius unasked, unless he had
come, as a stranger or visitor requiring attention, into
Catullus' neighbourhood ?

If Manlius' distress had arisen from the loss of his young
bride, Catullus would probably have said something more
distinct, and certainly would have sent in consolation something

'   *Maestius lacrimis Simonideis,*'

or something like his verses to Calvus on Quintilia's early
death (xcvi.).

1. **Quod mittis**, ' Insomuch as you send,' a prosaic phrase,
repeated v. 27, like ' *quod . . . . hoc fit quod*,' v. 33.

2. **Conscriptum lacrimis**, ' this poor little letter written in
tears,' instead of ink.

3. ' That I may lift you up, like a shipwrecked sailor cast
ashore out of the sea's foaming billows, and rescue you from
death's door.'

6. **caelibe**, ' unshared.'

---

[1] Cf. ' *mortis limine*,' v. 4.   There were ' *aquae*.' near Verona.

7. **scriptorum**, ' poets.'

8. **anxia pervigilat**, ' is kept awake all night with care.'

9. **Id** after the quotation (5-8) from Manlius' letter, as again 30 after the other quotation (27-9).

10. **Munera**, ' and look to me for the pleasures of love and song at once,' *i.e.*, love-poems.

12. **hospitis officium**, ' nor fancy that I am averse to my hospitable duties.' Another rendering is, ' remember without gratitude the kindness of your roof,' cf. LXVIII B. 28 (68) ; but this depends on the exploded opinion that the Manlius of this poem is the same as the Allius of the next.

14. **dona beata**, ' what the happy alone can give.'

15. **vestis pura**, ' the white toga of manhood,' the assumption of which made the youth his own master.

16. ' When my youth, in its flower, enjoyed a genial spring.' Cf. XVII. 14.

17. **lusi**, ' I loved and sang enough ' (cf. L. 2 note), ' and made myself known to the goddess who flavours the cup of passion with a sweet bitterness.' Cf. LXIV. 96, II. 10 note.

19. **hoc studium**, ' all my taste for this,' ' all my enthusiasm for this,' like ' *ea fama* ' = ' report of that,' ' *illa cura* ' = ' care for that,' but differing from *haec studia*, v. 26.

P. 53. 21. commoda, ' happiness.' Lines 19-24 are nearly repeated LXVIII. B. 52-56.

25. ' Since my brother died, I have routed from every corner of my mind these tastes and all pretty triflings of the spirit.'

33. **Nam** is often transitional, and here = ' with regard to your other request.'

36. **capsula**, ' small box ' of cylindrical shape, capable of holding some half-a-dozen rolls. Cf. *homo de capsula, ex*

capsula totus, of a man who looks as if he had just come ' out of a bandbox.'

37. **maligna**, ' niggardly.'

ingenuo, ' gentlemanly.'

39. **utriusque**, *i.e.*, both books and poems.

copia posta est, ' lay before you a store.' *Copiam ponere* seems ἅπαξ λεγόμενον, but not impossible. Munro reads ' *praesto est*,' the best of the emendations proposed.

40. **ultro deferrem**, ' I would have offered them unasked.'

LXVIII b.

This poem is connected in the MSS. with the preceding epistle to Manlius. It is, however, addressed to Allius, who must have been a different person, for no one bore *two* gentile names. The form, too, is not epistolary, but that of a set, indeed rather complicated, composition. Observe the artificial arrangement by which the parts of the subject are repeated in reverse order : Allius—Lesbia—Laodamia—Troy—fraterna mors—Troy—Laodamia—Lesbia—Allius. So, but more naturally, in the episode of LXIV., the order of treatment is : Ariadne — Theseus — Ariadne — Theseus — Ariadne. Though this poem is guilty of ornate expansion, and though it is wanting in Catullus' natural symmetry and direct simplicity of expression, yet it contains lines which the world will not willingly ' let die,' such as 15-22, 30-32, 93-4, 119-20.

3. **Ne**, ' lest Time, in his flight of unmindful generations, cloak, in the blindness of night, this friendly act.' For *ne* Ellis reads *nec* (with MSS.), although he rejects the latter in spite of similar evidence (or error) elsewhere. Cf. 151.
The thought here and in 151 *et seq*. is the same as that which constantly recurs in Shakspere's sonnets. Stone will moulder, brass will rust ; but verse will outlive both.

6. **carta anus**. Cf. ' *fama loquatur anus*,' LXVII. 10.

8. 'May Allius, even after death, grow greater and greater in renown.'

P. 54. 9. sublimis. 'Nor the high-flying spider weave his gossamer web, and ply his trade on Allius' uncared-for name.' *Sublimis*, cf. Hes. Εργ. 755, ἀερσιπότητος ἀράχνης.

11. **Amathusia.** Amathus, on the south coast of Cyprus, had a celebrated temple of Aphrodite, who is named from her city, as in *Erycina, Paphia* (so *Patareus,* Ἀθηναίη).

duplex, 'wily,' like *duplicis Ulyxei,* Hor. Od. I. vi.

12. **corruerit,** 'and how fiercely she convulsed me.' Cf. Lucr. v. 368 :

> '*Corruere hanc rerum violento turbine summam.*'

Possibly the word might mean 'fell upon me.' Cf. Hor. Od. I. xix. 9 : '*In me tota ruens Venus.*' Munro alters to *torruerit.*

13. **Trinacria rupes** = Aetna.

14. **lymphaque,** '*or* the water.' Cf. VII. 2 note.

15. **tabescere,** 'melt.' Cf. LXIV. 243.

17. **Qualis.** If this simile apply to the tears (which from *hic* 23 it would seem to do), then the latter part is an Homeric extension of the picture beyond the occasion (cf. Il. IX. 14 :

> ἵστατο δακρυχέων ὥστε κρήνη μελάνυδρος
> ἥ τε κ.τ.λ.) ;

for the 'relief of tears' can hardly be meant.

If the simile refer, like that of 23-5, to the welcome assistance given by Allius (and this seems to give a better sense), the *hic* 23 is rather hard. We should have expected *sic* or *ac.*

perlucens, 'gleaming,' as a mountain stream, seen from a distance, appears like a bright line ; or, in the common sense of the word, 'transparent.'

19. **valle,** 'rolled headlong down the sloping gorge.'

21. **lasso** is probably to be taken with *viatori*, for *lasso in sudore* involves a personification which belongs rather to the style of later Latinity.

22. **gravis**, ' crushing heat.'   Cf. II. 8, *gravis ardor*.

hiulcat, ' makes to gape,' *i.e.*, crack with dryness.   Cf. Verg. Geor. II. 363 :

> ' *Hoc, ubi hiulca siti findit canis aestifer arva.*'

23. **hic**, ' when I suffered thus.'

nigro, ' a hurricane black with clouds.'   ' *Ater turbo*,' Verg. Aen. v. 603.

25. **Jam . . . . jam**, ' at one time . . . . at another time.' Cf. Verg. Aen. IV. 175 :

> ' *jamque hos cursu, jam praeterit illos.*'

prece Pollucis, ' prayer to Pollux.'   Cf. Verg Aen. II. 31, ' *donum exitiale Minervae* ' = the gift to Minerva.

implorata (nominative), ' won by prayer.'

27. ' threw open a fenced field, and made a broad way through it.'   (Munro, *Journal of Philology*, No. 16, October 1879.)

29. **Ad quam** = ' at whose house.'   The connection of *domum—dominam*, and also the parallel words in the adieu 116 show that *dominam* is not Lesbia, who is never apparently so called, but the lady of the house, whose assistance was all important.

30. ' Hither my lustrous goddess softly drew, and on the polished threshold checked her glistening foot, rising on her creaking sandal.'   The creaking was a good omen.

32. **innixa**.   Cf. ' *pictis innixa cothurnis*,' Ov. Am. III. i. 31.

34. **Protesilaeam**, ' of Protesilaus,' the first Greek to leap ashore at Troy, and therefore (by an oracle) doomed to immediate death, which he met at the hands of a Trojan.

35. **inceptam frustra**, ' that house, begun never to be finished.'   Homer, in speaking of Protesilaus (Il. II. 601) has ἐλέλειπτο καὶ δόμος ἡμιτελής, ' the house had been left half complete,' *i.e.*, as wanting its lord and master ; and this would appear to have been rather misunderstood by Catullus. Froehlich reads *incepto* (i.e., *amore*), ' love begun but to be baulked,' which is almost as near to the MSS. *incepta*.

sanguine sacro, ' the blood of sacrifice.'

eros, ' our lords in heaven.'

37. ' May I set my heart too strongly upon nothing that is rashly to be undertaken against the pleasure of heaven ! '

Rhamnusia virgo. LXVI. 71, LXIV. 396.

P. 55. 39. jejuna, ' how fiercely the starved altar craves the blood of oblation.'

42. **una atque altera,** ' but one or two winters.'

44. **abrupto** is an old form of *abrepto* (Munro). If it be so here, then *conjugio*=*conjuge*. But *abrupto conjugio* may quite as well mean ' their union violently broken off.'

45. **Quod,** ' this severance (by death) of her husband (or, rupture of her marriage-bond), the Fates knew was not far distant, should he once have gone in arms to Troy.' *abisse* is read in most MSS., and is taken as ' perfect for future ' ; and then *Quod* refers, not (as above) to the general verbal idea of *abrupto conjugio*, but to *conjugio*, her husband, ' who, the Fates knew, would depart in death very soon.' But this forces both the tense and meaning of *abisse*.

scibant. Cf. LXIV. 320 *custodibant*, LXXXIV. 8.

50. **acerba cinis,** ' untimely pyre of men and of all manliness.' But for *virtutum* see LXIV. 52 note.

51. **Quae vel et id.** MSS. *vetet id.* Munro *taetre id.* Ellis *Qualiter id.* ' Troy, that brought the same untimely pitiful death even on my brother too.'

52-60 are nearly repeated from LXVIII A. 19-24.

58. **compositum,** ' so far away, not laid to rest in the midst of familiar tombs, by the side of kindred dust, but buried in the abominable, ill-starred realm of Troy, you are imprisoned by a foreign land on the last margin of its soil.'

63. **libera otia,** ' take his ease unchecked in a peaceful bower.' Cf. Hor. Od. I. xv. 16 :

> ' *Nequiquam thalamo graves*
> *Hastas et calami spicula Gnosii*
> *Vitabis strepitumque.*'

67. **tanto,** ' in so mighty a whirlpool did love's tempestuous

tide engulf you, and bear you down into its sheer abyss—such an abyss as, in the Greek story, near the city of Pheneus, at the foot of Cyllene, drained the marsh and dried the rich soil ; that abyss, to have dug which, breaking through the marrow of the mountain, is the glory of the falsely-styled son of Amphitryon.' Heracles was son of Jove and Alcmena, the wife of Amphitryon.

P. 56. 70. siccare is Schrader's certain correction of MSS. *siccari*, which makes nonsense. The ' oozy soil ' does not come into the comparison, the only point of which is the vastness of the barathrum.

audit = ἀκούει = ' has   the   repute,'   as   *male audire* = ' to have a bad reputation,' but the construction with the infinitive is a remarkable Grecism.   So *falsiparens* is an imitation of ψευδοπάτωρ.

73. **monstra,** ' when with his unerring arrow he struck down the monstrous Stymphalian birds, at the tyrannical bidding of an unworthy taskmaster,' *i.e.,* Eurystheus.

74. **deterioris eri.**   Cf. Odyss. XI. 621, πολὺ χείρονι φωτὶ Δεδμήμην, ὁ δέ μοι χαλεποὺς ἐπετέλλετ᾿ ἀέθλους.

78. **tuum,** MSS.   Heyse emends
   Qui tamen indomitam ferre jugum domuit,
' which taught you, though indomitable, to bear the yoke.' *Tamen* then intensifies *indomitam* (see Munro's note on Lucr. III. 553). Ellis' *dominum domitum* misses the point, which is the depth and strength of *Laodamia's* love.

79. ' Not so dear to a life-weary father is the head of a late-born grandson, his only daughter's nursling, who has come at last, after long delay, to inherit his grandsire's wealth, and has given a name to be entered in the witnessed tablets ; who banishes the unnatural joys of the mocked next-of-kin, and scares the bird of prey from the hoary head.'

83. **derisi.**   Cf. Hor. Sat. II. v. 55 :
   ' *Captatorque dabit risus Nasica coronae.*' [1]

84. **volturium** was the nickname given to legacy-hunters, who wait, like vultures, by the side of the dying.   Cf. **Plaut. Trin.** 100 :
   ' *Turpilucricupidum te vocant cives tui :*
   Tum autem sunt alii qui te volturium vocant.

---

[1] Al. *Corano.*

86. **compar**, ' mate.' *improbius*, ' more unconscionably.'

87. **decerpere**, ' snatch kisses with nipping bill.'

88. **multivola**, ' than the most passionate-hearted woman.' ἅπαξ λεγ.

89. **tu**, Laodamia. *furores*, ' fevered love.'

aut nihil aut paulo = literally ' if not in nothing, then in little.' Cf. xxii. 4 note.

96. **furta**, ' frailties,' v. 100. *verecundae*, ' decorous.'

97. **stultorum**, ' the slaves of jealousy.'

P. 57. 99. **in culpa**, ' on account of her lord's infidelity.'

contudit iram (Hertzberg), ' smothered her burning wrath.' Cf. Hor. Od. iv. iii. 8 : ' *tumidas contuderit minas*.' The MSS. read *quotidiana*, or *cotidiana*, emended by Lachmann to *concoquit iram*.

100. **omnivoli furta**, ' the frailties of Jove in his all-grasping desire.' *Furta* is Haupt's reading for MSS. *facta*. Cf. xii. 7.

101. **quia nec**, ' But—since it is wrong even to compare men with gods—drop the thankless task of the palsied sire.'
Between 101 and 102 a loss of verses has been supposed, the estimates of which vary from 2 to 18 vv. The connection of thought is not quite simple, but seems to be this : Catullus has been urging himself to forgive his mistress' errors, by quoting to himself the precedent of Juno. If the queen of heaven can forgive her husband, sure a poet can forgive his mistress. Then he checks this comparison as profane, and, taking a lower key, calls on himself not to play the part of the ' *comicus stultus senex*,' constantly suspicious and unhappy.

103. **tamen**, ' besides.' Cf. Munro on Lucr. v. 1177.

deducta, *i.e.*, like a bride.

107. **unus**, Lachmann with a few MSS. It seems more appropriate than *unis*, which is against the spirit of 95 *et seq*.

108. **dies** is rather out of place. Cf. lxiv. 9, lxvi. 18. *lapide candidiore*, ' with a brighter stone.' cii. 6 note.

109. **quod potui**, ' it is all I can give.' Cf. Verg. Ecl. iii. 70.

111. **vestrum.**[1] ' That the name of your family may not be overswept with mouldering rust by this day or to-morrow or all the days to come.' Compare

> ' To-morrow and to-morrow and to-morrow.'

114. **Antiquis piis**, ' to the good in old times.'

115. **tua vita** = ' your beloved.' Cf. XLV. 13.

116. **domina**, ' the mistress of the house.' Who she was is obscure, perhaps the same as *tua vita* ; and then the latter will be Allius' wife. Cf. 28 note. Or, if she was not the same as *tua vita*, then Allius, and, through him, Catullus were both alike indebted to a certain lady (*domina*) who lent them her house, there to meet their loves : cf. 29.

117. **terram dedit aufert**, MSS. *te et eram dedit Afer*, Munro ; *rem condidit Anser*, Ellis ; *dedit auctor*, Rossbach ; *nobis taedam dedit Anser*, Baehrens ; *terram dedit Anser*, Heyse. *Terram dedit* = ' gave me firm ground.' *Aufert* is manifestly corrupt, and very probably contains a proper name, the owner of which will, in that case, be the friend who introduced Catullus to Allius. *omnia bona*, LXXVII. 4.

LXX.

This poem is imitated from Callimachus, Epig. XXVI.

1. **mulier**, ' mistress.

2. **petat**, ' come in person to woo.'

3. **cupido**, ' to a lover's eager hearing.'

4. Cf. Soph. Frag. :

> ὅρκους ἐγὼ γυναικὸς εἰς ὕδωρ γράφω.

Sir W. Scott :

> ' Woman's faith and woman's trust—
> Write the characters in dust,
> Stamp them on the running stream,
> Print them on the moonlight's beam.'

---

[1] That *vester* sometimes in Catullus = *tuus* Munro affirms. Cf. XXXIX. 20, XCIX. 6, LXVI. 91 note.

LXXII.

P. 58. 1. **Dicebas quondam,** ' Once you used to say.'

2. **tenere,** ' clasp as husband.'   LXIV. 29, *Tene Thetis tenuit.*

3. **dilexi.** ' Then I felt for you, not the fondness of the crowd for a mistress, but the love of a father for his sons and the husbands of his daughters.'   LVIII. 2, ' *Plus quam se atque suos amavit omnes.*'

5. **impensius,** ' burn more prodigally,' ' though the knowledge heaps fuel on my fires.'

6. **vilior et levior,** ' you are far cheaper and more tawdry in my eyes.'

7. **Qui potis est.** ' You ask, how can that be ?   Because lovers, so sinned against, are forced to love more, but to wish less well,' ' feel less kindly.'

8. **bene velle.**   LXXV. 3.

LXXIII.

1. **quisquam.**   For the use of a pronoun of the third person with a verb in the second person, cf. Verg. Aen. IV. 625 :

' *Exoriare aliquis nostris ex ossibus ultor,*'

Hor. Od. III. xxvii. 50 :

' *O deorum
Si quis haec audis,*'

and in the dramatists, '*Aperite aliquis actutum ostium.*'

Desine quisquam, literally ' Cease any one.'   ' Perish any man's desire to deserve well of any ; perish every fancy that perchance some one may be won to gratitude.'

3. **ingrata,** ' all services are unrequited, and it is now no pleasure to do kindnesses, but rather increase of weariness and suffering.'

4. **Jam juvat** is supplied by Munro.

5. **urget,** ' persecutes.'

6. **modo,** ' a little while ago.'

unum atque unicum, ' one and only.' Cf. Sappho (quoted by Ellis) :

ὅττινας γὰρ
Εὖ θέω, κῆνοί με μάλιστα σίνονται.

LXXV.

1. **Huc deducta,** ' so straitened by your frailty.'

2. **officio suo,** ' so beggared by its very devotion.'

4. **omnia** in a bad sense, like πανοῦργος, ' though you drain sin to the dregs.'

LXXVI.

Compare VIII.

1. **benefacta,** ' in the retrospect of his good actions.'

2. **pium,** ' that he has done his duty.'

3. **sanctam fidem,** ' never profaned the holiness of truth.'

4. **numine,** ' sanction.' Cf. LXIV. 135.

P. 59. 7. cuiquam, ' all the blessings men can wish or confer on a single friend.'

9. **credita,** ' lent.'

11. **animo offirmas,** ' take your stand in resolution ' : for the intransitive use of the verb cf. VIII. 19, *obdura.* Munro would read *animum.*

istinc, ' and both rescue yourself from that unhappy fall, and cease,' &c.

teque . . . . et. Cf. CII. 3. For the position of *-que* compare XXXI. 13, LVII. 2, and Munro's Lucretius II. 1050 note.

14. **qualibet,** ' choose your means, but do this thoroughly.'

15. **pervincendum,** ' this point you must carry.' Cf. Cic. ad Att. II. i. 8, ' *restitit ac pervicit Cato.*'

17. **vestrum,** ' if pity be your attribute.'

18. **extrema in morte,** ' on the verge of death itself.' Cf. Verg. Aen. II. 447, ' *Extrema jam in morte* ' ; so LXIV. 217, ' *in extrema fine senectae.*'

19. **puriter,** ' blamelessly.' XXXIX. 14 note.

20. **pestem perniciemque,** ' outroot this killing canker.'

21. **subrepens** (cf. LXXVII. 3), ' crawling stealthily.'

torpor, ' lethargy.'

LXXVII.

This Rufus is probably M. Caelius Rufus, the correspondent of Cicero, and Catullus' rival in the favour of Lesbia. From Cicero's defence of him we learn most about Clodia's profligacy.

P. 60. 3. **subrepsti.** LXXVI. 21. For the form, see on XIV. 14.

4. **omnia bona.** LXVIII. B. 118. = Catullus' happiness with Lesbia.

6. **nostrae pectus amicitiae.** The passages quoted by Ellis, ' *fidae pectus amicitiae* ' (Mart. IX. xiv. 2), ' *almae pectus ami- citiae* ' (Stat. Sil. IV. iv. 102) are not parallel, as they are simply cases of descriptive genitive. Here the notion is, ' the breast my friendship leaned upon.' *Pestis* is an obvious suggestion.

LXXXII.

3. **ei,** monosyllabic, as in the dramatists.

4. **seu quid.** Cf. XIII. 10 note : ' or than that dearer treasure —if there be such—than eyes.' For the sentiment, compare Herrick :

> ' Thou art my life, my love, my heart,
>   The very eyes of me.'

LXXXIII.

1. **viro.** If (as is certain) Lesbia be Clodia, this will be Metellus Celer.

2. **fatuo.** ' This the insensate fool enjoys most heartily.'

3. **nihil sentis.** 'You have no perception.' Cf. XII. 3, XVII. 20.

4. **sana.** 'If she forgot me and said nothing, her heart would be whole ; as it is, her carping and her talking at me not only prove that I am in her mind, but—a much more potent fact—that she is burning with passion.'

6. **uritur.** Cf. LXI. 173.

LXXXIV.

Although the pronunciation of the aspirate, at the end of the Republic, seems, according to Cicero (Orator XLVIII., &c.), to have varied according to quickly changing fashion ; and although a difference was made between the vulgarity of aspirating vowels and aspirating consonants unduly ; yet extravagance in both appears to have been condemned as a popular error. Arrius, it is to be remarked, errs in both ways, and Catullus affirms the error to have been traditional in his less than undistinguished family. Hence the vulgarity of speech attaching to Arrius was similar to that now found in the uneducated provincial or the cockney.

1. **chommoda,** ' whinnings ' ; and so *hinsidias,* ' hambush.' *Commoda* is a military term.

si quando, ' whenever.'

3. **mirifice,** ' thought himself a prodigy of pronunciation.'

4. **quantum poterat,** ' with all his force.'

5. **credo.** ' Well he might.'

7. **requierant,** ' our ears had a general holiday.'

8. **leniter et leviter,** ' smoothly and softly spoken.'

10. **horribilis,** ' then came the chilling news.'

LXXXV.

' Combien Ovide et Martial, avec leurs traits ingénieux et façonnés, sont ils au dessous de ces paroles négligées, où le cœur saisi parle seul dans une espèce de désespoir.' Fénelon (quoted by Munro).

LXXXVI.

P. 61. 1. multis, ' in the judgment of many.'

candida, ' I grant her lustre, stature, shape—these qualities I simply concede, one by one.'

3. venustas, ' no gracefulness, no pearl of wit in all her great person.'

4. salis. Martial VII. 25, Lucr. IV. 115-8, Hor. A. P. 271.

5. cum, ' first, she is fairer than the fairest from head to foot ; still more she is the usurper of all the graces of all.'

LXXXVII.

This poem seems incomplete, as wanting balance, or antithesis, of thought.

4. ex parte mea, ' as I have shown on my side in my love of you.' Cf. XVII. 18.

XCII.

2. dispeream, ' Perdition seize me, if Lesbia loves not me ! '

3. totidem mea. ' Because my numbers tally,' an expression taken from dice, or some other game of chance.

deprecor, ' cry her down with diligence,' ' abominate her.' Cf. Aul. Gell. VI. 16.

XCIII.

1. Nil nimium, ' I am not at all over-anxious.'

2. albus an ater. Cf. Cic. Phil. II. xvi, ' *Vide quam te amarit is, qui albus aterne fuerit ignoras.*'

XCV.

P. 62. Catullus' friend, and companion in Bithynia (x. 29), C. Helvius Cinna, appears to have been a poet of the Alexandrine school. His chief poem was the ' Smyrna,' mentioned here, dealing with the love of Myrrha and Cinyras. Its obscurity was such that great glory accrued to the critics who were able to explain it (Philargyrius on Verg. Ecl. IX. 35). Virgil seems to have respected Cinna's poetical power :

' *Nam neque adhuc Vario videor nec dicere Cinna Digna.*'

Only two consecutive lines of Cinna remain :

> ' *Te matutinus flentem conspexit Eous,*
> *Et flentem vidit paulo post Hesperus idem.*'

These lines seem to have suggested Tennyson's

> ' Her tears fell with the dews at even ;
> Her tears fell ere the dews were dried ;
> She could not look on the sweet heaven,
> Either at morn or eventide.'

3. **Hortensius.** Cf. LXV. 2. Ovid. Tr. II. 441 :

> ' *Nec minus Hortensi nec sunt minus improba Servi*
> *Carmina.*'

Aul. Gell. XIX. 9, condemns both Hortensius and Cinna :

> ' *Hortensius invenusta et Cinna illepida* . . . . *fecerunt.*'

Munro, wishing the conrrast throughout the poem to be between Cinna and Volusius, would read ' *Hatrianus* ' = ' the native of Hatria,' in the marshy district at the mouths of the Po.

5. **Satrachi,** a Cyprian river, connected with the tale of Myrrha.

cavas, ' deep-bedded.'

6. **cana,** ' hoar centuries,' *i.e.*, of the distant future.

pervolüent, ' turn the pages.' Cf. II. 13.

7. **Volusi.** XXXVI. 1.

Paduam. ' At the Padua, their very birthplace.' The *Padua* was an effluent of the Po.

8. **scombris,** ' furnish slack wraps for mackerel.'

9. **monumenta,** ' memorials,' ' remains.'

The *lacuna* seems to require the name of some Greek poet, and has been variously supplied : *Phanoclis* (Rossbach), *Philetae* (Bergk), *Phalaeci* (Munro). Ellis reads *sodalis* (from x. 28). Some (inferior) MSS. read *laboris.*

10. **Antimacho,** ' swollen Antimachus,' the lengthiest of epic poets, a contemporary of Plato.

XCVI.

On the death of Quintilia, wife of Calvus. **Compare Propertius** II. xxxiii. 89, 90 :

> ' *Haec etiam docti confessa est pagina Calvi,*
> *Cum caneret miserae funera Quintiliae.*'

3. ' When in fond regret we recast old loves, and weep for the friendships we bade farewell to long ago.' Ellis reads *quo desiderio*, apparently in apposition to *dolore* ; but this yields a harsh construction. *Qui* would be as near MS. *que*.

4. **missas.** Munro prefers *amissas* with Statius.

XCIX.

mellite, ' honied.' Cf. XLVIII., ' *Mellitos oculos tuos, Juventi*,' and III. 6.

3. **non . . . . tuli**, ' my deed cost me dear.' LXXVII. 9.

amplius horam, ' for more than an hour I was impaled on the top of the cross.' Cf. Verg. Ecl. III. 105 :

> ' *Tres pateat caeli spatium non amplius ulnas.*'

5. **purgo**, ' excuse myself.'

6. **tantillum**, ' ever so little of your cruel anger.'

vestrae. Cf. LXVIII B. 111 note.

8. **abstersisti** (*abstersti*, Ellis). ' You moistened your lips with many a drop, and rubbed them clean with every finger, lest any infection from my mouth should remain, as if it had been an unclean she-wolf's revolting slaver.'
For elision between the first and second half of the Penta-meter see Appendix I. H. *ad fin.*

P. 63. 10. **lupae** might have the not uncommon meaning of *meretricis* here ; but this is not necessary.

11. **infesto**, ' cast me over to the mercy of my cruel foeman, Love.' Ellis reads *infestum* : see CXVI. 4 note.

13. **jam**, ' presently.'

15. **proponis.** CIX. 1.

CI.

See General Introduction II., p. xxiii.

4. **advenio . . . . ut . . . . alloquerer :** for sequence of tenses cf. CXVI. 3.

7. **interea** is difficult. It seems to mean, 'till I can do more.' Rossbach emends to '*in terra hac.*' The gifts were perhaps a lock of hair, flowers, &c.

10. **ave atque vale**, the formula of farewell to the dead. So Aeneas says, at Pallas' funeral, Aen. XI. 97 :

> ' *Salve aeternum mihi, maxime Palla,*
> *Aeternumque vale.*'

CII.

1. **tacito . . . . cujus . . . . animi.** 'If a true friend ever entrusted aught to the silent keeping of another, whose deep-seated loyalty was known to the core, you both shall find me sworn by their oath, and must believe me to have become the very god of silence.'

3. **illorum**, not *tacitorum quorum fides nota sit* (Ellis), but the two true sworn friends, between whom the secret is held. Munro alters to *tacite*, and refers the plural *illorum* to the generic notion contained in *fido amico*, a construction of which of course there are plenty of examples (cf. LXIV. 146 note) in both Greek and Latin. But this seems to spoil the point of '*tacito—Harpocratem*' ; and v. 2 would be rather a feeble amplification of *fido*, whereas it goes excellently with *tacito* in sense, making both the *amici* to be *fidi*, and so leading up to their union in *illorum*. For *tacito* used practically as a substantive, cf. LXIV. 176 note.

meque . . . . et. Cf. LXXVI. 11, *teque . . . . et.*

4. **Harpocratem.** = the god of silence (LXXIV. 4).

puta. Remark the rare collocation of imperative with indicative (*invenies*).

CVII.

1. **Si cui quid . . . . proprie.** 'If ever answer came to anxious prayer, when hope was gone, then is it welcome, in the truest sense, to the soul.'

P. 64. 5-8. For the form of these lines, cf. IX. 5 and 10-11.

6. **lucem . . . . nota.** Cf. LXVIII. B. 108 (148). Cf. Hor. Od. I. xxxvi. 10 :

> ' *Cressa ne careat pulcra dies nota.*'

7. **hac me est optandus vita.** So MSS. 'Who is more ideally blest in this life than I,' ' more to be envied.' Ellis reads,

> ' *ab dis*
> *Optandum in vita dicere quis poterit ?* '

Remark that Catullus uses *ego* and *nos* quite indifferently— not only here, but elsewhere ; but not *tu* and *vos* (yet *vester* = *tuus*, cf. LXVIII. B. 111).

CVIII.

1. **Comini.** This man has been identified, very probably, with P. Cominius, of whom Cicero speaks (pro Cluent. XXXVI.), ' *quo accusante defendi C. Cornelium* ' ; and this Cornelius may have been Catullus' friend, addressed in CII. 4.

populi arbitrio. ' If the people were to choose what death to inflict on your white but sin-stained age.'

3. **inimica bonorum,** ' the assailant of virtue.'

4. **exsecta.** Lachmann : cf. *effossos*. Ellis reads *exerta* = ' protruding,' which has perhaps a little more MS. authority, but not much meaning.

CIX.

1. **Jucundum . . . . perpetuumque.** ' You hold out to me the promise that this our mutual love shall be full of joy and never fail.' *Proponis*, XCIX. 15.

5. **perducere,** ' continue unbroken.'

CXIV.

Mentula (XXIX. 13) is identified with *Mamurra*, the ' fraudulent bankrupt of Formiae ' (XLIII. 5). As a favourite officer of Caesar, he seems to have employed his opportunities to amass wealth. Cicero, in a letter to Atticus (VII. vii. 6), speaks of Mamurra's wealth, with bitterness. His luxury, however, ('*primus parietes aedium marmoreis laminis praetexit, solido marmore columnas erexit,*') and his debauchery (XXIX., XLI.) seem to have left him always poor. From this poem and the next it appears that he obtained a *saltus* (*i.e.*, an assignation of 800 *jugera* of land) near Firmum, a town of Picenum ; but that only a small portion of this estate was lucrative. Compare CXV. :

> '*Mentula habet instar triginta jugera prati,*
> *Quadraginta arvi ; cetera sunt maria.*
> *Cur non divitiis Croesum superare potis sit,*
> *Uno qui in saltu tot bona possideat—*
> *Prata, arva, ingentes silvas latasque paludes*
> *Usque ad Hyperboreos et mare ad Oceanum.*'

Catullus satirises here his greed, his lasciviousness, and his poverty.

1. **Firmano saltu** (*Firmanus saluis*, MSS.), ' on the strength of his Firman allotment.'

3. **omne genus,** indeclinable and used adverbially : ' flying game and fish of every kind, meadows, cornlands, and ground game.'

4. **fructus,** ' he exceeds his returns by his expenditure.'

5. **concedo.** ' Therefore I grant he is rich, if you will grant that he wants everything : let us admire the many acres, so long as the master lacks one measure.'

6. **modo.** There is a play on the two senses of *modus* : (1) a ' measure of land,' (2) moral ' measure,' ' self-control.' The final syllable of *modo* is shortened in the hiatus. Cf. Verg. Ecl. VIII. 108, Aen. VI. 507, LV. 4, x. 27.

CXVI.

P. 65. 1. **studioso** (Munro would read *studiose*). ' Though my mind is often diligent in the chase, as I search how I may send to you poems of Callimachus, that by their means I may make you gentle to me, and prevent your striving in hostility to shoot your shafts full upon my head—now I discover,' &c.

2. **Battiadae,** LXV. 16.

3. Remark the collocation of tenses, *requirens uti possem—qui lenirem neu conarere—video.* The explanation seems to be that *requirens = qui requirebam*, as CI. 2-3, *advenio ut donarem* suggests that the purpose of Catullus' visit was formed in the past.

4. infeste (*infesta*, MSS.). Ellis reads *infestum*, which he takes as passive—'the object of hostility'—as in XCIX. 11 (against the best MSS.). *In usque*, IV. 24.

7. contra, 'your hopes shall be baulked : your shafts I brush aside with a fold of my cloak, but mine shall pierce you through, and you shall pay for your sin in pains.'

dabis = *dabi'*. Catullus nowhere else makes this elision, so common (not only in earlier poets, but) in his contemporary Lucretius.

[The following Appendices comprehend not only the selected Poems, but Catullus' works as a whole.]

APPENDIX I.

THE VERSIFICATION OF CATULLUS.

A. More than a third of Catullus' poems are written in the HENDECASYLLABIC metre. This metre is ascribed to the invention and known by the name of PHALAECUS, and one epigram of his is extant in the Anthology. It was used by Sappho, Anacreon, and (mixed with other metres) by Callimachus and Theocritus. It is the metre of part of the Athenian drinking-song:

> ἐν μύρτου κλαδὶ τὸ ξίφος φορήσω.

There are about 542 hendecasyllables in Catullus, and the scheme is:

$$
\begin{array}{ll}
(a) & \acute{-}\ -\ \mid\ \acute{-}\ \smile\ \smile\ \acute{-}\ \smile\ \acute{-}\ \smile\ \acute{-}\ \asymp \\
(\beta) & -\ \smile\ \mid\ -\ \smile\ \smile\ -\ \smile\ -\ \smile\ -\ \asymp \\
(\gamma) & \smile\ -\ \mid\ -\ \smile\ \smile\ -\ \smile\ -\ \smile\ -\ \asymp
\end{array}
$$

The poems written in this metre are I.-III., V.-VII., IX., X., XII.-XVI., XXI., XXIV., XXVII., XXVIII., XXXII., XXXIII., XXXV., XXXVI., XXXVIII., XL.-XLIII., XLIV.-L., LIII.-LVIII.

(a) is by far the commonest form, and is rigidly followed by the only other great master of hendecasyllables, Martial.

(β) occurs about 33 times : I., VI. (?), XXI., XXXII., XXXV. (*bis*), XXXVI. (*bis*), XXXVII. (*bis*), XL., XLI. (*bis*), XLII. (*septies*), XLV. (*quater*), XLVII., XLIX. (*bis*), L., LIV., LVII.

(γ) occurs 34 times : I., II., III., XII., XXVI. (*bis*), XXXII. (*quater*), XXXV. (*ter*), XXXVI. (*ter*), XXXVIII. (*bis*), XL. (*ter*), XLI. (*bis*), XLII. (*ter*), XLV. (*ter*), XLIX. (*bis*), LIII., LIV., LV.

In LV. after the base (or first foot) a spondee is found, in place of the usual dactyl, in 15 vv.

One verse (XL. 1) is perhaps hypermetrical : but v. note.

The two cases of hiatus, XXXVIII. 2, LVII. 7, are probably due to corruption of the text : see notes.

B. Iambics.

(i.) There are in Catullus 55 Trimeters (iv., xxix., lii.), in which the pure iambic foot alone is used, with the exception of lii. 2, 3, both of which verses begin with a spondee. The tribrach in xxix. 23 (4th foot) is almost certainly a false reading. In iv., xxix. the coincidence of verbal and metrical accent is remarkable (except iv. 5, 6, 9, xxix. 15, 21). For *Caesura* see (iii.) below.

(ii.) One poem (xxv.) is composed of Iambic Tetrameters catalectic, in which vv. 3, 4, 5, 7, 9, 10, 13, have a spondee in the first place, and vv. 5, 13 a spondee in the fifth place, or rather first place of the second half of the verse.

(iii.) In the Scazon or Choliambic (= 'Limping Iambic ') metre of Hipponax, employed by Callimachus and Theocritus, but little used by Latin poets before Catullus, are written viii., xxii., xxxi., xxxvii., xxxix., xliv., lix., lx.—in all 131 vv. The pure scheme

$$\acute{\smile}\,{-}\,\smile\,{-}\,\acute{\smile}\,{-}\,\smile\,{-}\,\acute{\smile}\,{-}\,\smile\,{-}\,\smile\,{-}\,{\approx}$$

occurs only 13 times ; 29 vv. have a spondee in the first place, 13 vv. have a spondee in the third place, and 74 a spondee in both first and third places. A tribrach $\smile\,\smile\,\smile$, allowed by Martial in the third or fourth place, is only found once (xxii. 19) in the second place ; and once (lix. 3) the third foot is a dactyl. In xxxvii. 5 the first foot is a spondee (*confūtvere*),[1] not a dactyl (*confŭtŭere*). ' In Catullus' iambics and scazons, which have the hepthemimeral caesura, the end of the second foot must coincide with the end of a word.' (Munro.) iv. 4, xxix. 22 are only apparent exceptions, for there the preposition is separable from the verb.

C. Glyconeo-Pherecratean.

(i.) The Priapean [2] metre is a system (= stanza) composed of

---

[1] This was kindly pointed out to me by Mr. Munro.

[2] Inscriptions on the images of the garden-god, Priapus, were written in this metre. Of such *Priapea* a specimen, ascribed (but improbably) to Catullus, is subjoined :

CARMEN XIX.

Hunc ego, juvenes, locum villulamque palustrem
Tectum vimine junceo caricisque maniplis,
Quercus arida rustica conformata securi,
Nutrivi magis et magis ut beata quotannis.
Hujus nam domini colunt me deumque salutant
Pauperis tuguri pater filiusque,

one *glyconic* followed by one *pherecratean* verse. The *synapheia* is observed, *i.e.*, there is no metrical pause between the end of the first and the beginning of the second verse, and so, should a glyconic end with a vowel, the vowel must be elided, if the pherecratean open with a vowel. This system, in which XVII. (26 vv.) is composed, is generally printed as one long line—but see on (ii.) and (iii.) below. The scheme is

| *Glyconic.* | *Pherecratean.* |

$$ \smile \,\_\, \_ \, \smile \, \smile \, \_ \, \smile \, \_ \, | \, \_ \, \smile \, \_ \, \smile \, \smile \, \_ \, \cup $$

In this poem, however, the base (or first two syllables, or first foot) of the glyconic is a spondee in 9 cases ; that of the pherecratean, also, is twice a spondee.

(ii.) In XXXIV. (24 vv.) three glyconics precede the pherecratean, and the synapheia is observed throughout the system. The base of the glyconic is 8 times spondaic, thrice iambic ; that of the pherecratean is once iambic.

(iii.) The epithalamium (LXI.) is composed in a system of four glyconics and a pherecratean, in which of course the synapheia is observed. The apparent exceptions to the law of the synapheia, in which a vowel or short syllable precedes ' Io Hymen Hymenaee io ' are removed by the pronunciation of the first *io* as ' *yo*,' which is more than probably correct. In v. 223 *omnibus* ends the verse, and the next begins with a vowel : but Catullus may have followed ancient usage in making the final syllable long, or (more probably) such an emendation as the interchange of *insciis* and *omnibus*, or the substitution of *obviis* for *omnibus* is required, in this, the only exceptional case in 235 vv. It is to be remarked also that the name ' Aurunculeia ' is divided between two glyconics. The base of a glyconic is 13 or 14 times a spondee, that of the

> *Alter assidua colens diligentia ut herba*
> *Dumosa asperaque a meo sit remota sacello,*
> *Alter parva ferens manu semper munera larga.*
> *Florido mihi ponitur picta vere corolla*
> *Primitu', et tenera virens spica mollis arista ;*
> *Luteae violae mihi luteumque papaver,*
> *Pallentesque cucurbitae et suave olentia mala ;*
> *Uva pampinea rubens educata sub umbra.*
> *Sanguine hanc etiam mihi—sed tacebitis —aram*
> *Barbatus linit hirculus cornipesque capella,*
> *Pro queis omnia honoribus haec necesse Priapo*
> *Praestare et domini hortulum vineamque tueri.*
> *Quare hinc, o pueri, malas abstinete rapinas ;*
> *Vicinus prope dives est negligensque Priapus.*
> *Inde sumite ; semita haec deinde vos feret ipsa.*

pherecratean is twice so. One pherecratean (v. 25) replaces the usual dactyl by a spondee.

D. Catullus has written two Sapphic poems (XI., LI. = 40 vv.), and follows the original metre ; so differing from Horace who elaborated for himself an almost rigid system, capable of few variations.[1] Comparing LI. with the original poem of Sappho, we find that Sappho twice begins a verse with trochaic syzygy ($-$ $\smile$ $-$ $\smile$), Catullus once (13) ; three times ends a verse with a trochee, Catullus twice ; twice breaks up a word between the third verse and the Adonic($-$ $\smile$ $\smile$ $-$ $\simeq$) which concludes the system, Catullus never ; nine times she has caesura after a later syllable than the fifth, Catullus twice ; thrice ends a verse with a monosyllable, and Catullus [thrice. In XI. he begins a verse with a trochaic syzygy twice, once ends a verse with a trochee, three times divides a word between two verses, and eight times has the late caesura. Hence we may fairly conclude that the scheme of both Sappho and Catullus admitted two forms,

$$ter \begin{cases} (\alpha) & - \smile - - - \quad \smile \smile - - - \\ (\beta) & - \smile - \smile - \quad \smile \smile - \smile \smile \\ & \qquad\qquad\qquad - \smile \smile - \simeq \end{cases}$$

of which (α) alone is Horatian ; that both preferred (or at least freely admitted) the late caesura, which is much rarer in Horace ; that the monosyllabic ending, so much avoided by Horace, was not unwelcome to them ; and that synapheia, and the consequent division of a word between two verses (of which only three examples are found in Horace), was normal with them. Like the hexameter, therefore, in the hands of Virgil, the Sapphic under Horace's treatment seems to have been Romanised—that is to say, to have become less elastic and more regular ; but the lyric metre suffered much more and gained much less than the epic metre in its admission to the ' Latinitas.'

E. The CHORIAMBIC metre (*Sapphic sixteen-syllable, or greater Asclepiad*), employed by Sappho and Alcaeus, and, after Catullus, once or twice by Horace—who, as usual, more rigidly, requires the end of the two first choriambi to coincide with the end of a word—is only represented by XXX. The

---

[1] It is to be remarked, however, that Horace's later Sapphics are much freer than the earlier.

verse consists of a dissyllabic base (a spondee, except in v. 9, where it is a trochee), followed by three choriambs, and ended by two short syllables. The scheme is

$$\acute{-} \; \smile \; \acute{-} \; - \; \smile \; \smile \; \acute{-} \; \; \acute{-} \; \smile \; \smile \; \acute{-} \; \; \acute{-} \; \smile \; \smile \; \acute{-} \; \smile \; \asymp$$

F. The 'Attis' (LXIII.) is written in a metre which seems to have been peculiar to poems of which the subject was the worship of Cybele. This metre, with less than his usual success in his imitations of classical metres (unfortunately so brief), has been employed by Lord Tennyson in 'Boadicea.' But the failure is more than pardonable, for the origin and development of the verse are still wrapped in obscurity. We are told by Hephaestion—our great metrical authority—that the system originally consists of an *Ionic Tetrameter Catalectic*, and that its name GALLIAMBIC has arisen from its special employment. The simple scheme would then be

$$\smile \; \smile \; \acute{-} \; - \; | \; \smile \; \smile \; \acute{-} \; - \; \| \; \smile \; \smile \; \acute{-} \; - \; | \; \smile \; \smile \; \acute{\asymp}$$

Such a verse, however, is not found in this poem. If, however, we replace the *Ionic a minore* by an *Ionic a majore* in the first or third place, thus :—

$$\smile \; \smile \; - \; - \; \; - \; \smile \; \smile \; - \; - \; \| \; \smile \; \smile \; - \; - \; \; \smile \; \smile \; \asymp$$
$$- \; - \; \smile \; \smile \; - \; - \; \| \; - \; - \; \smile \; \smile \; \; \smile \; \asymp$$

we can scan v. 18 ;[1] and this suggests a clue. Granting that two short syllables may be the metrical equivalent of one long syllable, and *vice versa*, we obtain the following scheme, which will scan every line :—

		a					*β*			

1. $\smile \; \smile \; - \quad - \quad | \; \smile \; \smile \; - \; - \| \; \smile \; \smile \; - \quad - \quad | \; \smile \; \smile \; \asymp$
2. $\acute{-} \quad - \quad - \; \smile \; \smile \; | \; \smile \; \smile \; - \; - \| \; - \quad - \quad - \; \smile \; \smile \; | \; \smile \; \smile \; \asymp$
3. $\smile \; \smile \; - \quad - \quad | \; \smile \; \smile \; - \; - \| \; - \quad - \; \smile \; \smile \; - \; | \; \smile \; \smile \; \asymp$
4. $\smile \; \smile \; \smile \; \smile \; \smile \; | \; \smile \; \smile \; - \; - \| \; \smile \; \smile \; - \quad - \quad | \; \smile \; \smile \; \asymp$
5. $\smile \; \smile \; - \quad \smile \; \smile \; - \quad \smile \; - \; - \| \; \smile \; \smile \; - \quad - \quad \smile \; \smile \; \asymp$
6. $- \quad - \quad - \; \smile \; \smile \; - \quad \smile \; - \; - \| \; - \quad - \; \smile \; \smile \; \smile \; \smile \; \asymp$
7. $\smile \; \smile \; \smile \; \smile \; - \quad - \quad \smile \; - \; - \| \; \smile \; \smile \; \smile \; \smile \; - \quad \smile \; \smile \; \asymp$

Thus the first half of vv. 1, 2, 3, answers to *a*, scheme 5 ; the second half to *β*, scheme 3 : v. 77 answers wholly to scheme 3 : v. 22 to scheme 2 : and so on. One difficulty remains. This metre is said to be subject to *anaclasis*. The exact force of this word is still a subject of conjecture ; but in this usage

[1] But Mr. Munro thinks both 18 and 54, the only verses in which the $\smile \; \smile \; \acute{-} \; -$ occurs in the first place, unmetrical.

it seems to refer to the phenomenon seen in scheme 5, 6, 7, where a short syllable, apparently belonging to the second Ionic, seems to have ' broken itself back,' or ' bent itself back,' so as to become inserted before the last long syllable of the first Ionic ; the same thing also occurring in the latter half of the verse. But the simpler explanation of the fact (as revealed by the present poem) is to refer this phenomenon to a resolution of — into ⌣ ⌣, followed (though this is a metrical license requiring illustration) by a converse reunion or consolidation of another ⌣ ⌣ (the one ⌣ obtained by the resolution, the other ⌣ previously existing next to it in the verse), into a new —. Whatever be the theoretical explanation, the above scheme will make the scansion of every verse in this poem practically clear.

G. Two poems (LXII., LXIV.) contain 474 HEXAMETERS. In both poems, Catullus' treatment of the hexameter differs from that of Lucretius, as falling more largely under later Greek influence. Both of these poets, who published their poems very much about the same time, are inferior in versification to Virgil, who, however, has occasionally imitated some of their metrical peculiarities. Both Lucretius and Catullus wrote single verses rather than paragraphs—that is to say, the end of a clause generally coincides with the end of a line : the monotony, and also the wordiness, which this practice caused, was avoided by Virgil, and an immeasurably greater variety in effect was obtained by him, when (in the *Georgics* and the *Aeneid*) he wrote passage by passage, not verse by verse, distributing his periods among several lines with an artistic arrangement of the pauses. The *Eclogues* are naturally nearer to the older treatment of the hexameter than the longer poems. While we admit, as we must, the comparative want of variety shown by an examination of the rhythm of Catullus' hexameter, as judged by the standard of Lucretius and still more of Virgil, we must, however, remember that the latter poets wrote, the one more than seven thousand verses, the other more than twelve thousand, Catullus not five hundred ; and that monotony of rhythm in a poem of sixty or even of four hundred lines, is a different thing from such monotony in works ten or twenty times longer. It is only by deliberate comparison that the rhythm of Catullus' hexameter is found to be monotonous.

The following is a detailed account of the facts of the hexameter in Catullus :—

1. The first two feet are cut off from the rest of the verse

(e.g., ' *Nutricum tenus*,' LXIV. 18), 5 times in LXII., 28 times in LXIV. Virgil [1] only uses the ruder rhythm exceptionally, and in passages where he imitates Catullus or Lucretius : in the latter it is quite common.

2. In the third foot the caesura $-\smile\,|\,\smile$ (instead of the more ordinary $-\,|\,\smile\,\smile$) occurs 7 times in LXII., 28 times in LXIV. This is commoner in Lucretius, and is frequent in Virgil, especially in the Eclogues.

3. *Bucolic caesura.* The fourth foot closes with the end of a word (generally a spondee) 27 times in LXII., 247 times in LXIV. This is a favourite rhythm (if not quite so frequently found) in Lucretius ; but—although occurring about 240 times in the Eclogues (which contain 829 vv.)—it is generally avoided by Virgil in his other poems.

The *trochaic rhythm* in a dactyl in the 4th foot (e.g., *saepe levi somno suadebit | inire susurro*) is un-Greek, and is never found in Catullus (once only in Cicero, according to Munro, and rarely in the most finished parts of Lucretius). Virgil employs it (not reckoning the cases when the last short of this dactyl is a monosyllable) 18 times in the Eclogues (829 vv.) ; 40 times in the Georgics (2188 vv.) ; and 135 times in the Aeneid (9895 vv.) ; and it is perhaps still more frequent in Ovid.

4. Catullus belonged to the σπονδειάζοντες : 6 times in LXII., and 26 times in LXIV. only one dactyl is found in a verse, in the fourth or fifth foot, and twice (LXIV. 3, 44) the last five feet are all spondees. There are in LXIV. 27 dispondaic endings, of which 8 are preceded by a dissyllable containing two shorts ($\smile\,\smile$). Dispondaic endings are comparatively rare in Lucretius, and a trispondaic ending is unknown. In Virgil spondaic endings are imitations from the Greek or perhaps Alexandrine affectations. If the last word is a tetrasyllable in Virgil it is also a proper name (so 10 times ; exc. Ecl. iv. 49, Aen. III. 549) : not so in Catullus, who in LXIV. has 22 dispondaic tetrasyllabic endings. When a dispondaic ending is not also a tetrasyllable, it violates the usual law of the Latin hexameter which requires metrical ictus and verbal accent to correspond in the last two feet of the verse. This irregularity occurs 5 times in LXIV., and at least 13 times in Virgil.

[1] I find, however, that in the Eclogues this rhythm is far from exceptional ; it is rarer in the Georgics, but still as frequent as in Catullus ; and the same may be affirmed of the Aeneid.

5. **Catullus** ends a verse with a *monosyllable* twice, LXII. 45,
LXIV. 315 ; Virgil 28 times ; Lucretius often—all violating the
law which requires the coincidence of verbal accent and
metrical ictus at the close of the verse. One (LXIV. 55) *two
dissyllables* (not dispondaic) break the same law ; in the
Georgics thrice, at least, and a dozen times in the last books
of the Aeneid. A *tetrasyllable* (not dispondaic) occurs twice
in LXII. (*hymenaeus*), the same word being found in a similar
position in LXIV. twice, and *calathisci* once. Virgil has *hymenaeus* at the end of a verse 10 times, *hyacinthus* 5 times :
but also *ululatu*, *lacrimisque*. These also involve a discordance of ictus and accent, and (before the last two Greek
words) a lengthening of a short syllable. Virgil of course
freely ends with similar tetrasyllables when they are proper
names. Once in LXII., twice in LXIV., the last word is *pentasyllabic*. Such endings (as also tetrasyllabic endings not requiring discordance of ictus and accent) are much liked by
Lucretius. More than a dozen pentasyllabic proper names
end Virgil's verses : add to them *ancipitemque* (Aen. v. 589),
quadrupedantum (XII. 614).

6. Of *elisions between fourth and fifth* foot there are 2 in
LXII., 9 in LXIV. These are not rare in Lucretius or Virgil
(*-que* is generally the elided syllable). *Elisions between fifth
and sixth feet* appear once in LXII., 5 times in LXIV. : they
are not at all avoided by Lucretius, and he is occasionally
imitated by Virgil, but rarely, in this respect. Catullus,
generally, is less harsh in his elisions in his hexameters than
in his other metres.

7. There is one Hypermeter in Catullus (LXIV. 298) as there
is one in Lucretius (v. 849) ; Virgil has about a score, the
last syllable being in all but two cases *-que.*

H. In Catullus, alone among Latin poets, the ELEGIAC re-
tains its original form, its Greek freedom, ease and elasticity.
In other hands, even in those of Propertius, but more than
all in the hands of Ovid, this metre became Latinized, and
underwent a change, similar to (but far greater than) the
change undergone by the hexameter as finally represented in
Virgil, or the Sapphic or Alcaic in Horace. The fundamental
originality of the Roman genius nowhere reveals itself so
clearly, to just examination, as in the use which it made of
what it borrowed or rather annexed, from the literature of
Greece. The elder tragedy, the elder comedy, speculative

philosophy, and the simple lyric, were soon left alone as incompatible with the native mind. But the epic and the elegiac and the epigram, like new provinces, could be conquered, could adopt Roman laws, submit to and survive a Roman reconstruction. A loss of freedom could be compensated by dignity, a loss of ease by symmetry, a loss of spontaneity by precision, a loss of nature by art. The transformation of a province and of poetry under Roman rule meant death to the old forms, but regeneration into new forms of perfection. At the same time, in both cases, some room might still remain for regret ; and we cannot but regret that others did not arise to continue, after Catullus, the freer growth, the more fluent and natural and less artificial maturity, of the Greek elegiac. For he has left some whole poems and many passages which show, like Caesar's plans, what might have been but for the 'Ides of March.'

Of Catullus 642 elegiacs remain (LXV.-CXVI.). Ovid's rules, such as the close of a thought with a couplet, the avoidance of elision, especially in the latter half of both the hexameter and the pentameter, the preponderance of dactyls, the ending of the couplet with a dissyllable, which must be either noun or verb, and the like, were not observed by Catullus. In the hexameter he has 9 *monosyllabic* endings, 9 *tetrasyllabic*, 9 *dispondaic*, 2 *pentasyllabic* (LXVIII. 105, XCVII. 5). One hexameter (CXIV. 3) consists of six spondees. In the pentameter there is one *monosyllabic ending* (LXVI. 8), 83 *trisyllabic* endings, 98 *tetrasyllabic*, 17 *pentasyllabic*, 1 *heptasyllabic* (LXVIII. 72) ; and 34 *adjectival* endings. Elision occurs between the first and second halves of the pentameter 16 times ; hiatus thrice.

J. The few peculiarities of Catullus' PROSODY are :—

(α) The lengthening of a short final vowel before two consonants in THESIS : *Propontida trucem* IV. 9, *impotentia freta* 18, *nefaria scripta* XLIV. 18, *modo scurra* XXII. 12, *ultima Britannia* XXIX. 4 ; in ARSIS, *si pote stolidum* XVII. 24, *gelida stabula* LXIII. 53, *nulla spes* LXIV. 187.

(β) That a short final syllable is lengthened thrice before *hymenaeus* LXII. 4, LXIV. 20, LXVI. 11. See also LXI. 223 note.

(γ) Hiatus occurs LXVI. 11, *novo auctus*, and (shortening the preceding long vowel) LV. 4 *tĕ in*, CXIV. 6 *modŏ* (abl.) *ipse*. See also X., 27 note, and supra A. *ad fin.*

(δ) *s* is once elided, CXVI. 8

APPENDIX II.

THE DICTION OF CATULLUS.

One of the greatest charms of Catullus lies in the simplicity and naturalness of his language, which are in great contrast to the later artificial Latin style. In this 'inimitable spontaneity' he is 'the most Greek of all the Latin poets.' He is free from Grecism, however, as he is free from everything artificial or archaic or affected, both in vocabulary and in syntax. However difficult the metre in which he writes, however subtle the thought he would convey, he is never intricate and never obscure. His words seem to have fallen of themselves into metre without leaving their natural order,[1] and would make good prose—if they were not poetry. His language, in the epigrams, lyrics, and elegiacs, is little removed from ordinary speech. He is full of familiar phrases ; he is fond of the diminutives [2] of affectionate or merry talk ; he uses the tongue of the wits of the town, the lips of the lover of real life. Even his Greek words were those heard in common conversation. In the truest sense, he followed

> *Usus*
> *Quem penes arbitrium est et jus et norma loquendi.*

1. FAMILIAR EXPRESSIONS in Catullus are :

a. *Indefinite phrases.*

I. 8, quicquid hoc libelli, qualecunque quidem.
VI. 15, quicquid habes boni malique.

---

[1] Except only XLIV. 9, LXVI. 18, 41, 65, LXXXVIII B. 28, 108.

[2] 'I hold it to be one of the most grievous defects of the literary diction established in the Augustan age, that it almost banished from the language of poetry those diminutives which are a characteristic, not only of Catullus' diction, but of the letters to Atticus and of the verse of Plautus & Terence : it made the lyric of the heart impossible.'—MUNRO.

a. *Indefinite phrases*—continued.

XXXVII. 4, quicquid est puellarum.
XXX. 13, quicquid est domi cachinnorum.
LXVIII A. 28, quisquis de meliore nota est.
II. 2, quantum est hominum venustiorum.
IX. 10, quantum est hominum beatiorum.
XLV. 5, quantum qui pote plurimum perire.
V. 13, tantum basiorum.
XIV. 7, tantum impiorum.
XXIV. 2, non horum modo sed quot aut fuerunt,
         aut sunt aut aliis erunt in annis. XXI. 2, XLIX. 2.
II. 6, carum nescio quid.
VI. 4, nescio quid febriculosi scorti.
XXXVIII. 7, paulum quid libet allocutionis.
VI. 14, ni tu quid facias ineptiarum.
XIII. 10, seu quid suavius elegantiusve est.
XLII. 14, aut si perditius potest quid esse.
XXII. 13, aut si quid hac re tritius videbatur.
LXXXII. 2, aut aliud si quid carius est oculis.

b. *Colloquial idioms.*

III. 13, vobis male sit, X. 18, maligne, XIV. 10, bene ac beate.
V. 3, unius aestimemus assis.
XVII. 17, nec pili facit uni.
VII. 2, sint satis superque.
X. 6, quid esset jam Bithynia, quomodo se haberet ?
 ,, 9, id quod erat.
 ,, 11, cur quisquam caput unctius referret.
 ,, 17, unum beatiorum.
XXII. 10, unus caprimulgus aut fossor.
XXXVII. 16, tu praeter omnes une de capillatis.
X. 29, fugit me ratio.
XI. 20, ilia rumpere.
IX. 2, milia trecenta (=plurima)—*passim.*
XVII. 5, ex tua libidine.
 ,, 18, ex sua parte.
III. 17, tua opera.
XVII. 12, nec sapit pueri instar.
XXIX. 23, eone nomine.
XXXVI. 16, acceptum face redditumque.
XXVIII. 8, refero datum lucello.
XLIV. 4, quovis pignore contendere.
LXI. 93, si jam videtur.
LXIV. 277, ad se quisque discedebant.
LXVII. 16, sive id non pote sive pote.
XCII. 3, quia sunt totidem mea.
XXXII. 1, amabo.

c. *Single words belonging to popular idiom.*

I. 4, nugae.
XXIX. 8, columbus.
II. 9, ipsa (mistress).
LVIII. 4, quadrivium.
  ,,   ,, angiportum.
XXVIII. 5, vappa.
LXI. 142, glabri.
  ,, 138, cinerarius.
  ,, 126, concubinus.
LXVIII B. 84, volturius.
XVII. 21, stupor.
X. 3, scortillum.
LIII. 5, salaputium.
LVI. 5, pupulus.
LXVII. 21, sicula.
XCVII. 6, ploxenum.
XLII. 13, lutum.
  ,,   ,, lupanar.
  ,, 5, pugillaria.
XXVIII. 12, verpa.

pass. basiare, basia.
IV. 11, conturbare.
X. 30, parare (buy).
XVII. 19, suppernare.
XXIX. 16, expatrare.
  ,,   ,, elluari.
  ,, 17, lancinare.
  ,, 7, perambulare.
VII. 12, fascinare.
XXV. 6, involare
          (steal).
LXXXIII. 5, gannire.
XXV. 2, conscribillare.
XXVII. 2, inger.
XXXII. 2, meridiatum.

VI. 4, febriculosus.
XXIX. 6, superfluens.
VII. 11, curiosus.
XXXVII. 16, semitarius.
XLIV. 4, suburbanus.
XXXII. 10, pransus.
XXXVII. 1, contuber-
  nalis.

d. *Fashionable epithets*[1] *of style, conduct, &c.*

XXII. 9, bellus,   -   - sordidus, XII. 5.
L. 3, delicatus,   -   - stolidus, XVII. 24.
XII. 9, disertus.
XXII. 2, dicax.
XIII. 10, elegans,   -   inelegans.
XXII. 8, facetus, facetiae, infacetus, XLIII. 8 ; infacetiae, XXII. 14,
                       XXXV. 19.
I. 1, lepidus, lepores,   illepidus, XXXVI. 17 ; ineptiae, XIV B. 1.
XIV. 2, jucundus,   -   [injucundus.]
  ,, 16, salsus, sales,   - insulsus, X. 33.
[commodus]   -   - incommodus.
                    molestus, X. 33.
[sapiens]   -   - insipiens, XLIII. 8.
XXII. 2, venustus, -   invenustus, XII. 5.
  ,, 2, urbanus,   - inurbanus ; ruris plenus, XXXVI. 19.
  ,, 12, scurra,   - fossor, XXII. 10 ; caprimulgus, XXII. 10 ;
                    pernicies, XXVII. 6 ; pestis, XLIV. 12 ;
                    venena, XIV. 19.

---

[1] In ordinary language, changes of fashion affect epithets (adjectives, &c.) more than anything else. Catullus' adjectives in general are given below 7, his adverbs 6, his verbs 8.

a. *Nouns in* -or *and* -io *belong rather to ordinary prose than to poetry, but Catullus has*

XII. 12, aestimatio.
XXXVIII. 5, allocutio.
XLV. 9, approbatio.
LV. 6, ambulatio.
VI. 11, inambulatio.
„ „ argutatio.
VII. 1 (pl.), basiatio.
XXXV. 5 (pl.), cogita-
tio.
XXI., esuritio.
XXXII. 8 (pl.), fututio.
XXI. 8, irrumatio.

LXI. 127, locutio.[1]
XLVII. (pl.), vocatio.
XLVIII. 6, osculatio.
LXI. 45, conjugator.
LXIII. 50, creatrix.
LXI. 2, cultor.
LXIV. 300, cultrix ;
LXIII. 72.
XLI. 4, decoctor.
LXIV. 41, frondator.
XXII. 10, fossor.

LXIII. 59, genitor.
„ 50, genitrix.
XIV. 25, lector.
„ 9, litterator.
X. 13, praetor.
LXIV. 204, rector.
XXXVIII. 8, sessor.
LIX. 5, ustor.
XLIV. 11, petitor.
XXIX. 11, imperator.

2. Catullus employs DIMINUTIVE (i.) *nouns,* (ii.) *adjectives,* (iii.) *verbs,* (iv.) *proper names.*

i.

amiculus, XXX. 2.
articulus, XCIX. 8.
auricilla, XXV. 2.
auricula, LXVII. 44.
axulus, XVII. 3.
bracchiolum, LXI. 181.
calathiscus, LXIV. 319.
capillus, XXV. 1.
capsula, LXVIII A. 36.
catulus, XLII. 9.
corolla, LXIV. 284.
cuniculus, XXV. 1.
femella, LV. 7.
flosculus, XXIV. 1, &c.
furcilla, CV. 2.
gemellus, IV. 27.

hortulus, LXI. 92.
labellum, VIII. 18.
lacrimula, LXVI. 16.
lapillus, XXIII. 22.
latusculum, XXV. 10.
lectulus, L. 15.
libellus, I. 1.
lucellum, XXVIII. 6.
medullula, XXV. 2.
mentula, XCIV. 1, &c.
munusculum, LXIV.
103, &c.
ocellus, III. 17, &c.
palmula, IV. 4.
papilla, LXI. 105.
ponticulus, XVII. 3.

puella, II. 1, &c.
puellula, LVII. 9, &c.
pupula, LXIII. 56.
pupulus, LVI. 5.
ramulus, LXI. 22.
sacculus, XIII. 8.
salillum, XXIII. 19.
sarcinula, XXVIII. 2.
scortillum, X. 3.
solaciolum, II. 8.
sicula, LXVII. 21.
tabella, L. 2.
tigillum, LXVII. 39.
versiculus, XVI. 3.
villula, XXVI. 1.
zonula, LXI. 53.

ii.

albulus, XXIX. 8
aridulus, LXIV. 316.
aureolus, II. 12.
bellus, *pass.*
bimulus, XVII. 13.
eruditulus, LVII. 7.
floridulus, LXI. 193.
frigidulus, LXIV. 131.
gemellus, IV. 27.
imulus, XXV. 2.

integellus, XV. 4.
lacteolus, LV. 17.
lassulus, LXIII. 35.
languidulus, LXIV.
331.
misellus, III. 16, &c.
mollicellus, XXV. 10.
molliculus, XVI. 3.
pallidulus, LXV. 6.
parvulus, LXI. 216.

perlucidulus, LXIX. 4.
pusillus, LIV. 1.
tantillus, XCIX. 6.
tinnulus, LXI. 13.
tenellulus, XVII. 15.
tremulus, XVII. 13.
turgidulus, III. 17.
turpiculus, XLI. 103.
uvidulus, LXVI. 63.
votulus, XXVII. 1.

iii.

conscribillare, XXV. 12.   pipilare, III. 10.   ustulare, XXXVI. 8.
postulare, LXVI. 42.

iv.

Ipsithilla, XXXII. 1.   Septimillus, XLV. 13.   Veraniolus, XII. 17.

3. In the LOVER'S VOCABULARY are (i.) terms of endearment, (ii.) terms descriptive of passion.

i.

mea puella, II. 1 ; mulier mea, LXX. 1.	vita amabilior, LXV. 10.
deliciae, II. 1.	vita atque anima dulcius, LXVIII B. 66.
desiderio meo nitenti, II. 5.	lux mea, LXVIII B. 160.
suos amores, X. 1, *et passim.*	me carior ipso, LXVIII B. 119.
mei lepores, XXXII. 2.	carius oculis, LXXXII. 2, &c.
ocelle, XXXI. 2 ; L. 19.	mellitus, III. 6, &c.
mea vita, XLV. 13 ; LXVIII B. 115.	

ii.

gravis ardor, II. 8.	uritur intimo flamma, LXI. 172.
cum penitus maestas exedit cura medullas, LXVI. 23.	perdite amare, XLV. 3.
ignes interiorem edunt medullam, XXX. 15.	perire, XLV. 5 ; deperire, XXXV. 12.
misellus, XLV. 21, &c.	facit delicias libidinesque, XLV. 24.
cura, LXIV. 94.	*Add* LXIV. 87-101.
illi non minus ac tibi pectore	

4. Catullus used words of GREEK origin very rarely, and chiefly in his longer poems ; and all of those employed by him are found elsewhere. The following list will be found almost (if not quite) complete :—

ambrosia, XCIX. 2.	cista, LXIV. 260.	Hesperus, LXII. 20.
amaracus, LXI. 7.	conchylus, LXIV. 50.	hyacinthinus, LXI. 93.
apheliotes, XXVI. 3.	crocinus, LXVIII B. 94.	hymenaeus, LXI., LXII. 4.
barathrum, LXVIII B. 78.	cymbalum, LXIII. 29.	
	Daulias, LXV. 14.	leaena, LX. 155.
barbarus, LXVI. 46.	elleborus, XCIX. 14.	labyrintheus, LXIV. 115.
bombus, LXIV. 265.	ephebus, LXIII. 63.	
calathiscus, ,, 320.	epistolium, LXVIII. 1.	mitra, LXIV. 69.
carbasus, ,, 228.	grabatum, X. 22.	mnemosynum, XII. 13.
carpatina, XCVIII. 4.	gymnasium, LXIII. 60.	
catagraphus, XXV. 7.	gyrus, LXVI. 6.	moechus, XI. 17.
chorus, LXIII. 30.	Hamadryas, LXI. 23.	nothus, XXXIV. 15.
chorea, LXIV. 288.	hendecasyllabus, XII. 10.	onyx, LXVI. 83.
cinaedus, X. 24.		

orgia, LXIV. 260.
paedicare, XXI. 4.
palaestra, LXIII. 60.
palimpsestus, XXII. 5.
papyrus, XXXV. 2.
parthenice, LXI. 194.
pathicus, XVI. 2.
pelagus, LXIII. 16.

phaselus, IV. 1.
plateae, XV. 7.
podagra, LXXI. 2.
raphanus, XV. 19.
stadium, LXIII. 60.
strophium, LXIV. 66.
Tempe, LXIV. 36.
thalamus, LXI. 192.

Thyias, LXIV. 392.
thyrsus, LXIV. 257.
thiasus, LXIII. 28.
tympanum, LXIII. 21.
typanum, ,, 9.
zona, II. 13.
zephyrus, XLVI. 3.

(ii.) Catullus uses *Greek Forms of Inflexion*, in dealing with Greek proper names, side by side with Latin forms, and apparently on no principle (not even that of metrical convenience, *cf.* Propontida, IV. 9 : Athon, LXVI. 46.)

a. *Greek nominative singular :*

Acme, XLV. 10 ; Aganippe, LXI. 30 ; Cybele, LXIII. ; Hebe, LXVIII B. 76 ; Minois, LXIV. 61 ; Nereine, LXIV. 29 ; Phryx, LXIII. 22 ; Scyros, LXIV. 36 ; Zephyritis, LXVI. 57.

b. *Greek genitive singular :*

Cybeles, LXIII. ; Arsinoes, LXVI. 54 ; Locridos, *ib.*; Phasidos, LXIV. 3.

c. *Greek dative singular :*

Pelei, LXIV. 383 (but Peleo, 337, Pelei *gen.*, 279 ; Erecthei, 231, Thesei, 121) ; Minoidi, LXIV. 248 ; Tethyi, LXVI. 70 (but *gen.* Thetidis, LXIV. 19 ; *dat.* Thetidi, 21) ; Hydrochoi, LXVI. 94.

d. *Greek accusative singular :*

Acmen, XLV. 1 ; Booten, LXVI. 67 ; Amphitriten, LXIV. 11 ; Attin, LXIII. 42 ; Athon, LXVI. 46 ; Thesea, LXIV. 246 ; Pelea, 21 ; Propontida, IV. 9 ; Ancona, XXXVI. 13 ; Amathunta, *ib.* 14 ; Minoa, LXIV. 86 ; Callisto, LXVI. 66.

e. *Greek vocative singular :*

Amastri, IV. 13 ; Socration, LXVII. 1 ; Theseu, LXIV. 70 ; Peleu, 27.

f. *Greek nominative plural :*

Nereidĕs, LXIV. 15.

g. *Greek accusative plural :*

Cycladas, IV. 7 ; Sacas, XI. 6 (but Arabes, 5) ; Thyiadas, LXIV. 392 ; Tempe, 36 ; pelage, LXIII. 16 (?).

h. *Greek genitive plural :*

Chalybum (Χαλύβων), LXVI. 48 (probably).

5. SPECIAL FORMS. (i.) Catullus is free from *archaisms*, unless the term must be applied to the following small list :

citarier, LXI. 42.
comparier, LXI. 65.
componier, LXVIII B. 101.
vincier (al. nitier), LXI. 68.
deposivit, XXXIV. 8.

recepso, XLIV. 19.
tetulit, LXIII. 47, 51 ; LXVI. 35.
face, XXXVI. 16 ; LXIII. 82 (?).

alis, LXVI. 28 ; alid, XXIX. 15.
coetu (dat.), LXVI. 37.
uni=unius, XVII. 17.
suopte, LI. 10.

(ii.) *Contracted forms* are

abstersti (?), XCIX. 9.
cessasti,   ,,   12.
duxti, XCI. 9.
luxti, LXVI. 21.
misti, XIV. 14.
nosti, LXVII. 37.
promisti, CX. 3.

promisse, CX. 5.
subrepsti, LXVII. 3.
tristi, LXVI. 30.
desissem, XXXVI. 5.
siris, LXVI. 91.
cognossem, XCI. 3.
servisse, LXVII. 3.

violasse, LXXVI. 3.
putastis, XVI. 3.

prendi, LV. 7.
comprendis, LXII. 35.

juerint, LXVI. 18.

(iii.) *New Compounds*. Although the earlier Roman poets freely formed new compound words, the language seems to have lost this power (a loss wisely regretted by Horace, A.P. 55) at the close of the Republic. In Lucretius there are about fifty newly-coined words, in Catullus less than twenty ; and in both cases most of these words were little or never used by subsequent classical writers. Catullus has

buxifer, IV. 13.
clarisonus, LXIV. 126.
coniger,   ,,   106.
ederiger, LXIII. 23.
falsiparens, LXVIII B. 72.
fluentisonus, LXIV. 53.
flexanimus, (?) LXIV. 331.

inobservabilis, LXIV. 116.
justificus, LXIV. 407.
laserpicifer, VII. 4.
multivolus, LXVIII B. 88.
nemorivagus, LXIII. 72.

omnivolus, LXVIII B. 100.
pinnipes, LV. 17.
plumipes, ,, 19.
properipes, LXIII. 34.
silvicultrix, LXIII. 72.

erifuga, LXIII. 51.
unigena, LXIV. 301.

6. Catullus' ADVERBS (see footnote to 1 (*d*) above) are arranged below according to their terminations :

-ă.	praeterea.	illic.
ita.	sinistra.	illuc.
-ā.	ultra.	istinc.
antea.	*c.* (cf. *-m.*).	posthac.
contra.	hic.	sic.
frustra.	hinc.	tunc.
interea.	huc.	*-d.*
postilla.	illinc.	haud.

-ĕ.

aliunde
ante
bene
deinde
denique
facile
fortasse
forte
impune
inde
male
paene
persaepe
prope
quoque
repente
rite
saepe
temere
ubicumque
undique
usque
usque quaque

-ē.

amplifice
antique
assidue
beate
belle
benigne
certe
clare
cupide
eximie
[hodie]
infeste
jocose
laboriose
late
lepide
libere
longe
maligne
maxime
mimice
mirifice

misere
moleste
novissime
penite
peraeque
perdite
praecipue
probe
proprie
pudice
pulcre
sane
sincere
sumptuose
tarde
valde
venuste
vere

-i.

brevi
heri
ibi
qui
ubi

-l.

nihil
procul
semel
simul

-m. (cf. -c.).

clam
etiam
jam
nequiquam
nunquam
palam
quam
quondam
ubinam
unquam
usquam

equidem
identidem
indidem

item
quidem
saltem
tandem
tantundem

certatim
confestim
furtim
passim
praesertim
statim
ubertim

dudum
iterum
nimirum
nimium
nondum
parum
paulum
plurimum
primum
quantum
rursum
solum
tantum
tum

-n.

non

-ŏ.

modo
postmodo

-ō.

adeo
alio
continuo
ideo
immo
merito
omnino
oppido
paulo
porro
praesto
principio

protelo	semper	foris
quo	super	magis
sero	turpiter	nimis
subito	igitur	satis
ultro		

		adversus
	-s.	penitus
	acerbius	radicitus
-r.	amplius	rursus
audacter	diligentius	
continenter	gravius	
inaniter	impensius	*-t.*
insolenter	improbius	ut
leniter	lenius	post
leviter	libentius	
libenter	minus	
miseriter	plus	*-u.*
nuper	potius	diu
pariter	prius	
perniciter	verius	
pudenter		*-x.*
puriter	foras	vix

7. The ADJECTIVES employed by Catullus—except those mentioned above—are given below according to their terminations :

-us.	gratus	mundus
	indignus	nescius
aequus	infirmus	novus
albus	ingratus	nudus
altus	inimicus	obscurus
amarus	iniquus	omnivolus
bonus	immundus	opacus
caecus	improbus	parcus
canus	impius	parvus
carus	impurus	paucus
cavus	inscius	primaevus
certus	justificus	probus
clarus	laetus	procerus
conscius	laetificus	proclivus
curvus	laevus	profundus
densus	longus	rarus
dignus	magnanimus	raucisonus
dirus	malus	redivivus
durus	merus	saevus
ebrius	mirificus	sanus
ferus	mirus	septemgeminus
fidus	multivolus	serus
flavus	multus	severus

siccus
solus
tardus
torvus
totus
truncus
vagus
vastus
veridicus
verus
vesanus
vivus
unanimus

-bus.

acerbus
superbus

-ĭcus.

antiquus
impudicus
pudicus

-ĭcus.

unicus

-cus.

priscus
spurcus

-ticus.

rusticus
trirusticus

-dus.

algidus
aridus
avidus
candidus
cupidus
egelidus
fervidus
floridus
foedus
frigidus
gelidus

gravidus
horridus
illepidus
languidus
lepidus
limpidus
liquidus
lividus
lucidus
pallidus
placidus
putidus
putridus
rabidus
rapidus
rosidus
sordidus
splendidus
squalidus
stolidus
tepidus
turbidus
umidus

-ndus.

errabundus
fandus
fecundus
furibundus
jucundus
nefandus
tremebundus
secundus
verecundus

-eus.

aequoreus
aëreus
aureus
caeruleus
ferreus
flammeus
laneus
ligneus
luteus
niveus
pineus
purpureus

roseus
saxeus
virgineus

-ius.

anxius
caesius
dubius
egregius
eximius
medius
nimius
patrius
regius
saucius
varius

-arius.

balnearius
nefarius
semitarius

-lus.

aemulus
rutilus
tinnulus
tremulus
vetulus

-culus.

ridiculus
turpiculus

-mus.[1]

cognitissimus
electissimus
extremus
imus
infimus
optimus
primus
proximus
summus
supremus
ultimus

---

[1] Only found as superlatives.

-nus.

abiegnus
fraternus
geminus
magnus
malignus
maternus
nocturnus
obscenus
paternus
plenus
pronus

-anus.

humanus
suburbanus
urbanus

-enus.

alienus
serenus

-ernus.

aeternus
hesternus

-īnus.

anguinus
divinus
matutinus
peregrinus
supinus
taurinus

-tinus.

pristinus

-rus.

amarus
avarus
ignarus
immaturus
maturus

-sus.

adversus [1]
diversus [1]

excelsus
invisus [1]
insulsus
lassus
laxus
obesus
russus
salsus
semi-rasus

-osus.

aestuosus
araneosus
arundinosus
cuniculosus
curiosus
ebriosus
febriculosus
formosus
frondosus
imaginosus
jocosus
laboriosus
morbosus
muscosus
nervosus
ostriosus
pilosus
spinosus
spumosus
studiosus
sumptuosus
tenebricosus
torosus
ventosus
verbosus

-tus.

aegrotus
altus
angustus
avitus
castus
facetus
faustus
funestus
ignotus

incultus
infacetus
infestus
injustus
indistinctus
indomitus
intactus
invenustus
invictus
invitus
irritus
justus
lautus
lentus
maestus
molestus
mutus
robustus
scelestus
stultus
vegetus
venustus

-tus. [1]

acceptus
acutus
apertus
aptus
auctus
auspicatus
beatus
capillatus
citatus
citus ·
comatus
contentus
cunctus
delicatus
dentatus
destinatus
disertus
diversus
doctus
expeditus
expolitus
incitatus
inquinatus

[1] Originally past participles.

minutus
notus
perditus
pileatus
praeruptus
praetextatus
quietus
recoctus
reconditus
rectus
redimitus
sanctus
secretus
semi-lautus
sollicitus
spurcatus
tacitus
tritus
unguentatus

-ntus.

opulentus
truculentus

-uus.

annuus
assiduus
continuus
fatuus
ingenuus
menstruus
mortuus
mutuus
perpetuus
semi-mortuus
vacuus
viduus

-ivus.

furtivus

-r (er, -fer, -ur).

ater
aurifer
coniger
dexter

integer
laserpicifer
letifer
miser
noctifer
piger
prosper
pulcer
ruber
sacer
sagittifer
satur
scaber
sinister
taeter
tener

-s.[1]

anceps
caelebs
compar[2]
discors
expers
iners
mas
par[2]
particeps
pinnipes
plumipes
praeceps
princeps
properipes
tardipes
vecors
vetus

-es.

dives
sospes
teres

-is.

brevis
caelestis
communis
dulcis
grandis

immitis
inanis
incolumis
lenis
levis
lĕvis
mitis
mollis
omnis
perennis
pinguis
suavis
silvestris
sublimis
tenuis
tristis
turpis
vilis
viridis

-alis.

aequalis
aequinoctialis
genialis
jugalis
litoralis
mortalis
nuptialis
penetralis
regalis
sesquipedalis

-elis.

fidelis
crudelis

-ĭlis.

subtilis
gentilis

-ĭlis.

difficilis
facilis
humilis
rasilis
similis

---

[1] After consonant stems. [2] *s* dropped.

sterilis

-bilis.

amabilis
flebilis
horribilis
inobservabilis
memorabilis
miserabilis
nobilis

-tilis.

volatilis

-ns.

amens
clemens
demens
frequens
inelegans
immerens
impotens
ingens
insipiens
insperans
omnipotens
pestilens
praesens
potens
recens
vemens

-ns.[1]

albicans
ardens

constans
elegans
flagrans
flavens
florens
fragrans
frigerans
fulgens
furens
gaudens
lacrimans
lactens
laetans
languens
micans
mugiens
neglegens
nitens
olens
obliviscens
perlucens
praeterpidans
properans
pudens
radians
semi-hians
spūmans
sudans
superfluens
valens
viridans

-er.

acer
alacer

celer
uber

-or.

[deterior]
immemor
memor

-x.

duplex
multiplex
redux
trux
vindex

-ax.

audax
dicax
fallax
mendax
minax
procax
rapax
salax
tenax
vorax

-ix.

felix
infelix

-ox.

ferox

8. Catullus' VERBS follow (i.) INCEPTIVES, (ii.) FREQUENTA-
TIVES, (iii.) PREPOSITIONAL. Peculiarities in the use of these,
particularly the last (iii.), distinguish the special vocabularies
both of Greek and of Latin poets.

(i.) INCEPTIVE VERBS :

acquiescere
contremiscere

crescere
deflorescere

expallescere
exardescere

---

[1] Originally present participles.

incandescere
increbescere
languescere
miserescere
mollescere

mutescere
notescere
oblivisci
requiescere
senescere

silescere
tabescere
vanescere
vigescere

(ii.) FREQUENTATIVES :

adventare
aspectare
auctare
auscultare
captare
circumcursare
citare
cogitare
delectare
expectare
flagitare

fluitare
frequentare
exsultare
insultare
jactare
labefactare
mersare
noscitare
ostentare
prospectare
quaeritare

quassare
respectare
sectari
spectare
tepefactare
trusare
venditare
ventitare
versari
vexare
volitare

(iii.) PREPOSITIONAL VERBS :

a-, ab-, abs-.

abesse
abducere
abhorrere
abire
abjicere
abjungere
abluere
abripere
abrumpere
abscondere
absorbere
abstergere
abstinere
absumere
abuti
amittere
auferre
avehere
avertere
avellere

ad-.

accidere
accipere
accolere
acquiescere

accubare
addere
adesse
adhortari
adimere
adipisci
adire
adjurare
adjuvare
admirari
adoriri
advenire
advocare
advolare
afferre
afficere
affigere
affirmare
agnoscere
alludere
alluere
alloqui
ammovere
annuere
apparere
appetere
applicare
approbare

aspectare
aspernari
aspicere
asservare
attenuare
atterere
attingere
attrahere
attribuere

anti-.

antistare

circum-.

circumcursare
circumdare
circumsilire
circumsistere

co-, con-.

coacervare
cogere
cogitare
cognoscere
coire
colligere

collocare
collucere
comesse
commemorare
commendare
commingere
committere
commodare
comparare
compellare
comperire
complecti
componere
comprecari
comprendere
comprobare
concedere
conciliare
concinere
concipere
conclamare
concoquere
concredere
concutere
conferre
conficere
confiteri
confutuere
conjungere
conqueri
conscelerare
conscendere
conscindere
conscribere
conscribillare
consequi
conserere
conservare
considere
consolari
conspicere
consternere
constituere
construere
consurgere
contegere
contemnere
contendere

contingere
contorquere
contrahere
contremiscere
conturbare
convellere
convenire
convocare
corripere
corruere

de-.

decedere
decerpere
declarare
declinare
decurrere
dedere
dedicare
deducere
deesse
defendere
deferre
defetisci
deflectere
deflorescere
defricare
degere
delabi
delectare
demanare
demere
demetere
demittere
demonstrare
deperdere
deperire
deponere
deprecari
deprendere
derelinquere
deridere
derigere
descendere
deserere
desiderare
desinere
desistere
despicere

despondere
despuere
destinare
detinere
devincere
devocare
devolvere
devorare

di-, dis-.

diffindere
diffundere
diffutuere
digredi
dilacerare
diligere
diluere
dimittere
dirigere
discedere
discernere
discerpere
discruciare
discupere
disperire
dispicere
displicere
dissolvere
distinguere
divellere
dividere

e-, ec-, ex-.

ecfodere
ecfutuere
edere
educare
educere
efferre
efficere
efflare
effluere
effugere
effundere
egredi
ejicere
elevare
eluere
emergere

emori	*in-.*	*ob-.*
emulgere	ignoscere	obdurare
eniti	imbuere	obesse
eripere	imminere	objurgare
eruere	impellere	oblectare
evertere	implicare	oblitterare
evirare	implorare	oblivisci
evitare	inaurare	obloqui
evolvere	incandescere	obscurare
exagitare	incedere	obserare
exardescere	incendere	obsidere
excedere	incidere	obstare
excipere	incingere	obstinare
excitare	incipere	obterere
excruciare	incitare	obtingere
excutere	incohare	occidere
exercere	incolere	occupare
exesse	increbescere	offerre
exigere	incurvare	offirmare
exire	indicare	operire
exorior	indicere	oppetere
expallescere	inducere	opplere
expatrare	ineptire	opponere
expedire	inferre	opprimere
expellere	inflectere	ostendere
expendere	infundere	ostentare
experiri	ingenerari	
expetere	ingerere	
explere	ingredi	*per-.*
explicare	inhibere	
expolire	injicere	perambulare
exposcere	inniti	percellere
exprimere	instare	percurrere
expromere	instituere	percutere
exsecare	instruere	perdepsere
exsequi	insultare	perdere
exsilire	invenire	perducere
exsolvere	invidere	perferre
exspectare	invisere	perfundere
exspirare	invocare	perhibere
exspuere	involare	perire
exstare	inurere	perjerare
exsternare	irrigare	perlucere
exsultare ·	irrumare	permiscere
exsuperare		permulcere
extenuare		pernumerare
exturbare	*inter-.*	perpeti
extollere		perscribere
exurere	interficere	persequi
	interire	persolvere

perspicere
pertundere
perurere
pervenire
pervigilare
pervincere
pervolvere

por-.

polliceri
polluo
porrigere

prae-.

praecerpere
praedicare
praedicere
praeesse
praefari
praeferre
praegestire
praeoptare
praeponere
praeportare
praetrepidare
praevalere
praevertere

praeter-.

praeterire

pro-.

procedere
procreare
procumbere
procurrere
prodere
prodesse
prodire
proferre
proficere
proficisci
profundere
progignere
promittere
propellere
proponere

proscindere
prosequi
prosilire
prospectare
prospicere
prosternere
prostituere
protendere

re-.

reboare
recedere
recipere
recolere
recordari
recrepare
recumbere
recurare
reddere
redimere
redire
reducere
referre
reflagitare
reflectere
refringere
refulgere
reglutinare
relegare
religare
relinquere
remittere
remorari
remugire
remunerari
renidere
renovare
reperire
reponere
reposcere
requiescere
requirere
residere
resolvere
resonare
respectare
respergere

respondere
restituere
restringere
reticescere
retinere
retonare
retrahere
revertere
revincire
revisere
revocare

se-.

secedere
secubare
sevocare

sub-.

subducere
subire
sublevare
substernere
succendere
succumbere
suffigere
summittere
suppernare
supponere
surrepere
surripere
suscipere
suscitare
suspendere
suspirare
sustollere

super-.

superare
superfluere
superimpendere
superirrigare
supervehere

trans-.

tradere
transferre
transire

The few isolated peculiarities of Catullus' *syntax* will be found in the Notes.

INDEX I.

Nominum et Locorum.

INDEX II.

Notarum.

abhorret, XXII. 11.
abibit, sic, XIV. 16.
ablative of quality, LXIV. 50.
abrupto = *abrepto,* LXVIII B. 44.
accubans, LXI. 171.
accusative, cognate, VII. 9.
acino, XXVII. 4.
aditum ferens, LXI. 26.
ad sensum constr., LXIV. 146.
aequales, LXII. 11.
aere citatis, LXIII. 18.
aestuante animo, LXIII. 47.
albus an ater, XCIII. 2.
aliquid, I. 4.
alite bona, LXI. 19.
altera mille, V. 8.
amaraci, LXI. 7.
amariores calices, XXVII. 2.
amicitiae pectus, LXXVIII. 6.
amplius horam, XCIX. 3.
analytic perfect, XVII. 2.
animis mutuis, XLV. 20.
antistans, IX. 2.
applicans collum, IX. 8.
arenae *collective,* VII. 3.
aspirate mispronounced, LXXXIV.
at *in imprecation,* III. 13.
at, *with ironical objection,* LXVI. 21.

atque, LXV. 24.
attraction of case in predication, XLIV. 1.
aucte, LXIV. 26.
auctūs hymenaeo, LXVI. 11.
audit, *with infinitive,* LXVIII B. 70.
auricilla, XXV. 2.
auspicatiorem, XLV. 26.
ave atque vale, CI. 10.
avertere, LXIV. 4.
axulis, XVII. 3.

barbara, LXIV. 265.
beatas, LI. 15.
bombos, LXIV. 264.
Book, Roman, XXII. 6.

caelesti numine, LXVI. 7.
caesio, XLV. 7.
cana saecula, XCV. 6.
capsula, LXVIII A. 36.
carta, XXII. 6.
  „   anus, LXVIII B. 6.
catagraphos, XXV. 7.
cavas, XCV. 5.
cavě, L. 18.
celebrabant, LXIV. 260.
Chalybum, LXVI. 48.

PRINTED IN GREAT BRITAIN BY ROBERT MACLEHOSE AND CO. LTD.
THE UNIVERSITY PRESS, GLASGOW